DATE DUE

MAY 2 8 02			

CHILDREN AS PAWNS

Children as Pawns

The Politics of Educational Reform

Timothy A. Hacsi

HARVARD UNIVERSITY PRESS

Cambridge, Massachusetts

London, England · 2002

To Sandra Lee Skinner

Library of Congress Cataloging-in-Publication Data
Hacsi, Timothy A.
Children as pawns : the politics of educational reform / Timothy A. Hacsi.
p. cm.
Includes bibliographical references (p.) and index.
ISBN 0-674-00744-1 (alk. paper)
1. Education and state—United States.
2. Educational change—United States.
3. Educational evaluation—United States.
I. Title.

LC89 .H215 2002
379.73—dc21   2001051485

Contents

Acknowledgments

Researching and writing a book is a lonely process; it is also one in which the author builds up personal debts to those who helped. In this case, my debts are relatively few but deep. Carol Weiss mentored the postdoctoral program in evaluation that brought me to Harvard. A few months into my stay, Carol posed a question: Would I consider writing a history of evaluation? That idea gradually transformed into this manuscript, which is certainly not a history of evaluation, but does blend history and evaluation in a way that I believe says something useful about education. Carol has provided me with any number of insights, though of course she cannot be blamed for my particular interpretations of specific evaluations in these pages. It is the simple truth to say that this book would not exist without her prompting, support, and vast knowledge of evaluation.

During the two years of my fellowship at the Harvard Children's Initiative, I was blessed with wonderful colleagues and thoughtful administrators. My fellow Fellows from 1997–1999, Tracy Huebner, Anthony Petrosino, and Patricia Rogers, were (and are, when we get the chance) a delight to work with. We pushed one another's thinking about evaluation, I hope in good ways; I also hope they learned at least half as much about evaluation from me as I did from them. Kay Merseth, then director of HCI, helped make it a great place to be, in addition to being supportive of all our projects, including this one. Mary Askew was not only the best administrator one could hope for but also an inspiration. Her devotion to the well-being of children is immense and helped inspire us all to do good work. Finally, Allan Brandt told me about the fellowship, and his support undoubtedly helped me get it. I am truly grateful for that, for many reasons, and for his friendship.

I have had the special good fortune of working with Elizabeth Knoll as my editor at Harvard University Press. She has been a source of fruitful ideas, constant support, and accurate critiques, and I appreciate each of those things greatly. The book is much the better for her involvement and, as important, the process has been enjoyable throughout; as those of you know who have written anything of length with an editor's involvement, that is not always the case. Julie Ericksen Hagen copyedited the manuscript beautifully, for which I am also grateful.

The readers for Harvard University Press provided me with a great deal of helpful advice. Maris Vinovskis gave the manuscript the kind of reading authors dream of: very positive, and full of useful advice on how to improve it. Time and circumstance have kept me from following his suggestions as fully as he—and I—might have liked, but even so, his advice made this a smarter and more readable manuscript than it was when he first saw it. I especially enjoyed a discussion we had about the manuscript, and other things, at a conference in late 2000, and I appreciate the chance to thank him here. An anonymous reader for the press also gave me useful feedback, especially concerning my choice of topics, and I am grateful to that person as well.

Although they have not had any direct involvement in this project, I would be remiss if I did not thank the professors I had as an undergraduate at Oberlin College, and in the graduate history program of the University of Pennsylvania. I am particularly grateful to Michael Katz and Gary Kornblith, both of whom were models of careful research, collegiality, and social responsibility. Neither is the least to blame for any flaws in this volume, but they each have some responsibility for the things that are right in it.

A number of people helped, either by talking with me at length or by reading a chapter or two and giving me feedback. I would especially like to thank Mary Askew, Debra Block, Sherman Dorn, Tracy Huebner, Anthony Petrosino, Sandra Skinner, Carol Weiss, and Sheldon White. On a personal note, family and friends were invaluable, especially Jacqueline Hacsi, Jon Walters, Karen Skinner, Nancy Skinner, Linda Skinner-Austin, John Austin, and Alida Austin.

The best thing about coming to Harvard had nothing to do with academics. In the very early stages of researching this book I met Sandra Skinner. Sandy was patient when I had to work on this at night (and was a fountain of information on a number of issues concerning disadvantaged children), and she kept me focused on what really matters when I wasn't happy with the manuscript. As these words are being written our baby, Lilly, just turned one month old. This book is dedicated to Sandy, with love and gratitude.

Introduction

How can we improve our schools?

Ever since the publication of *A Nation at Risk* in 1983, the state of America's schools has been the subject of public concern, media scrutiny, and political outrage.[1] Virtually everyone agrees that the nation's schools have problems, but they disagree about the nature and extent of those problems. The list of proclaimed flaws is long, and sometimes contradictory: bad teachers, indifferent students, disinterested parents, faulty curriculums, a lack of morality or religion, destructive teacher unions, rigid bureaucrats, too much federal interference, not enough federal support, unequal funding methods, and more. The proposed solutions are equally varied, and range from relatively simple to mind-numbingly complex: better teacher training, vouchers, accountability through high-stakes testing, changes in school governance, standards, more money for schools, charter schools, and dozens of other ideas large and small are advocated by interested parties. Despite years of discussion, and several waves of school reform in individual schools, school districts, and state governments, the question remains: How can we improve our schools?

Any intelligent discussion of "improving" education leads to questions about what it is that we want public schooling to achieve. Do we want to provide real opportunity for all children? Do we want to give whatever help is needed for children who start school behind or who struggle in school to "catch up," or do we want to provide superb education for the children who seem most ready to move forward quickly? Do we want to train children to be good citizens, or to have a certain moral view of the world? (And if so, which one?) Do we want to prepare children to be good workers as adults, or to be independent thinkers? In an ideal world we

1

would be able to do many of these things well, but in the real world where resources are limited and different groups compete for attention and funding, choices between these various goals are constantly being made.

This is not to say that our schools have deteriorated disastrously, having fallen from some earlier era when they were far superior to today's schools. There was no such Golden Age. Historian Michael Katz points out that *A Nation at Risk's* claim that American students were not learning as well as they had in earlier eras "has reappeared periodically since the 1870s." Instead, it is the aims of schools that have changed: they have become more ambitious. One version of educational history argues that in the nineteenth century the main goal of schools was to provide children with a good education; in today's terms, it was excellence. But schools then were usually more about providing a specific moral view of the world to all children—and a solid education to some—than about educational excellence for all.[2] Since the nineteenth century the central goals of public schooling have shifted back and forth, shaped by events and concerns in the broader society. Over the first half of the twentieth century, rapidly increasing numbers of students stayed in school longer, and high school graduation went from a rarity to an expected occurrence, first for middle-class white children and then for virtually all children. Schools focused on providing a general education to (almost) all, and tracked students into college-prep, vocational, and other streams. In the 1950s the cold war between the United States and the Soviet Union, and especially the launch of Sputnik, led to a belief that America's schools had failed and subsequently to a focus on improving how science, math, and foreign languages were taught. The focus shifted to educating the "best" students. During the 1960s and early 1970s the civil rights movement, President Lyndon Johnson's Great Society, and several prominent court cases focused attention on the perceived failure of schools in view of the lack of equity among different groups' educational opportunities. As a result, the focus shifted from teaching the "best" students to providing equal access to groups that had faced discrimination. In the 1980s an uneven economy, an increased sense that global economic competition required a highly educated workforce, a revived cold war, and the publication of *A Nation at Risk* combined to shift concern about public schools back from equity to excellence.[3]

In recent years, some reformers have proposed trying to strike a balance between equity and excellence. Today schools face a new and daunting challenge: providing *all* children with a strong, solid education. This is a truly lofty goal. Any claims that we managed to do this once upon a time are wrong. This has never been attempted before, and it is not clear that we, as a society, are really ready to try now. We talk a good game, but only time will tell if we are serious. Even assuming we are prepared to strive for good schools everywhere that meet a variety of student needs, we still have to figure out *how* to reach this goal.

Understanding what we know—and what we do not know—-about what works in schools seems to me not just a good beginning but in fact a necessary one. This book is intended as a step in that direction. It describes the policies we have followed on five different educational issues. Each case study—Head Start, bilingual education, class size, social promotion, and school financing and funding—also describes the major evaluation evidence on that particular topic. When I say "what we know about what works," it is this evaluation evidence that I am talking about, mixed with what I hope is a fair amount of common sense. (More about what evaluation is and why it matters in a moment.)

I began this work with a number of assumptions about education that should be made explicit at the start. I believe schooling is extremely important, not just for the children who attend schools but for the future of our society. I do not, however, believe that schools can address society's major problems either effectively or rapidly. Many of the perceived problems of schools are actually societal problems that play out in schools as well as in many other arenas. This is certainly true of violence in schools, for example; it is also true of racism, and sexism, and inequality, from a liberal perspective, and of sexual activity and immorality, from a conservative perspective. While school officials would be derelict if they did not try to address these problems as they affect schooling, they cannot hope to *solve* them, because these are issues that run throughout society, and they require solutions that do the same. Despite these limitations, I believe that schools can and should play a role in creating a more fair and just society. I also believe our schools can make serious, ongoing efforts to educate *all* children. In fact, it seems to me that doing so would be the greatest contribution schools could make to our society, and the best way they could go about helping to address our society's larger problems.

I should say something here about my background. I am a historian, chiefly interested in such issues as welfare, urban history, families and children, and education. I have worked in a number of interdisciplinary settings, particularly at the University of Chicago and Harvard University, splitting my time and energy between history and policy issues. I also spent two years as a postdoctoral fellow at the Harvard Children's Initiative, where I worked on evaluation under the guidance of Carol Weiss. I recently finished coediting a volume on evaluation approaches with my colleagues from the fellowship, Tracy Huebner, Anthony Petrosino, and Patricia Rogers. The book you are holding was my main project during that fellowship, stemming from a suggestion by Carol that I write about the history of evaluation. The book gradually changed into something else, as book projects have a way of doing, and it has become a book about education policy, with significant evaluations playing a key role in the discussion of those policies.

This book, like most, is aimed at several audiences. My primary audience is individuals concerned with the state of public education in the United States who hope to gain some insight into how it can be improved. Obviously this includes teachers, school officials, parents, and people who help shape education policy at the district, city, state, and federal levels. What this book is *not* is a technical study of hundreds of evaluations aimed chiefly at evaluators. Nor is it a detailed educational history intended largely for historians. Even so, while some aspects of the stories told herein may be familiar to academics, especially in education and history, they should find much that is new as well. I also hope evaluators will find much of interest here, both in terms of how evaluations compare to policy and in understanding the kinds of evaluations needed to influence public policy.

What exactly, you may be asking, is evaluation? In general, educational evaluation seeks to judge the worth of a program or policy, or to understand how that program or policy functions, or, more ambitiously, to study both *how* and *how well* it works. For example, a curriculum for helping first graders learn to read could be evaluated to understand how it functions (how teachers employ it, how students understand it) or to see how it compares with another curriculum (which program helps more students become good readers?). Evaluation can focus on what happens in a single classroom, or it can look at an entire school or school district, or it can look at some aspect of schooling as it occurs in many different places. A school district policy requiring elementary schools to double the amount of time children spend learning math could be evaluated with any number of questions in mind. Evaluators could examine whether teachers actually implemented the policy, what other subjects lost ground as a result, whether student test scores in math increased, and whether students who received the extra time studying math gained an advantage that lasted into later years of schooling.

But of course there is more than that to evaluation, much more, and you will need to know some things about evaluation to understand the details of my arguments and judge them for yourself. The following chapters describe a number of specific evaluations, such as Project STAR, a randomized experiment on class size conducted in Tennessee in the late 1980s. They also describe a number of reviews of the evaluation literature on specific topics, such as two meta-analyses of the effects of social-promotion decisions on later student achievement. Finally, underlying much of the discussion are questions about how and when evaluation evidence gets used. After all, politicians and policymakers have many factors to take into account; how and when evidence plays any role at all, much less a significant one, is far from clear.

So what are randomized experiments? What on earth is a meta-analysis? To most readers, these phrases fall somewhere between vaguely familiar and confusing (and probably boring) jargon. But knowing why each of these approaches is powerful, as well as where and how they and other evaluation approaches can be flawed, is central to understanding this book. To help the reader make sense of the sources I use to judge the educational policies described here, a somewhat detailed description of evaluation is in order. And since I am a historian, I feel compelled to explain them by saying a little about the history of evaluation as a field.

Many people have played an important role in the development of educational evaluation, but a few must be mentioned in even the briefest of descriptions. To begin at the beginning means describing the work of Ralph Tyler, who rose to prominence in educational research circles in the 1930s and 1940s and has been referred to as the "father of educational evaluation." Tyler began writing about evaluating student progress in 1929, and he advanced the field in many ways. His views on evaluation developed from the then-traditional idea that evaluation should appraise how *students* were doing to the more modern belief that evaluation should examine the quality of educational *programs*. This meant that for Tyler, testing should be used to determine whether teaching had achieved its goal of students' learning specific things. If testing showed that it had not, the results could be used to improve teaching rather than to simply rank students.[4] In Tyler's view, evaluation had a handful of major purposes, including regularly checking the effectiveness of education and consequently making recommendations for improvement; it should also examine the theories underlying education.[5] These goals have remained central to educational evaluation ever since, though how well evaluators have actually implemented them is hard to say.

For most of the 1950s, schools faced little outside pressure. Most evaluations were funded by local school districts, community chests, or foundations, and were concerned with local issues.[6] Everything changed when the Soviet Union launched its Sputnik satellite in 1957, thus adding a new twist to the cold war that had already raged for a decade. The space race was on, and the United States was starting off seemingly far behind. The cold war had a major impact on education, as the belief that the American educational system needed to be improved spread rapidly among the public, politicians, pundits, and educators themselves. Critics had been assailing the American educational system for years, but Sputnik's launch helped convince the nation (inaccurately) that American schools were behind the Soviet Union's. The federal government responded by passing the National Defense Education Act in 1958. The NDEA expanded testing in schools and called for new programs in science, math, and foreign languages. Projects to develop new curriculums began as a result, especially in the sciences, and curriculum projects that were already under way received a huge boost. This was especially important for the development of evaluation, because the new curriculums would have to be evaluated to ensure that they were better than older curriculums. Evaluation was evolving, as Ralph Tyler had advocated, from measuring individual results to studying the effectiveness of new curriculums compared with older curriculums in the same field.[7]

In 1963 two important pieces were published that can, in hindsight, be viewed as signposts indicating when educational evaluation began moving along two very different pathways. The first publication, which was extremely influential in the 1960s, was *Experimental and Quasi-Experimental Designs for Research* by Donald Campbell and Julian Stanley. The central goal of their work was to understand and address the danger of bias in evaluation. To take a very basic kind of bias, suppose twenty children were assigned to an "experimental" group to receive a new math curriculum, while another twenty children were assigned to a "control" group that received the standard math curriculum. Suppose that after one year the experimental group scored far higher (on average) than the control group on a math test. This might be taken as proof that the new curriculum was better than the old one. But suppose that further examination showed that the children in the experimental group had been superior math students compared with the children in the control group at the *start* of the year, when the assignments were made. This would have biased the results. Another obvious form of bias would be teacher quality: suppose the teacher providing the new curriculum was widely considered a superb math teacher, while the teacher providing the standard math curriculum to the control group was completely untrained and, for good measure, not very good at math. In such a case, the evaluation would not really have tested the quality of the curriculums, because other important factors would have been very different between the experimental group and the control group, and were not taken into account by the evaluators.

Campbell and Stanley's work presented a powerful argument for doing randomized experiments as a means of dealing with the problems created by bias. In a true experiment, you begin with a statement of objectives, perform rigorous measurements, and then use statistics to analyze the results. The rigor of experiments comes from sampling. The subjects of the experiment are randomly placed in two or more groups. So long as the number of subjects being randomized is not too small, each group will be equivalent on the kinds of factors that can affect how well or poorly they will respond to treatment. If randomization is performed properly, then the pre-treatment difference between the groups is zero. For example, income level, racial background, parental education level, and other relevant factors should be the same overall in each group. If this is so, then differences between the groups on the post-treatment tests can reasonably be attributed to the treatment they received—in other words, to the program or policy that is being evaluated. Experiments in which subjects are randomized into treatment and control groups are at the heart of evaluation in a number of fields; for example, that is how decisions are made about whether or not drugs should be approved for legal use.

It is important to note that in education there can sometimes be political or practical problems with having a no-treatment control group. If a program is assumed by educators to be a good thing, they may see giving it to some children but not others as unfair and morally unacceptable. But this is hardly an impassible barrier to experiments, since two or three different programs could be compared to one another, rather than to a control group receiving no special treatment. As Robert Boruch points out,

"What works better?" can be a more interesting and useful question than "Does it work?"[8] However, when randomization is used outside of the laboratory, to study social programs or schools, it can be very difficult to implement.[9] How feasible, and how desirable, randomized experiments are in education has been debated for several decades, and it remained an important issue in the late 1990s.

The second important publication of 1963 was "Course Improvement through Evaluation" by Lee Cronbach. It was Cronbach's first seminal article; his influence evolved much more gradually than Donald Campbell's, but in educational evaluation he became extremely influential in the 1980s and 1990s. Cronbach, who was trained in educational psychology, argued that recent approaches to the evaluation of education were misguided. He wondered how to move away from "the familiar doctrines and rituals of the testing game." Cronbach called for evaluators to think of evaluation as a process of gathering information. Rather than worrying overly much about outcomes, evaluators examining a course should try to understand how it "produces its effects and what parameters influence its effectiveness." Cronbach was interested in outcomes, but he was more concerned about whether or not evaluators were asking the right questions about the influence of the programs they studied. He wanted data collected that would aid in *improving* courses, not just in judging them as good or bad.[10] In a sense, he was far less ambitious about what individual evaluations might do than were Campbell and Stanley, at least in terms of their ability to definitively determine the results of an educational program. But in another sense, he was far more ambitious: he wanted evaluation to lead to better education (much as Ralph Tyler had advocated) by developing a richer and more complicated understanding of education, rather than by simply placing a stamp of approval on the programs that were deemed to work well.

The early and mid-1960s were a time of great optimism, fueled in part by a booming economy; rarely has the nation been so confident that government could solve even the most intractable societal problems. President Lyndon Johnson's Great Society combined poverty, health care, and educational programs in a "War on Poverty" with no lesser goals than to end poverty and racial discrimination in American society. Many of the programs were targeted toward disadvantaged children. One of the central legislative acts of the War on Poverty was the Elementary and Secondary Education Act of 1965 (ESEA). The ESEA's Title I (now known as Chapter

I) provided nearly $1 billion to schools with high concentrations of impoverished children. ESEA was the first federal educational program to send money directly to local schools, and it has continued to play a powerful role in public education ever since.[11]

Because vast amounts of money were being spent on these new programs in the mid-1960s, some in Washington believed that it was important to evaluate them to ensure that the money was not being wasted. Senator Robert Kennedy played an important role in amending the ESEA, adding requirements that school districts receiving Title I money conduct annual evaluations to determine what effects the program was actually having. (Milbrey McLaughlin has shown that Kennedy hoped, in vain as it turned out, that evaluation reports on Title I programs would give parents the ability to make sure the programs actually helped their children.) Johnson's social programs played a central role in spurring the development of evaluation in other fields as well, such as criminal justice and health, through the expansion of programs and legislation requiring—and funding—evaluations of those programs and policies.[12] The evaluation needs of the Great Society programs also weakened psychology's central place in evaluation methodology. Ernest House points out that after the ESEA was passed, the practitioners of, and methodology of, evaluation became much more diverse.[13]

In short order the allure of true experiments began to fade, as both the goals and the methods used to evaluate educational programs changed in the late 1960s and early 1970s. To some extent, these changes occurred because several highly prominent evaluations seemed to have failed. When educators and evaluators tried to evaluate Title I programs, for example, they found that their methods were not up to the task, just as Lee Cronbach had written in 1963. There were a number of reasons for these failures. The standardized tests that existed were of little use, as it turned out, since they were designed to rank students of average ability, not to illuminate the needs and achievements of disadvantaged children who were far behind in school.[14] In fact, the major program evaluations that followed within a few years of the Great Society's founding seemed to show that none of the programs being studied were making any difference for their participants. Not surprisingly, everyone involved found this disheartening, and while some observers believed it showed the ineffectiveness of the programs being evaluated, many others believed that what it actually showed was the weakness of evaluation methods.[15]

Part of the problem was that randomized experiments turned out to be very difficult to implement. As practiced in the 1960s, they also failed to address a number of important questions about *how* programs were functioning. Most studies found that programs had had "no effect," but this left a number of important questions not just unanswered but unasked. For example, what exactly *were* the programs that had had "no effect"? Many of the programs under study actually varied quite a bit from place to place; that was certainly the case with Head Start, for example. The kinds of evaluations being done did little to describe what these programs actually entailed. Furthermore, they provided no real information on whether the programs were being implemented as intended—or implemented at all.[16] The disappointing results of major programs, and the Coleman Report's discouraging findings (discussed briefly in Chapter 5), led to a widespread belief that social programs did not work, that in effect "nothing worked" when the government tried to address poverty and related social problems. But an alternate view was that most evaluations were not asking the right questions, or that evaluation methodology was unable to discover the positive effects that programs were actually bringing about.

At the same time, the late 1960s and early 1970s saw the first major wave of theorists and practitioners developing new ways of thinking about evaluation, many of whom brought ideas from other fields into evaluation. Individuals who would go on to become giants in the evaluation field, such as Michael Scriven and Carol Weiss, wrote influential articles in this period. As often as not, they argued for innovative new approaches that called for dramatic changes from earlier evaluation methods. In 1967 Scriven, a philosopher, distinguished between "formative" evaluations that placed emphasis on developing information to help programs improve, and "summative" evaluations that focused on studying the worth of a program; Scriven considered the latter to be more important. This emphasis fit fairly well with Campbell and Stanley's emphasis on describing program outcomes.[17] Taken together, Cronbach's 1963 article and Scriven's 1967 article presaged many of the debates that would be ongoing in evaluation over the next thirty years. Their work showed that there were many possible roles for evaluation, and many different ways to think about evaluation. Evaluators could focus on improving a program or determining its effects; they could use an experimental approach or qualitative methods; evaluations could be performed by the program itself or by outside evaluators; and so on and on. This helped spur other evaluators to try to "define the various dimensions or kinds of evaluation."[18]

In the 1960s, some of the most influential and prominent evaluators held to a "rational choice" model about how evaluation results would influence policy. They believed they could supply clear-cut answers about which programs worked and which did not, and decisionmakers (chiefly in government) would support the former and close down the latter. But this did not happen. For one thing, most prominent evaluations of major social programs found that the programs had little impact, and the evaluations themselves were generally so riddled with methodological flaws that their findings were not very reliable. At the same time, evaluators were finding that decisionmakers rarely acted specifically on evaluation results, even when the results seemed to point in one direction or another.

Carol Weiss, then a sociologist at Columbia University, published a series of articles in the early 1970s explaining that the decisionmaking process was far more complicated than the rational choice model presumed. Programs existed in a political arena, after all, and Weiss showed that what might seem obvious and rational to evaluators (such as closing or changing a program that evaluation showed did not work) was in fact neither to the people in power. Decisionmakers had many factors to take into account, and what a program's evaluation showed was only one factor—and far from the most important in most cases. As Weiss wrote, bureaucrats and policymakers were "not irrational; they have a different model of rationality in mind."[19] In later years, Weiss continued to provide insights into how evaluations influenced decisionmakers. One of her most compelling arguments was that evaluation evidence (and social science research more generally) often had an indirect, gradual impact. "Policymakers often hear about research indirectly as findings and conclusions seep into conferences, consultant briefings, conversations, field reports, the media, mail, and so forth."[20]

In the 1970s the fragmented field of evaluation transformed into a recognizable profession with the usual markings. Major journals and monograph series appeared, such as *Evaluation Review* and *New Directions for Program Evaluation*. Two professional evaluation organizations were formed in 1976, and a decade later they merged to create the American Evaluation Association. Universities began to offer graduate courses in evaluation methodology, and a handful of prominent universities developed full-fledged programs in evaluation. Evaluation as a professional field needed a knowledge base to give it legitimacy and coherence, and it created one by taking methods from all the social sciences and making its own blend.[21]

Probably the most dramatic change in educational evaluation in the 1970s and 1980s was in the kinds of questions being asked by evaluators. In the 1960s, as we have seen, the main question of interest had been "What impact did the program have on its recipients?" This question was now joined—and in many instances superseded—by a host of new questions, often driven by a new vision of programs as complicated affairs with many interested parties. In this period a number of evaluators moved away from the emphasis on what Scriven called summative evaluations, which focused on program *outcomes*. Instead, evaluators argued for a variety of ways to examine the *processes within programs*. Evaluators became interested in questions concerning how programs were being implemented. For example, was the program actually doing the kinds of things it claimed? What were staff members doing with the program's clients? Did participants show up regularly, and how did they feel about the services they were receiving? Understanding programs became as important as showing what their impact on recipients had been. The focus shifted from outcome studies to generating knowledge that helped evaluators understand what a program was doing, and that could be used to improve programs.[22] Lee Cronbach played a major role in this development.

Another issue receiving increasing attention in evaluation was the relationship between the cost of a program or policy and its results. While it is possible to put some educational goals in monetary terms (for example, the increase in lifetime earnings associated with finishing high school rather than dropping out), many desirable educational and social outcomes are not easily weighed in these terms. Two different approaches, cost-benefit analysis and cost-effectiveness analysis, have been used on occasion in educational evaluation, though they remain relatively rare. Cost-effectiveness analysis in particular examines both program effectiveness and program expense, and provides policymakers with more information than is generally provided by evaluations. Since policymakers make decisions within a limited budget, information on the cost-effectiveness of various programs is obviously useful.[23]

One of the most important developments in evaluation in the late 1970s and early 1980s was the creation of a new approach to reviewing studies known as meta-analysis. Literature reviews that examined earlier evaluations in a specific field had long been used to sort out conflicting evidence. Reviewers examined dozens (sometimes hundreds) of studies to see what the weight of the evidence showed. Such reviews can provide crucial knowledge beyond that offered by any individual study. As Richard Light and David Pillemer write, "For science to be cumulative, an intermediate step between past and future research is necessary: synthesis of existing evidence." Meta-analysis provides the best way of developing such syntheses. Gene Glass was a major innovator of meta-analysis, which is a way of reviewing existing studies on a specific issue. It goes beyond earlier approaches to reviewing studies, which described the studies or categorized them as showing positive results, no results, or negative results, instead using statistical techniques to combine all the included studies. All the studies on the topic are sought out, and those of sufficient quality are then analyzed together. An *effect size* is calculated for each study, which shows how much impact the program or policy actually had. Effect sizes allow the results from numerous disparate studies, which were originally presented in various formats, to be compared with one another, pooled, and analyzed together. Whereas many large, prominent studies showed little or no program effects in the 1960s and early 1970s, meta-analyses have often found that interventions do have some effect. This finding has gone against the belief that "nothing works" in social programs, which was widely held in the 1970s and has been repeated, somewhat blindly, in the media and political circles ever since.[24] Meta-analysis has become widely accepted, though several important scholars have expressed their doubts about its value, particularly if it is not done very carefully.[25] Like other evaluation techniques, the quality of a meta-analysis depends on how well it is conducted. Meta-analyses have a certain authority in many people's eyes because of their statistical nature; some experiments and some meta-analyses deserve to be held in high regard, while others do not.

Evaluation changed a great deal in the process of becoming a definable professional endeavor over the last third of the twentieth century. Some of its major thinkers have chosen now and again to reflect on what those changes brought about, usually with mixed feelings about how much progress has actually been made. In 1991 Michael Scriven noted that evaluation had "come a long way" since the 1960s, but that "the territory of good evaluation practice is still extremely small."[26] Theoretical and methodological advances continued to be made throughout the 1990s and will no doubt continue to be made in the future. But most evaluations are still conducted by people with little or no formal training in evaluation, with too little in the way of resources, and for too short a time frame, and there is no reason to think this will change anytime soon.

This does not mean that most evaluations are "bad." They usually provide useful information for program managers, staff, or other stakeholders about how well a program is being implemented and some of the impact it is having on clients. What they generally do not do is show exactly which aspects of the program are crucial to success, or whether the theory underlying the program is correct, or how strong the program's results (if any) are on different kinds of clients. In other words, most evaluations meet neither Campbell's desire for convincing causal conclusions nor Cronbach's desire for knowledge that can be generalized to other, similar programs. They are, in many cases, useful to people directly involved with the program being evaluated. They do not provide the kind of evidence that can reasonably be used to help shape policy decisions at the state or federal levels.

Evaluation is difficult in most circumstances, and when the thing being evaluated is education it becomes even more challenging, since education is extremely complex. Attempted reforms and new programs enter into organizational settings (schools) that have multiple interacting layers; these settings are not only complicated, they are also generally resistant to any significant change. Because of this, educational reforms and programs under evaluation are often found to be less than fully implemented, making determining their effectiveness even more difficult: how, after all, do you evaluate a program that is only half there? Even when the reform or program has been fully implemented, evaluating schools and what occurs in them is a tremendously difficult task. As House wrote in 1990, "For complex entities like educational programs, there are multiple and often conflicting criteria of merit. There is immediate retention versus long-term recall, knowledge of facts versus critical thinking, more history versus more math."[27]

One of the central questions about evaluation is how results are used by decisionmakers, including politicians. It is now generally recognized that there is some direct use of evaluation evidence (known as "instrumental use") along with the kinds of "enlightenment use" that have long been recognized.[28] But if most evaluations are of less than stellar quality, how do the users of evaluation determine whether or not the evidence they are paying attention to is solid and reliable? Along with the good news that evaluation evidence is being used in multiple ways comes the risk of the *misuse* of evaluation. One way this can occur is through policy implementation of evaluation results that is so changed by the political process that the actual policy ignores, or even goes against, what the evaluation results actually demonstrate to be appropriate. As Chapter 3 shows, there is convincing evidence that smaller classes increase student achievement, if the classes are small enough and other factors—teacher quality, for example—remain the same. But the most ambitious example of class-size reduction, done in California, has (unintentionally) led to large numbers of experienced teachers leaving urban schools for suburban schools. Urban schools have been forced to employ unqualified teachers, who in many cases do not do a good job. Thus, the *specific way* smaller classes have been created in California might actually harm some of the children in them. The concept of enlightenment, by which evaluation results eventually make their way into the knowledge and assumptions of politicians and policymakers, does not really depend on the evaluation's level of excellence. Given enough publicity, any evaluation—good, mediocre, or awful—can enter into the public and political mind as "proven."

The next five chapters will trace policy decisions made on several topics over recent decades, and examine the nature of evaluation results on those five topics. The quality of evaluation evidence varies considerably from one issue to another, as does the nature of the relationship between that evidence and policy. In some cases, evaluation evidence does offer clear messages about "what works" in education, and in other instances the evidence says little with real confidence. Policymakers sometimes use evidence to help shape policy, though they may or may not use it correctly. In other instances, policymakers—and the public—are confused as to what the evidence has to say, or opposing sides on an issue both claim that "research shows" they are right and their opponents wrong. Indeed, one of the telling findings of this volume is that, despite often ignoring evaluation evidence, politicians and policymakers of all stripes want to claim that research is on their side.

Professional evaluation uses terms and methods that may seem unfamiliar to almost everyone outside the field, but many of its issues are familiar. For example, evaluators have to decide what exactly to focus on in the program or policy they are evaluating; they have to prioritize among many things. They may do so on their own, or in consultation with program managers or staff, or they may simply focus on what they are told to focus on, which may or may not be what the program is actually about. All of us face decisions that require us to set priorities, and these decisions involve judgments similar to those required of evaluators. Consider a family with a high school student trying to decide which college to attend (going to college in itself having been a prior decision). Parents might look at factors such as cost, their perception of the various schools' quality and prestige, and how close the schools are to their home. The student would probably share some of these criteria (though closeness to home might be an advantage in parents' eyes and be undesirable to the student). And the student might use other criteria, such as impressions from campus visits, whether the schools have fraternities and sororities, the quality of the schools' sports teams, or even the male-female student ratio of each school. Which issues should receive greater weight is another evaluative decision.

Each chapter in this book focuses on an important education issue, and on a few key evaluations that examine the actual results of the policy or program. On some of the topics, such as Head Start, there are dozens or even hundreds of individual evaluations. This book makes no attempt to describe each and every evaluation; doing so would lead to an extensive laundry list that would, in the end, be worth less than the sum of its parts. Evaluations might be strung together showing that one Head Start center encouraged parental involvement, several others increased student achievement in first grade, and a handful more improved student health, for example. But other evaluations would likely contradict those: at one Head Start center parental involvement might not actually help children, or student achievement might not seem to improve, or Head Start might fail to offer health care effectively. What would one make of this?

Furthermore, the quality of the evaluations varies greatly, so their results would have to be placed in the context of each study's methodology and rigor: how it showed what it showed, and how much those results could actually be trusted. And they would provide information about what happened in a few Head Start centers, not what happened in most. Such findings can be very useful for the specific local programs being evaluated in each case, but that does not mean they have much meaning for similar programs in other places, and it is exactly *that* kind of information I am trying to provide—information that applies, or could reasonably be expected to apply, to most or all settings.

This goal led me to focus on three types of evaluations. The first are evaluations that have large numbers of subjects and are conducted in multiple settings. For example, an evaluation that includes a thousand language-minority students at several dozen schools in four or five different states is more likely to provide useful information than is a more modest evaluation of one or two bilingual or immersion programs.

The second type of evaluation reviewed in this book employs a longitudinal design, meaning it follows children for a long period of time to examine the long-term effects of programs. A study of Head Start that follows children through sixth grade obviously provides more information about how attending the preschool program influences student achievement than does an evaluation that tracks children only into the first grade. These two qualities, evaluations that have large sample sizes (preferably thousands of students) and evaluations that follow students for many years after they leave the program under study, are both relatively rare. But they do occur, and they are not mutually exclusive. Several studies described in this book do both.

Finally, the third type of evaluation evidence featured in this volume is the review, which combines many studies to see what the bigger picture reveals. Reviewers determine standards that guide the type of evaluation included in their review; for example, a reviewer of Head Start might be interested in its effect on student achievement, and therefore only include evaluations that examined that as an outcome. Along with the issue studied, there are issues of quality. A reviewer might include only studies that had some sort of comparison group, so that there is some reason to believe each evaluation's results are reliable. The most effective method of review is meta-analysis, which uses statistical methods to combine the results of numerous different evaluations.

I do not mean to denigrate the vast majority of evaluations, which are smaller in scope than the evaluations I describe here. Nor is the attention I pay to experiments, quasi-experiments, and reviews (particularly meta-analyses) meant to devalue qualitative evaluation. In fact, many of the evaluation questions I find most interesting require a qualitative approach, or at least an extensive qualitative component. But qualitative evaluations and modest evaluations of whatever methodology, for all the important things they can tell various stakeholders, generally do not provide the kind of information that school districts, states, and the federal government should use when making decisions.

I have chosen five different, though sometimes related, educational issues for the following chapters. Chapter 1 focuses on Head Start, a preschool program for disadvantaged children that virtually everyone who ever picks up this book will have some knowledge of, though what they think they know may turn out to be wrong, or at least more limited than they had believed. Similarly, most of us have at least some ideas about bilingual education, the topic covered in Chapter 2. I knew that bilingual education was a highly political topic when I began this book, but I had no idea just how political; nor did I know how complicated it was. Chapter 3 focuses on the question of whether smaller classes lead to improved student achievement. Many readers will probably think, "Of course they do," while others may doubt that it would matter, assuming that factors such as innate student ability, family background, and teacher quality shape student achievement almost completely. As it turns out, the important questions are: *when* do smaller classes matter, *how small* do they have to be, *how much* difference can they make, and *for whom?*

Chapter 4 describes the tumult over social promotion, the practice of promoting children from one grade to the next whether they have learned much or not. This policy is easy to attack in a nation where (in theory, at least) people are expected to earn what they get, and where competition is not merely allowed but is believed by many to lead to highly desirable social outcomes. But in a democracy that claims to give all children opportunity despite their origin, the question of whether to promote struggling students or not leads to a much more complex issue: how to help students when they are falling far behind. Finally, Chapter 5 examines the evidence for whether the amount of money spent per student influences student achievement; this too leads to the much more complicated question of *how* and *when* more funding makes a difference. And questions of money tie back into each of the other issues covered. Head Start has never been funded at a high enough level to cover all eligible children, or to provide a truly high-quality preschool environment for the children who are enrolled. Teaching children when they come to school speaking little or no English is hard and expensive, whether it is done in their native language, in English, or in a mixture of the two. Reducing class size is directly dependent on vastly increased resources: more money to hire more teachers, and more money to create more classrooms. Similarly, serious efforts to end social promotion require money to provide special help for children who are being held back or are in danger of being held back.

I chose these five topics for several reasons. First, I wanted to look at issues that most or all school systems have to address. While alternatives to public schools have been talked about at great length in recent years—in terms of vouchers, privatization, and charter schools—my main interest was in questions that schools are already dealing with, such as language-minority children, class size, and funding. (For that matter, charter schools, private schools, and public schools managed by private companies also have to deal with the issues I discuss in this volume.) Second, I wanted to look at issues that have a fairly extensive body of evaluation. That was another reason to not examine vouchers, for example. There is now very little evidence about whether they actually have much impact, and there was even less when I began this study in late 1997. Third, I decided to avoid curriculum issues and instead focus on issues that affect children's education broadly, rather than specifically focusing on math or reading skills. (Of course some curriculums are better than others, but I think the debates between different curriculums are less interesting, and less important, than do adherents on both sides of those debates.) While there are any number of other educational issues of interest, the five I examine have a powerful influence on how schools function and how children learn, and there is enough evaluation evidence on each to tell us important things.

Education is a political realm, and almost every aspect of it is contested in America today. Some of these contests are reflected in the topics chosen for this book. Is it the federal government's job to help prepare disadvantaged children for school? And when it tries, does it do a good job? What level of government—local, state, or federal—should bear the main burden of financing public schools, and what financial role should the other levels play? Should funds be provided for boards of education, superintendents, and principals to do with as seems best to them, or should state governments and the federal government target money to specific issues or programs? Should immigrant children be taught English gradually while also being taught in their native language, or should they be immersed in English? Who should control what is taught in school? What is to be done with children who are failing? Numerous arguments about the proper nature and structure of education go on every day, in government, the media, and local communities.

In most situations, evaluations play a small (or nonexistent) role in policymaking at the state and federal level. The political nature of education means that other forces—ideology, fear of raising taxes, bureaucratic inertia, class and racial conflict, among others—play the leading role in the creation and maintenance of policy. Sometimes, however, evaluation evidence can come along at the right time and place and play a major role in the shaping of policy.

Despite evaluations' generally limited influence, advocates and opponents of particular educational reforms often announce loudly that the evidence is on their side. "Research shows" that "my view" is right is one of the most commonly heard phrases in debates over educational policies. So is, "most experts agree" with "my" opinion. Almost inevitably, *both* sides of any specific debate say that the research is on their side, and that the experts say they are right and their opponents are wrong. This occurs when the evidence is fairly clear (it is rarely crystal clear) for one side and both sides still say that research supports them and not their opponents, and it occurs when the evidence is murky and conflicted. In the first case, one side is right and the other wrong; in the second case, *both* sides are wrong.

The problem for teachers, parents, and policymakers is knowing what the best evidence actually says without first having to learn a great deal about social science research methods and then reading every study under the sun. In the following pages, I try to sort out just what the evidence does have to say on these five issues, how it has been used, and when it has been ignored. I have tried to be as unbiased as possible, but of course real "objectivity" on these kinds of issues does not exist. Even so, the evidence has changed my opinion rather markedly on two of these topics, and modified it on the other three. I hope readers will come to this book the same way I came to my research: willing to learn some things that may not fit what they thought to be true, in the interest of improving our schools.

1

What Difference Does Head Start Make?

Once we evaluate Head Start in terms of appropriate rather than inappropriate criteria, we will discover that Head Start has been far more successful than its critics would have us believe . . . [O]ver the years Head Start has been our nation's largest deliverer of health services to poor children. Also underappreciated is Head Start's pioneering effort in parent involvement . . . [and] related to the parental involvement phenomenon is the success Head Start has had in improving services to children.

—Edward Zigler, 1979

In fact, Head Start has been a gigantic dud. Experts on both the left and the right agree that it generates no measurable, permanent gains.

—Orlando Sentinel Tribune, 1993

Is Head Start a program that gives a boost to children before they enter school, perhaps even part of the answer to the problem of poverty in the United States, or is it instead "a gigantic dud," a politically popular program that does little good? Just what is Head Start, and what does it do for children? Perhaps it is best to begin with the basic facts. Head Start is a preschool program serving poor children ages three to five. It began as a summer program in the mid-1960s, but quickly developed into a school-year program that children attend for one or two years, usually in half-day sessions throughout the school year. The program stresses play and conversation, and focuses on pre-reading skills through storytelling and the labeling of items in the room. Head Start enrolls children from families living in poverty and provides its children with comprehensive care that includes a variety of health and nutritional services along with the educational component. From the program's inception, Head Start's basic philosophy has been to use the resources of the community and seek extensive parental involvement. Head Start is best understood as a program for disadvantaged families; it aims to help poor children directly as well as indirectly by trying to give their parents a boost as well. This is done in several ways. Local Head Start policy councils have always been run by parents, and parents of current or former students make up a significant portion of Head Start staffs.

Head Start has been a popular program throughout its existence, though that popularity has wavered at times, particularly among politicians. The program's popularity has fluctuated partly because the evidence about its results has been spotty, and also because it has undergone several attacks from conservative politicians. By and large, however, media coverage has been glowing, and public opinion has strongly supported Head Start. People believe that it helps children get ready for school, and the children in Head Start programs are widely seen as deserving of aid. Most Head Start centers have long waiting lists; despite its popularity the program has never managed to serve more than half of all eligible children, and for much of its history Head Start actually enrolled less than one-fourth of eligible children. There have also been many Head Start variants and add-ons, such as Follow Through and Even Start. This chapter focuses on the core Head Start program itself.

When critics of Head Start have claimed that the program does not actually help children, their charges have gotten considerable media coverage. Such criticisms have sometimes weakened Head Start politically, though they have never managed to destroy it. Supporters have responded that the program has been proven to work, and politicians of both major parties, as well as the public, have tended to agree with that assessment. But what does the actual evidence say about Head Start? What do we know about what it does and does not do for the children who participate? And can we trust what we think we know? Just who is right, Head Start supporters who claim it is one of the most successful social programs in the nation's history, or critics who claim it doesn't help poor children at all?

Preschool Education Prior to Head Start

Head Start was hardly the first program in the United States that tried to educate young children before they entered public school. Formal schooling for children under the age of five has a long, uneven past in the United States. One form, known as infant schools, began in Scotland in 1816 and spread to the United States in the late 1820s, as many European institutional and educational ideas did during the eighteenth and nineteenth centuries. In the 1830s, infant schools flourished in some large northeastern cities, including New York, Boston, Philadelphia, and in some smaller cities, particularly in Massachusetts. They were for children from poor families, and they took in children from a year and a half until they were old enough to attend public school. Some infant schools emphasized play, but others tried to teach their three- and four-year-old children to read. The popularity of infant schools was relatively short-lived, however, and by 1860 few children younger than five were attending school of any kind.[1]

Much more familiar now than infant schools, the first kindergarten in the United States was opened in 1856 by a German immigrant. Kindergartens were originally intended for the children of wealthy families, but over the last third of the nineteenth century social reformers used them to prepare children from poor families for school. Kindergartens became commonplace late in the nineteenth century, and they sometimes enrolled children well under the age of five. In the 1890s, public school systems began to include optional kindergarten for five- and six-year-old children.[2] Various other kinds of preschool programs and nurseries gained popularity across the twentieth century, sometimes only temporarily. But it was not until the creation of Head Start in the 1960s that a government-funded preschool program spread nationwide.

Planning Head Start

Head Start was different from its predecessors in a number of ways. It developed in a very specific intellectual and political context, which needs to be understood by anyone hoping to make sense out of the path the program has followed since its inception. Programs dealing with children are shaped in part by ideas about what exactly children are and how they develop. In the early 1960s, developmental psychology was a field in motion.

The belief that heredity controlled what people were and how they acted, which had dominated psychology over the first half of the twentieth century, had come under fire in the late 1950s as psychologists became increasingly aware of the importance of environment. J. McVicker Hunt's *Intelligence and Experience,* published in 1961, helped shape views of child development for much of the 1960s. Hunt was a psychology professor at the University of Illinois who had served as president of the American Psychological Association. His book was intended for a wide audience, and it got one. Hunt disagreed with the long-held belief that intelligence was fixed and inherent, instead arguing that there was a growing body of evidence that showed intelligence—which, like many others, Hunt assumed could be accurately measured by IQ tests—was actually quite malleable. He regarded IQ "as a phenotype, like height or weight, for which the genes set limits of potential development but which is finally developed through encounters with the environment."[3] Hunt spent almost half the book discussing the work of Piaget, and also described other studies done in the 1950s. Hunt concluded that it was reasonable "to consider that it might be feasible to discover ways to govern the encounters that children have with their environments, especially during the early years of their development, to achieve a substantially faster rate of intellectual development and a substantially higher adult level of intellectual capacity."[4] In other words, giving some young children a better environment could make them "smarter" for the rest of their lives. It was an optimistic argument for an optimistic time. Even better, it was clothed in the mantle of science.

Another idea gaining currency in the early 1960s, also destined to play a role in the creation of Head Start, was that there were "critical periods" when human beings were most sensitive to environmental experience. *Stability and Change in Human Characteristics,* written by Benjamin Bloom and published in 1964, argued that these critical periods occurred when humans were undergoing periods of rapid growth. And when did people grow more rapidly than in early childhood? Bloom's argument helped shape the idea that children under the age of four or five would be most susceptible to the kind of environmental aid Hunt talked about, and the media ran with the story that with proper timing, a well-planned intervention could dramatically increase a child's IQ.[5]

Ideas about the nature of American society were also changing, and these changes helped shape social policy. President Lyndon B. Johnson's War on Poverty programs (including Head Start) grew out of the realization in the early 1960s that there was still serious, extensive poverty in the United States. This should have been obvious to everyone in the 1950s, but it was most definitely not obvious to either politicians or the middle class, due in large part to the tremendous postwar economic expansion. In addition, the groups with high poverty rates were African Americans, Hispanics, and people living in rural areas, all of whom were practically invisible in media coverage and public discussions of American life in the 1950s. Exactly how President John F. Kennedy became aware of American poverty is not clear. But there was an antipoverty program being planned in 1963, and after Kennedy's death late that year, Johnson went forward with it. It was in his January 1964 State of the Union address that Johnson first used the phrase "war on poverty."[6]

One of the fundamental assumptions of the War on Poverty was that education could diminish, and eventually end, poverty in the United States. The original poverty programs developed in late 1963 consisted of education and job training targeted at teenagers and young adults, and did not include a preschool program. The first major event of the "War" was the Economic Opportunity Act of 1964, which provided for job training through the Job Corps, mobilization of the poor to help themselves through the Community Action Program, and a domestic Peace Corps known as Volunteers in Service to America (VISTA). It also created the Office of Economic Opportunity (OEO), which was given considerable autonomy to develop additional programs.[7] Across the 1960s the War on Poverty either initiated or increased funding for a slew of social programs, including Medicare, Medicaid, food stamps, legal services, Head Start, Model Cities, and two major New Deal programs, Social Security and Aid to Families with Dependent Children. (When Ronald Reagan became president in 1981 and slashed social spending, it was the programs that had been newly created in the War on Poverty that suffered most, not the surviving New Deal programs.)

In February 1964 Johnson appointed Sargent Shriver to plan the War on Poverty. Shriver, the brother-in-law of the late President Kennedy, was a good choice. He had helped found the Peace Corps and had also been president of the Chicago Board of Education. From these experiences, Shriver was reasonably knowledgeable about the problems faced by people living in poverty, in particular the multiple problems faced by poor children. He believed that preschool, immunizations and medical care, and a healthy diet could make an important difference in the lives of disadvantaged children. Shriver was also apparently aware of research by Susan Gray, whose Early Training Project sought to improve young children's motivation to achieve and their aptitude for learning. Based on her work with dozens of African-American children from urban homes, Gray seemed to show that early intervention could increase the IQ of a child with a low IQ by ten points or more.[8]

Before the end of 1964, Shriver and the OEO found themselves with a budget surplus: $300 million had been allocated for the first year of the Community Action Program (CAP), and it became obvious to the OEO that not all of it would be spent by the end of fiscal year 1965. (CAP was controversial, and many city governments were unwilling to take part, more than a little due to the fact that some CAP programs had led protests against their own local governments.) Shriver asked his research team for suggestions on the best ways to use the surplus funds, and in the ensuing discussion learned that nearly half of the 30 million Americans living in poverty were children. It was clear that helping poor children would be more politically popular than helping poor adults, particularly if that help were provided directly to the children through schooling or health care, rather than indirectly, through their parents, as with Aid to Families with Dependent Children. Unlike poor parents, disadvantaged children were generally seen as victims deserving of aid, not as people who had made bad choices or were somehow otherwise responsible for their own problems.[9] For these reasons, a program targeted toward children seemed a good way to spend the surplus funds.

Just as the early and mid-1960s were an optimistic time in political circles, allowing the creation of the War on Poverty, which would have been unthinkable (and seen as unnecessary) in the 1950s, so too were they optimistic in child development circles. Hunt's *Intelligence and Experience* was just one of many arguments for a more flexible, and therefore optimistic, view of children's development, especially when it came to IQ. The belief that children's intelligence could be improved (or harmed) by environment was becoming widespread. So was the belief that there were critical periods when children could be most effectively influenced, for good or ill. Early childhood was seen as one such time. It is not surprising, then, that the belief that early intervention in the lives of disadvantaged children could dramatically raise their IQs flourished in the early 1960s, and wound up playing an important role in OEO's program for its surplus funds: a preschool program for disadvantaged children.

In late 1964 Shriver asked his staff for advice about how a preschool should function and what it should try to accomplish. By January 1965 Dr. Robert E. Cooke, pediatrician-in-chief at Johns Hopkins Hospital, had been chosen to gather a group of experts from various fields to plan a preschool program. In keeping with the rushed planning of the War on Poverty in general, the group had only a few months for its work. Cooke's selection as the head of the Head Start Planning Committee assured that the program would be comprehensive, focusing on health issues as well as educational ones. The committee could have modeled its proposal on already-existing nursery school programs, perhaps adding something here or there, but it did not. The overall composition of the Head Start Planning Committee virtually guaranteed a comprehensive preschool program in which education was not the only, or even the most important, aspect. Overall, the committee included four physicians and three psychologists, but just two experts in early childhood education.[10]

The Head Start Planning Committee did its work conscientiously, and presented a plan for an ambitious, comprehensive preschool program that went far beyond traditional conceptions of schooling. While not completely original, it was much closer to a new invention than most social programs, which tend to rely heavily on earlier efforts. Head Start would seek to develop children's cognitive skills, in keeping with ideas about boosting IQ, but it would also do a number of other things, and it proposed to do some of them in unusual ways. One of the main goals was to improve children's motivation. Another central—and unusual—goal, in keeping with the activism of the civil rights movement and the Community Action Program, was to involve parents in fundamental ways. The influence of committee member Urie Bronfenbrenner, a psychologist at Cornell, was crucial. Bronfenbrenner was in the process of developing his ecological approach to child development, which holds that to have a lasting impact on children, you must make changes in their daily environment. You could not simply take children and place them in classrooms for a few hours a day. Their families, and perhaps even their neighborhoods, needed to support the same goals as the intervention for it to have a real impact. From this perspective, which the Planning Committee adopted, parents *had* to be strongly involved for Head Start to work. And the committee's vision extended even further: Head Start would include health care examinations and immunizations, and its extensive parent involvement would at times function as job training. In addition, it would provide social services, mental health services, nutrition education, and even hot meals. Head Start would go far beyond earlier preschool programs, and it was not at all clear that cognitive factors were its most important part. As Edward Zigler (a Planning Committee member) and Susan Muenchow point out, the committee's recommendations did not even mention the idea of raising children's IQs.[11]

Head Start Begins

The Planning Committee recommended a relatively modest start for the program, so that it could be tested in a few places and then improved before widespread implementation was attempted. Not surprisingly, given the heady feel of the years before Vietnam became a political and societal nightmare, President Johnson and Sargent Shriver chose instead to start big, with a nationwide program enrolling hundreds of thousands of children in its first year. The president's wife, Lady Bird Johnson, agreed to serve as Project Head Start's honorary chairperson. The strong support of the president had guaranteed that the program would actually be created; the strong support of the first lady greatly increased media attention. Unfortunately, the president and the first lady both talked about the program as a way to raise children's IQs, and as a result the media did the same. The belief that IQs could be dramatically increased by early interventions spread more widely as a result, as did the mistaken idea that that was Head Start's goal. The subtlety of the Planning Committee's call for a comprehensive program was lost in the excitement.[12] Because of President Johnson's insistence on beginning Head Start on a grand scale, and subsequent funding increases, the program began in the summer of 1965 with 561,000 children enrolled. By late 1966 there were also almost 200,000 children in half-day programs that ran during the school year.[13]

How did a program that was being planned in January and February of 1965 get up and running, serving more than half a million children, by the summer of 1965? Through foresight, hard work, and with more than a little guesswork and chaos. Shriver chose Dr. Julius Richmond, then chief of pediatrics at a large university hospital and later to become the surgeon general of the United States, to direct Head Start. Richmond's most important decision was probably his conclusion that the staff-to-child ratio being considered, one adult for every thirty children, was unacceptable. Instead, a ratio of one to five, or one teacher and two adult aides for every fifteen children, was chosen.[14] Another equally important decision was reached in a more haphazard way. Jule Sugarman, soon to be named Head Start's associate director, was asked by Shriver what the program's per-child cost would be. Shriver gave Sugarman one hour to make an estimate, and Sugarman and a colleague came up with a cost of $180 per child for an eight-week summer program. That became the figure cited in press coverage, and by local communities applying for Head Start funds. Not surprisingly, Head Start was given the name "Project Rush-Rush" in Washington.[15] But the rushing was done with purpose. Sugarman made extensive outreach efforts to impoverished communities, encouraging them to apply for Head Start funds. He even enlisted prominent women in Washington to telephone community organizations, school boards, and church groups in the 300 poorest communities in the nation, and sent 125 federal interns into those communities to assist them in developing programs.[16]

Given the rush to find applicants across the nation, it was inevitable that early Head Start programs varied tremendously. Interestingly, the quality of Head Start programs in the mid- and late 1960s may have varied more on issues of childhood education than on health or parent participation. The desire to give local communities considerable leeway and the low number of early childhood educators on the Planning Committee meant that the planning documents contained only broad, general recommendations that offered limited guidance. There was no single, agreed-upon curriculum for Head Start centers to follow. Another problem caused by the program's quick start-up was a severe shortage of qualified teachers, particularly teachers ready to work for Head Start's low wages. As a result, in the summer of 1965 almost half of Head Start staff members nationwide had had no prior experience with preschools or with teaching poor children.[17]

Every Head Start center had its own way of implementing the program. One Los Angeles umbrella organization for a number of Head Start locales managed to hire reasonably qualified teachers in the first year; most of the new teachers had experience in preschool programs, and the rest were elementary school teachers. Six days of additional training were then provided for the teachers. Although the staff was unusually qualified, the programs in these Los Angeles Head Starts represented the variety of activities at Head Start programs elsewhere. Learning through the use of language, and through dancing and singing, was emphasized. Various forms of play were expected to help children develop learning and social skills. Teachers consulted with parents and other community members to understand the cultures, languages, and needs of the children's families and neighborhoods. June Solnit Sale relates a story that says a great deal about how Head Start's educational and social components hoped to function: "An observer could see disbelief in the faces of some of the neighborhood people when a nursery school teacher said to two children who were fighting, 'I know you must be angry, but I won't let you hurt each other'—then held the children apart and talked to them, and asked them to talk to each other, about their anger without meting out any punishment."[18]

Early Evaluations

Head Start enjoyed widespread political support right from the beginning, but how well did it actually work? It was a comprehensive program with a network of services intended to help children, and it was supported by a wide variety of people for a number of reasons. Raising IQ's was just one of its goals, and its planners did not really expect it to manage that feat, but even though this was far from the top of their list of goals for the program, it was what the public had been led to expect. It is therefore not surprising that the early evaluations of Head Start focused on IQ: it was a sexy topic, it was easy to measure, and if there actually was improvement it could be expected to have a long-term impact. Furthermore, it was one of the few goals of Head Start that evaluators knew how to study. As Edward Zigler has written in looking back, "We did not know what to measure." Finally, the important role played by psychologists in early evaluations of the program, along with the expectations created by politicians and covered extensively by the media, made IQ testing almost unavoidable.[19]

Like Head Start itself, the early evaluations of the program had little time for planning; the Head Start Planning Committee had debated whether to even include an evaluation component before eventually deciding to do so. The results of the early evaluations gained wide attention, boosting Head Start's profile even further and increasing public expectations for what it could achieve. From 1965 to 1968, a number of evaluations seemed to show that children who attended Head Start did in fact experience immediate, dramatic increases in their IQ test scores. In testimony before Congress in 1966, Sargent Shriver cited this early research as showing that Head Start had raised children's IQs by as much as ten points.[20] The evaluation findings during the late 1960s were not all in agreement, however. Some studies that followed children into kindergarten or first grade found that Head Start graduates started off more prepared for school than other children from comparable backgrounds, but they also found that this advantage "faded out" and other children quickly caught up. The impact of Head Start was real, but whether or not that impact *lasted* any significant period of time was another issue altogether. And what exactly that impact actually was remained far from clear. The work of Edward Zigler and Earl Butterfield showed that the same positive results found in the more positive evaluations of Head Start could come from higher motivation, rather than actual increases in children's IQs. Children who had higher expectations of success would do better on IQ tests not because their intelligence had grown, but because they were more willing and able to use their intelligence while being tested.[21]

With doubt increasing about the ability of Head Start to do what its *political* founders, President and Lady Bird Johnson, had claimed it would—raise IQs—plans were made for a major national evaluation. The Office of Economic Opportunity awarded the evaluation contract to the Westinghouse Learning Corporation in tandem with Ohio University in June 1968. Like everything else associated with Head Start in the early years, this evaluation was begun in a rush: it was to be completed by April 1969. Though Zigler and other highly placed officials had argued against it, IQ scores and school achievement tests were at the heart of the evaluation[22]—although this focus would have been difficult to avoid, given expectations about Head Start's ability to increase IQ. In addition, there were few trustworthy measures for the gains Head Start's managers actually expected it to provide. This was particularly true for Head Start's major goal, instilling social competence, which basically meant a child's day-to-day ability to function, to do well in school, to relate successfully to adults and other children. Finally, the rushed nature of the evaluation and the demand for quick results meant that it would be short-term study, not longitudinal. Although following children through school and seeing how Head Start children did in later years would have been the best way to study its impact, this was not an option. The Westinghouse/Ohio study's executive summary admitted its limitations: "The study did not address the question of Head Start's medical or nutritional impact. It did not measure its effects on the stability of family life. It did not assess its impact on the total community, on the schools, on the morale and attitudes of children while they were in the program." In other words, the evaluators admitted that their study did not

even try to examine most of the effects that Head Start's creators had intended the program to cause. Nonetheless, the study's authors believed
that the questions they had addressed "were the right questions to ask
first."[23]

The study began under President Johnson, but it was concluded and released under his successor, Richard Nixon, a Republican who was much
less enthusiastic about programs for the poor. Before release of the report,
the media began to hear that the results of the Westinghouse/Ohio evaluation of Head Start would be negative. At the same time, Congress was considering whether to reauthorize Head Start and other War on Poverty programs. Political battle lines were being drawn between a Congress that
supported most of the antipoverty programs and a president intent on
changing or eliminating many of them. In this contentious atmosphere,
the Westinghouse/Ohio working draft was released as a preliminary draft
on April 14.[24]

The Westinghouse/Ohio study looked at 104 Head Start centers and
nearly 2,000 children who had attended Head Start in its first three years of
existence. More than two-thirds of these children had attended summer
programs, while the remainder had gone to school-year programs. A comparison group was developed of almost 2,000 children who, like the Head
Start sample, were in either the first, second, or third grade at the time of
the evaluation. The study found no positive results from the summer Head
Start programs, but it did find small positive results for the first- and second-grade children who had attended school-year-long Head Start programs. The study recognized that Head Start did more than simply try to
improve cognition directly. However, the Westinghouse/Ohio report's executive summary—the only part of the massive volume that most journalists and politicians were likely to bother reading—lumped summer
and school-year Head Start programs together and stated that its "most
justifiable conclusion" was that Head Start had not produced any meaningful gains. It recommended that summer programs be phased out and
converted into full-year programs, which should in turn be improved in
the hope that they would become more effective.[25]

How good was the Westinghouse/Ohio study? Scholars rushed to re-
analyze the data. Urie Bronfenbrenner, a member of the Planning Committee, did so and concluded that the tangible benefits of Head Start did,
in fact, fade away in elementary school. He believed this was partly due to
the brief amount of time children were in most Head Start programs,

which was too short to have lasting results. In keeping with his ecological approach, Bronfenbrenner also credited the "fade-out" of Head Start's impact to the gap between what children experienced at school and what they experienced at home. Given Bronfenbrenner's status as one of Head Start's best-known founders, his acceptance of fade-out was another serious blow to the program.[26]

However, not everyone agreed that the Westinghouse/Ohio study's results were telling. A number of social scientists criticized the study on a range of issues, including the obvious question of whether or not studying IQ was an appropriate way to measure Head Start's success. In fact, the chief statistical consultant to the evaluation resigned in protest and refused to accept his pay, because he viewed the evaluation design as flawed and the study's conclusions as inaccurate.[27] Another criticism leveled at the report was that its sampling procedures had been faulty. One reanalysis of the data found that Head Start centers had been effective, particularly for African-American children in cities.[28]

Rather than worrying about the Westinghouse findings or arguing against their validity, some supporters of Head Start believed that the program had worked but that weak elementary schools had failed to build on its achievements. Others said the problem was that intervention needed to occur earlier, that by the time children were three, the effects of poverty had already dimmed their potential.[29]

Head Start in the 1970s: Survival and Supporting Evidence

The most significant result of the Westinghouse study was to shift Head Start away from summer sessions and toward school-year programs that gave children much longer exposure. By 1970 the majority of children in Head Start were in nine-month programs that ran concurrently with the public school year.[30] Another result of the Westinghouse study and the criticisms leveled at it was an attempt to broaden expectations beyond IQ measures. The Office of Child Development (OCD), which was the agency overseeing Head Start in the early 1970s, made social competence an official goal of the program. This included cognitive issues but also other matters, such as how children deal with their environment. The OCD commissioned three different efforts to develop an operating definition of social competence, in the hope it would become easier for evaluators to measure, but none of the efforts succeeded. Even with these changes, the

Westinghouse report, along with the change in the presidency from Johnson to Nixon, dramatically weakened political support for Head Start. By 1977 funding had decreased, the program enrolled only half as many children as it had in the 1960s, and Head Start was probably fortunate to still exist at all.[31]

Conservatives looking back in the 1980s on the War on Poverty claimed that it failed miserably. Most scholars studying the social programs of the 1960s, however, argue that they did not exactly fail; instead, it was believed they were never really tried. Certainly funding levels for the programs never approached what would have been necessary to have a strong impact on poverty. There were a number of reasons for this, including a rather simplistic view of how poverty functioned and how it could be ended. Most important, however, President Lyndon Johnson's increasing preoccupation with the Vietnam War took energy and support away from social programs. Head Start funding had already dropped from $350 million in 1967 to $316 million in 1968, before the Westinghouse study appeared. Once in office in 1969, Richard Nixon moved Head Start to the Department of Health, Education, and Welfare (HEW). When Edward Zigler replaced Jule Sugarman as overseer of Head Start, he learned of an Office of Management and Budget plan to gradually phase out Head Start over the next three years. Zigler's lobbying efforts and the program's grassroots support saved it. There was also some crucial support in the administration. Caspar Weinberger, secretary of HEW in the early 1970s, became a Head Start supporter after visits to some local programs. Weinberger helped keep the program afloat, aided by President Nixon's preoccupation with Watergate (a counterpoint to Johnson's preoccupation with Vietnam, which had weakened Head Start a few years before).[32] The only Democratic president of the 1970s, Jimmy Carter, supported Head Start. In 1977 Carter and Congress agreed on a $150 million funding increase, bringing the program's annual funding to $625 million. But there was a severe recession in progress throughout Carter's term. Even though he raised the Head Start budget nearly 75 percent, inflation was eating away at purchasing power, and the number of poor children was growing. In 1980, despite President Carter's efforts, fewer than 30 percent of eligible children were enrolled in the preschool program. Even though Head Start itself had not grown much during the 1970s, preschool was becoming more and more popular throughout society. The number of three- and four-year-old children enrolled in preschool had almost doubled between 1970 and 1980; of those attending preschool, just one-third of African-American children were in private preschool programs, compared with two-thirds of white children.[33]

Evidence supporting Head Start's effectiveness began to appear at the same time that Carter was trying to increase its funding. In 1978 the Consortium for Longitudinal Studies released evaluation results that confirmed the belief that IQ boosts were temporary and tended to fade away within a few years. But the consortium's findings also included long-lasting positive effects from Head Start. Children who had attended the preschool program were less likely to need special education classes (which tend to be very expensive), and they were somewhat less likely to be held back a grade than children who had not attended Head Start. These school benefits clearly lasted until at least age twelve. And this study was much more rigorous in nature than the Westinghouse report had been, with a good control group and a longitudinal design that followed the same children year after year.[34] The next year another study was released that followed 2,100 low-income children who had attended preschool in the 1960s and showed similar results, including the finding that Head Start graduates were only half as likely to become high school dropouts as were children from a comparison group. *Newsweek* wrote that the study "provides persuasive evidence that pre-school training pays remarkable personal and social dividends in later life." The *Washington Post* also described the study, claiming that it refuted the results of the Westinghouse report.[35]

The Winding Road of the 1980s: Political Attacks and the Perry Preschool Program

In early 1980 President Carter asked the secretary of Health and Human Services to create a panel to review Head Start and suggest future directions for the program. The committee was chaired by Yale psychology professor Edward Zigler, who had been a member of the original Head Start Planning Committee in 1965 as well as director of the Office of Child Development in the early 1970s. Other members included Dr. Robert Cooke, Urie Bronfenbrenner, children's advocate Marian Wright Edelman, Julius Richmond, Jule Sugarman, and the presidents of the National Head Start Association and the National Head Start Parent Association.[36] It would have been almost impossible to assemble a group more knowledgeable about Head Start, or more committed to its becoming as good a program as possible.

The committee found that Head Start was a success, particularly because of its role in providing health care to poor children. It also claimed (based on rather weak evidence) that Head Start's educational benefits did not "fade out," and that the program helped parents as well as children. But the committee acknowledged that there were also problems with the program. Inflation was weakening the quality of many Head Start programs by forcing cutbacks in staffing and services. Not enough technical assistance was being delivered to local Head Start grantees, due to a lack of sufficient staff at the regional level. Head Start teachers were poorly paid, and did not receive basic benefits such as health insurance or retirement plans. And Head Start was serving only 20 percent of eligible children.[37] The committee argued that protecting the quality of Head Start programs was its "first priority" in the future. It proposed performance standards to protect staff-child ratios and small class size in Head Start classrooms, and better pay and benefits for Head Start teachers. It also recommended a "controlled expansion" of the program to serve more children. The committee made a number of other proposals, all geared to improve the quality of Head Start programs and to reach more disadvantaged children. Finally, it said further evaluation was needed.[38]

In late 1980 a study was released that would gain more coverage in media and political debates over Head Start in the next fifteen years than any other—and it was not even an evaluation of Head Start itself. The 1980 report showed that children who had attended the Perry Preschool in Ypsilanti, Michigan, in the 1960s were doing noticeably better at the age of fifteen than counterparts who had not attended preschool. The results of the Perry Preschool program were covered widely by the media, in no small part because the Carnegie Corporation, which had helped fund the study, also helped publicize its findings. *Newsweek's* coverage was fairly typical. It reported that children who had attended Perry Preschool at ages three and four—all of whom were from impoverished African-American families—scored higher on reading, language, and math achievement tests than did children from a control group. They were only half as likely to need special education classes as the control group, and were less likely to exhibit delinquent behavior. For *Newsweek,* and for most other observers, the Perry results showed that preschool works. Other media reports made the same points, with some also highlighting the study's claims that spending money on preschool would save society money in the long run, because children would be less likely to need expensive special education classes and other social services.[39]

What was the Perry Preschool program, and what did its evaluation really show? How trustworthy were its findings? Did they apply to Head Start? To answer these questions we have to go back to the early 1960s, when David Weikart, the director of special services for the public school system of Ypsilanti, began a preschool program for disadvantaged children with state and local funds. The Perry Preschool program was designed as a longitudinal experiment to examine the impact of early intervention on disadvantaged children as they grew up. It began "as a local evaluation for a local audience." Children were chosen for the program partly because their families lived in poverty. Their parents averaged only a ninth-grade education. Half the families were on welfare, and almost half were single-parent households. In 42 percent of the families the parent or parents were unemployed, and most that were employed were unskilled and worked for low wages. The households were crowded, averaging seven people in a five-room house. All the families were African-American. Another basis for selecting children was that they had low scores on IQ tests given at age three, "in the borderline retarded range of 70 to 85."[40]

Perry took in 123 children over a five-year span, from 1962 to 1966. In 1962 a group of four-year-olds entered the program and received one year of preschool, while another group of three-year-olds entered and received two years of preschool. For each of the next three years, another group of three-year-olds entered and received two years of preschool. By combining children in preschool over a number of years, the project's designers believed that their results would indicate more about the potential of the approach than if they studied just one year's worth of students. Each year, children in the chosen sample were randomly assigned to either the experimental group (which attended preschool) or to the control group (which did not attend preschool). Actually, the assignment was not strictly random, because the project managers tried to match the experimental and control groups on the basis of their families' average socioeconomic status, their initial cognitive ability, and sex ratios.[41]

Of course, the word *preschool* can mean many things: a summer program or a nine-month program or a year-round program, a half-day program or a full-day program, a program concentrating on cognitive skills or one that tries to teach social skills or improve children's health. In Perry, children in the experimental group attended a preschool program weekday mornings, for a total of twelve and a half hours a week. There were also home visits to the child and mother that lasted one and a half hours a week. The program ran for approximately thirty weeks each year, from mid-October until the end of May. Each classroom had between twenty and twenty-five children and four teachers, for a teacher-child ratio of one to five or six. The program focused on cognitive achievement: its goal "was to help children acquire the intellectual strengths they would need in school."[42]

When its children were examined at age fifteen, the results of the Perry Preschool program were significant, though some were more visible than others. Children who had gone through the program had shown increased IQ scores during kindergarten and first grade, but these had faded by second grade. Even so, the impact of their temporarily higher IQ scores may have been powerful. Children who had gone through the program went to kindergarten with an average IQ of 95 instead of 84. Informal tracking of children in the minds of teachers, and in the view of the school system, often begins in the first months of kindergarten, so higher IQ scores, even temporary ones, may have a powerful impact on how children are viewed. They may also affect how children see themselves in relation to schooling. The study's authors argued that "the child's initial orientation towards school tasks would then be solidified by a greater commitment to schooling and by adoption of a student role consistent with school success." Beyond IQ scores, other notable improvements did not fade. Children who had attended preschool spent much less time in special education classes than did children in the control group. Children who had attended Perry Preschool were seen by their elementary school teachers as having higher school motivation than children in the control group. They also placed a higher value on the importance of schooling at age fifteen. Their parents reported that they were more likely to talk about what they were doing in school at age fifteen, compared with the reports of parents of children in the control group.[43] In other words, children who had attended the preschool were more interested in, and positive about, school than the children in the control group.

All of these things are significant, but how did preschool attendance influence actual school achievement, as measured by standardized tests and grades? In elementary school, children in the experimental group generally did better on school achievement tests than did children in the control group. At age fourteen they were still scoring higher on achievement tests than the control group. By the end of high school, 19 percent of the experimental group had received special education services for least one year, compared with 39 percent of the control group (the study contained some evidence that went beyond age fifteen). In addition, children in the experimental group exhibited less deviant behavior in school and less delinquent behavior than did children in the control group.[44] Almost any way one looked at the evidence, children who had attended Perry Preschool were better students than the children who had not gone to preschool.

The evaluation of Perry Preschool also included a cost-benefit analysis, which argued that the money spent on preschool resulted in considerable savings to society in later years. It claimed a whopping 248 percent return on the original investment in preschool; in other words, for every dollar spent on preschool, society as a whole saved $2.48. The majority of the savings came through an increase in the projected lifetime earnings of children in the experimental group, with additional savings coming from the reduced time children spent in expensive special education classes.[45]

Over the years since 1980, follow-up reports have added to the evaluation's findings; they are described briefly later in this chapter. The most impressive thing about the Perry Preschool program is its longitudinal nature: it examines results when the children are teenagers, young adults just out of high school, and twenty-seven-year-old adults. Unlike many longitudinal studies, in which subjects "drop out" and become difficult or impossible to find, Perry has had very low attrition. In addition, its findings are based on data from a number of sources, including IQ tests, school achievement tests, multiple interviews with the subjects and their parents, teacher ratings, and school records.[46] And unlike many educational innovations, the Perry Preschool classes were randomized. Because of all these factors, the Perry findings are widely (though not unanimously) regarded as rigorous and convincing. Perhaps the chief reason for doubt is the small number of children involved.

But another question about the Perry findings remains: Do they really apply to Head Start? There are obviously similarities between Head Start preschool programs and Perry, but there are also important differences. For one thing, the teachers in the Perry program were more highly qualified than the vast majority of Head Start teachers, and the teacher-student ratio was better. The Perry Preschool program also included home visits and, for most children, included two years of preschool. These are significant differences, and to say that the Perry study shows that Head Start works is inaccurate, as its authors have recognized. The Perry results may say little that is pertinent to many current Head Start programs. The programs are different in important ways, and some of those differences favor Head Start, such as its health component, its provision of social services, and its strong parental involvement. What the Perry results do show is that a high-quality preschool effort can have important long-term effects on disadvantaged children. In other words, the *potential* of Head Start to make a significant educational difference is real. Claims by the media or by politicians—who do not mention it but are clearly citing it, particularly when they give specific dollar amounts for what preschool "saves"—that the Perry results are a *vindication* of Head Start *as it exists* have little merit.

When President Ronald Reagan took office in early 1981, he intended to reduce government spending on social programs; neither the Perry findings nor the fifteenth-anniversary report on Head Start, described earlier in this chapter, mattered to the incoming administration. Reagan promptly proposed repealing the legislation that authorized Head Start and sending its funding to states as block grants, for each state to use as it chose. Reagan succeeded in slashing funding for a number of programs, but as it turned out, Head Start was not one of them. The program's supporters rallied to its defense, and the White House was flooded with calls and letters opposing the change. Head Start also received help from an unexpected source in the Reagan cabinet. Former secretary of health, education, and welfare Caspar Weinberger, who was Reagan's secretary of defense, had been a strong supporter of Head Start in the early 1970s, and he came to the program's aid again. By June 1981 Reagan had included Head Start within his limited safety net. It was still under fire, however. In December David Stockman, director of the Office of Management and Budget, proposed phasing out Head Start over four years and including the funds as part of a block grant to states. But because the program was popular with the public, much of Congress, and even members of Reagan's own cabinet, Head Start survived. In fact, overall spending for the program actually rose during Reagan's administration—but the number of children in the program rose more quickly. From 1979 to 1984 the number of poor children in the United States grew by 30 percent; partly because of this growth, the participation rate for Head Start fell by more than 220 percent over the same years. In addition, by 1989 Head Start's per-child spending had dropped by more than $400, adjusted for inflation. Head Start's program quality, which had been the chief concern of the fifteenth-anniversary report, was clearly damaged.[47]

The Consortium for Longitudinal Studies, mentioned briefly above, had released a report in 1978 that favored preschool education. The Consortium's main findings were released in 1983 and drew considerable attention from the media and from social scientists interested in early childhood intervention. Eleven different research groups concerned with early education, including the Perry Preschool evaluators and two Head Start researchers, had formed the consortium in 1975. The 1983 report described each of the groups' studies, all of which were longitudinal designs that followed their subjects for many years, and included a pooled analysis of all the data. Most of the children in the preschool studies were poor, and many were African American. Each of the studies used measures of intelligence, attitudes toward school, school achievement, teacher ratings, and self-concept to determine the results of the different preschool programs. In addition, some of the studies tried to develop or use newer, subtler measures. The pooled analysis showed an IQ increase that diminished in the early grades and vanished by the sixth grade. Math and reading achievement scores were improved in the early grades, but that increase also vanished by the sixth grade. However, the children who had attended preschool had better "achievement orientation" at age fifteen than did the control group, and their parents had higher aspirations for them. The results on children's likelihood of being placed in special education were striking: by high school graduation, just 13 percent of the experimental group had been placed in a special education classroom, compared with 31 percent of the control group.[48] This evidence seemed to confirm that some of the ongoing benefits found in the Perry Preschool evaluation existed in other programs, including some Head Start programs.

In late 1984, the Perry Preschool Program released the latest results of its ongoing evaluation, which had now tracked its subjects to the age of nineteen. The study's earlier findings were reiterated and built on with additional evidence. Children who had attended preschool had higher achievement test scores and fewer failing grades. They also had higher grade-point averages than children in the control group, though the difference was small, slightly above a C average for the experimental group compared with a C− average in the control group. The experimental group that had received preschool education had spent much less time in special education. Children who had participated in the preschool were more likely to have graduated from high school, and more had either gone to college or received later vocational training than had members of the control group. At the end of the interviews with the nineteen-year-olds, each was given a multiple-choice test designed to examine skills considered necessary for economic and educational success. The experimental group scored significantly higher on this test than did the control group.[49]

Although the study participants had been out of high school only a short while, the study found the experimental group more likely to be working steadily. They had also been employed more total months at ages eighteen and nineteen than the control group, and had had fewer months of unemployment since leaving high school. The study estimated that over the course of their lifetime those who had attended preschool would earn, on average, almost $25,000 more (in 1981 dollars) than would the control group members. They also estimated that members of the experimental group would receive, on average, almost $15,000 less in welfare benefits than would members of the control group.[50] The authors of the Perry Preschool evaluation also argued that the experimental group showed greater social responsibility than the control group. They were less likely to have been arrested, less likely to be sent to juvenile court, and had spent fewer months on probation than the control group. For example, 31 percent of the preschool group had been arrested or charged, as juveniles or adults, compared with 51 percent of the control group.[51]

Probably the most important thing in this updated version of the Perry evaluation, for both politicians and the media, was its continued economic analysis. The study's authors now claimed that the eventual savings gained from each dollar spent on preschool were far higher than their earlier estimate. They stated that for every dollar spent, an astounding $7.01 was saved by society. The bulk of predicted benefits came through greater earnings after the age of nineteen by children who had attended preschool, just as the 1980 report had claimed. Money was also saved because children who had attended preschool were less likely to need special education classes, less likely to commit crimes, and less likely to be on welfare.[52] As with the first Perry report, which followed children to the age of fifteen, the results were impressive but not necessarily relevant to what Head Start programs were achieving. In a chapter titled "The Lessons of Early Childhood Research," the authors of the Perry Preschool report argued that quality was the key to achieving long-term effectiveness from a preschool program.[53] But if they were right, the question remained: Did most Head Start programs have the kind of quality needed to produce the kinds of positive long-term outcomes found in the Perry study? The Perry Preschool report authors credited their study as the "cornerstone of a body of longitudinal research" that was having a "major impact on federal policies."[54] Whether that influence made sense, however, was another question. Perry had also played a significant role in the creation and expansion of preschool programs at the state level. By 1985 more than half of the nation's states had passed some sort of legislation providing for preschools, and a number of policymakers cited the Perry findings as having influenced them. Some state programs targeted at-risk children, seeking to identify them and provide help. A few state programs, most notably in California, worked hand in hand with Head Start; in most states, however, there was little coordination between state preschool programs and Head Start.[55]

The media had little doubt about the meaning of the Perry findings. *U.S. News and World Report* wrote, inaccurately, "the findings amounted to glowing endorsement of 'Head Start.'" The article cited the study's multiple findings, that children who had attended preschool were more likely to graduate from high school and to attend some form of higher education, less likely to be arrested or charged with a crime or to receive welfare payments than children in the control group.[56] That these findings for one specific preschool program, in one Michigan city twenty years earlier, were highly relevant to a national ongoing program was taken for granted, even though the design of the two programs was different in fundamental ways. They were both "preschool programs," and the media did not see beyond that title. To be fair, there were occasional doubts voiced in the media, but the type of coverage provided by *U.S. News and World Report* was by far the most widespread: Perry showed that Head Start works. Scholars and program people who should have known better made the same mistake. In a 1986 book on the Great Society's legacy, an essay entitled "Did the Great Society and Subsequent Initiatives Work?" stated that "in perhaps the most thorough analysis of early childhood programs, researchers found that" Head Start children had various advantages over other children. However, the results that were being cited were from the Perry findings when its children were nineteen years of age, not from a study of Head Start.[57]

Although Head Start survived during the Reagan presidency, it did so on a limited budget. Press coverage remained generally favorable. A *Los Angeles Times* editorial in February 1988 stated that "poor youngsters benefit immensely from solid preschool programs like Head Start. That is well-documented, but the problem is that there are not enough desks in Head Start classrooms for thousands of children in many cities."[58] It was—as usual—not completely clear what evidence of Head Start's success the author was referring to, but there could be no question about the waiting lists: far more parents wanted their children in Head Start classrooms than the government was willing to accommodate. In 1978, 25 percent of eligible children had been enrolled in Head Start. By 1987, it had fallen to below 19 percent. In April 1988, *Education Week* reported that only 16 percent of children eligible for Head Start were actually being helped. These program reductions happened at the worst possible time, just as the percentage of children who were living in poverty was rising from 17 percent of American children in the 1970s to an appalling 25 percent in 1983.[59]

There was some direct evidence in the mid-1980s that Head Start programs were having positive effects on the children who attended them. One review of several hundred studies concluded that Head Start children had better nutrition, were more likely to have been immunized, and enjoyed better health than comparable children who had not attended Head Start. Individual studies showed that Head Start children adjusted better to school than they probably would have otherwise, had fewer absences in later years of schooling, and were less likely to be held back ("flunked") than comparable children who had not attended preschool.[60] While these results were less compelling than the Perry findings, they were actually about Head Start programs themselves, and seemed to fit fairly well with what Perry showed. Similarly, a study in Maryland compared children who had attended Head Start with the school population as a whole and found that the children did better than they would have without Head Start, but they did not fare nearly as well as the overall school population. The study had been completed in the spring of 1985 by the educational accountability department of Maryland's Montgomery County school system and given to members of the board of education, "but attracted no additional attention." The study examined three groups of Head Start children, born in 1966, 1970, and 1974, in one of the nation's richest counties. As of 1983–84, when the children in the oldest cohort were high school seniors, their academic achievement was well below average, and they were three times as likely to be in special education as the "average" child in the county. And those Head Start graduates not in special education classes were far more likely to score poorly on standardized tests than the overall school population.[61] The report showed something anyone with common sense would know: even if Head Start gave disadvantaged children an important boost, it could not by itself give them the overall advantages enjoyed by upper-middle-class children.

Remember that Head Start was conceived as a program for both children and their parents. The *New York Times* reported that Head Start could have "dramatic effect on parents." "Many have gone to school, gotten jobs and have become more involved in their communities, according to Head Start officials, experts who have studied the program, and the parents themselves." Edward Zigler was quoted as saying, "I don't believe that 15 years later you would see the tremendous difference we are seeing just by having put a child in a preschool program for a year. There are no magic bullets." The powerful impact the program had on some parents was clear to everyone involved with the program (though it was not immediately evident exactly what "tremendous difference" Zigler meant). Parental involvement had been a key component right from the start, and it could be argued that it was one of Head Start's advantages over the Perry Preschool program. Head Start has built-in mechanisms for parental involvement: parents vote on all administrative decisions, including hiring teachers, and volunteer as teacher's aides. Through their involvement, many Head Start parents become more effective in their role as parents, and sometimes more effective workers and wage earners as well.[62]

Another obvious strength of Head Start is the health care it provides. Children receive dental exams, and are often then referred to clinics or private dentists for follow-up care. For many children, and even for many of their parents, this is their first contact with a dentist. One of the goals of the program is to bring the entire family into the medical system. An impressive 98 percent of Head Start children receive medical and dental screenings. The program also makes sure that children receive appropriate immunizations and undergo routine vision, speech, and hearing tests, and their height and weight are measured regularly. (Through the screenings, approximately 16 percent are diagnosed with a disability.) Good nutrition is also stressed, and all children in half-day programs receive at least one meal each day. While these kinds of services receive far less attention than test scores, they were a central part of Head Start's original mission, and they remain one of the program's most important functions.

Despite evidence of its successes, Head Start also faced many problems in the mid-1980s, some of which had been there from the beginning. Most obvious to some was the low pay for Head Start teachers. A government report by the inspector general of the Department of Health and Human Services in the mid-1980s showed that roughly 75 percent of all staff members collected unemployment compensation during off-season summer months. Staff members viewed this as reasonable and even necessary because of their low pay, but since the money for unemployment insurance came from program funds, the drain threatened the quality of services. In 1988, almost half of all Head Start teachers earned less than $10,000 a year. The average beginning salary of a Head Start teacher with a college degree was just $12,074. In part because of this disastrously low pay, in the mid-1980s annual staff turnover approached 50 percent.[63]

Presidents Bush and Clinton, and the Search for Full Funding

The Republican attitude toward Head Start changed dramatically during Vice President George Bush's 1988 campaign for the presidency, which featured repeated statements that he wanted to be the "education president." In keeping with that goal, Bush called for greatly increased funding for Head Start to make it available for all eligible four-year-olds. Once in the White House, President Bush did initiate an increase in Head Start funding. But his proposal in early 1989, authorized by the House of Representatives, fell far short of "full funding." Bush sought to raise Head Start funds by approximately 10 percent, pending Senate approval. The bill was accompanied by a report from a group of educators and business executives—the Committee for Economic Development—estimating that every dollar spent on Head Start and similar programs would save society five dollars in the long run.[64]

Along with increased funding came a crucial question: What should that money be used to do? President Bush wanted more children enrolled in Head Start, and wanted the money to help a higher percentage of eligible four-year-olds to attend, rather than bringing more three-year-olds into the program. It was certainly a reasonable goal to enroll all eligible four-year-olds for one year of preschool, before trying to increase the number of children who would receive two years of Head Start. But others argued that the additional funds should be used to improve the *quality* of existing Head Start programs so that the children who were enrolled would receive more effective help, rather than expanding extant preschools and creating new ones. There were a number of ways in which more money could improve existing quality, several of which involved teachers. Low teacher salaries could be increased, for example, or more teachers could be hired to address program deterioration over the years. In 1965 the staff-student ratio of Head Start across the nation had been one to five, but by 1989 it had fallen to one to ten. Another potential use of new money was to lengthen the school day. In 1989, 82 percent of children in Head Start were in programs with four-hour sessions, and some advocates proposed a shift toward full-day sessions.[65] In a May 1990 *New York Times* op-ed, two of the major figures in the Perry Preschool program, Lawrence Schweinhart and David Weikart, agreed with President Bush's desire to increase Head Start funding, but they disagreed with his desire to increase enrollment, believing that new funds should be used to improve quality. Weikart and Schweinhart recognized the need for expansion but argued that low annual salaries, averaging just $12,074 for Head Start teachers ($15,403 for teachers with college degrees), damaged the quality of many Head Start centers. In addition, they argued that research into the long-term effectiveness of Head Start was badly needed.[66]

President Bush continued over the next few years to seek more money for Head Start (though never approaching full funding), and also maintained his belief that increased funding should go to enrolling more four-year-olds. For fiscal year 1991 he asked for $1.9 billion, an increase of $500 million, and proposed using it to increase Head Start enrollment from 450,000 children a year to 630,000 students. Congress then suggested increasing funding by far more than Bush requested. It was the first time either Congress or the White House had suggested fully funding the program in earnest. Of course, authorizing funding targets did not mean that the targets would be met in later years, as Congress often appropriates far less actual money for programs than it authorizes. Head Start's funding for fiscal 1991 had been authorized at $2.386 billion, for example, but Congress had appropriated only $1.951 billion. On November 3, 1990, President Bush signed a bill authorizing $20 billion over the next four years for Head Start, which would have fully funded the program by 1994 if Congress had actually provided the money in its entirety (which Congress did not do).[67]

Both politicians and the media tend to have simplistic views of poverty, as well as of poverty programs. But sometimes one or the other takes a realistic view concerning what a program geared toward disadvantaged people, such as Head Start, can actually be expected to do. In February 1990 the *New York Times* pointed out that the past twenty-five years' experience had shown that the one-year program with little follow-up "cannot combat the ills of poverty." The article argued that Head Start did improve children's outcomes in some important ways, but also pointed out that the program had no lasting influence on standardized test results. The *Times* also stated that the "dismal quality of many schools" attended by Head Start graduates made it very difficult to sustain any advances the program caused.[68]

In 1990, Head Start's twenty-fifth anniversary year, the National Head Start Association's Silver Ribbon Panel reported on the program and found that some of the problems identified ten years before either remained or had grown worse. Teachers' pay was still low, and in some cases was below poverty level. Given that, it was no surprise that fewer than half of Head Start teachers had a college degree. Only 15 percent of Head Start programs were full-day programs, despite the growing number of children coming from single-parent families. And research, evaluation, and demonstration funds had fallen from 2.5 percent of the Head Start budget in 1974 to just 0.1 percent in 1989. Also in 1990, Congress made a serious attempt to improve the quality of Head Start programs. The Human Services Reauthorization Act of 1990 set aside 10 percent of new Head Start funds (adjusted for inflation) for the first year for program improvements, and 25 percent of new funds in following years for the same purpose. Half of the money set aside was to go to teaching, for improved benefits and salaries, in the hope of attracting more highly qualified staff. The other half was for improving facilities, training, transportation, and related issues.[69]

In January 1992 President Bush was running for a second term, and he once again used his support for Head Start to claim the mantle of "education President." (There was some irony to this, as his 1991 education proposals on Head Start had been widely criticized as inadequate.) President Bush's new proposal included an additional $600 million for Head Start, a 27 percent increase. Some newspapers, such as the *St. Louis Post-Dispatch*, pointed out that this increase fell far short of fully funding Head Start. The Children's Defense Fund claimed that such an increase would add fewer than 100,000 new children to Head Start. But whatever their attitude toward President Bush's proposals, newspapers across the nation showed support for Head Start itself. The *San Diego Union-Tribune* asked, "Can we afford it?" and then answered "Yes. If there is one poverty program that has demonstrated it can work, it's Head Start." The *Columbus Dispatch* noted, "Every survey has shown that this program for preschool boys and girls gives them a much-needed leg up when they begin regular school."[70] Neither paper went out of its way to explain what evidence it was discussing.

Throughout the 1992 presidential campaign, Democratic nominee Bill Clinton regularly attacked Bush for having offered "trickle-down education." Clinton pointed out that Bush had failed to fully fund Head Start, as Bush had repeatedly claimed he would do during his 1988 campaign. "America needs an education president who shows up for class every day, not just every four years," said Clinton.[71] It was no surprise that Bush and Clinton fought over which of them would be seen as the true champion of education, or that they used their support for Head Start as proof of their good intentions. Few education programs approach Head Start's widespread popularity. Media coverage of Head Start during 1992 was glowing. In April the *Los Angeles Times* wrote that "the nationwide program has received sustained applause since its inception in 1965, with study after study showing that every dollar spent on Head Start to help children get a good education can save $5 in government spending." A *New York Times* editorial in June called Head Start "the motherhood and apple pie of Government programs." Both newspapers were right about the program's popularity, though it is anyone's guess exactly which studies (besides Perry) the *Los Angeles Times* thought showed such successful financial savings.[72]

One of the signs that many people—both in the public and in high political office—believed Head Start worked was seen at the state level. Across the 1980s and early 1990s, state governments greatly increased their efforts to provide preschools for their citizens. This was driven in large part by Head Start's influence and popularity, and by the fact that Head Start still failed to reach the majority of eligible children in most states. In 1988, for example, the governor of Virginia proposed expanding the state's preschool offerings to reach all eligible four-year-old children by the mid-1990s. In January 1990 the governor of Oregon proposed amending the state constitution to earmark 30 percent of state lottery money to Head Start, to pay for making preschool available to every eligible child. Governor Goldschmidt claimed such a plan would be "the most significant—the most effective—anti-drug, anti-crime, pro-education strategy" in the nation. He pointed out that there were 11,000 eligible three- to five-year-olds in Oregon who were not in Head Start.[73] Head Start had even helped convince more affluent parents that preschool was important for their children as well. In the early 1990s in Massachusetts, for example, 76 percent of children in the state's richest communities were in a preschool program, while only 35 percent of children in poor communities were enrolled. In fact, children's access to preschool in general was closely related to the wealth of their community and where in the country they lived. One study found that preschool programs were fifteen times more available in affluent counties than in very poor counties. They were twice as available to poor or working class communities in the Northeast as they were to similar communities in the South, and throughout the nation poor and rural communities had far less access to preschool than did other communities.[74]

In his first State of the Union address, President Bill Clinton announced that Head Start would eventually save three dollars for every dollar spent. The *New York Times* pointed out that these promised savings were based on the Perry Preschool findings, not on evidence from Head Start itself, and that a number of critics doubted that any such savings would actually occur from increased Head Start funding. (Interestingly, they seem to have been based on the first Perry study, not on the more recent report that found savings of seven dollars for each dollar spent.) Whether President Clinton believed in his promise of savings or not, he clearly believed in supporting Head Start. He proposed to increase its funding by $10 billion dollars over four years, which was his single largest requested increase for a government program and accounted for roughly 10 percent of all the new "investment" spending he proposed for his first term.[75]

By early 1993, however, the media were beginning to question Head Start more often that they had at any time in the 1980s. *Time* magazine wondered whether it was actually a success, and expressed doubt about whether it would save so much money in the long run. *Time* described a recent investigation of Head Start conducted by the Department of Health and Human Services, which found that many Head Start programs were poorly run. It quoted Edward Zigler as estimating that "at best" only 40 percent of Head Start centers were "high-quality," and that "closing down 30 percent of them would be no great loss." Among the problems that *Time* cited were the low pay for teachers, which made attracting good staff very difficult, and the belief that positive effects quickly faded away. Even so, the magazine praised Clinton for being "on the right track" in recognizing the program's problems.[76] Another reason the media began to doubt Head Start was that several government reports showed that many local programs were poorly managed. A draft report from the inspector general at the Department of Health and Human Services questioned whether Head Start children were being properly immunized. The report found that only 28 percent of families were receiving most or all of the social services they needed, and only 43 percent of children were fully immunized. Another report questioned the ability of Head Start to expand rapidly, due to problems in finding adequate space and hiring qualified staff.[77] If Head Start could not even immunize children or direct them to appropriate social services, what reason was there to think it could have a major impact on their future? And if it could not expand effectively, why spend money on trying to serve more children?

Even more important in the growing assault on Head Start was the fact that a number of critics were speaking out loudly and forcefully. The *National Journal* stated that Head Start had "amazingly fervent bipartisan support," but also quoted Robert Rector, a policy analyst at the conservative Heritage Foundation, as claiming that "we have 25 years of lack of success in Head Start." Even so, the article claimed that most of the recent criticism Head Start had faced had actually come from supporters, who were looking to improve its quality and make it more accessible to the low-income families it served. These supporters felt that President Clinton's strong belief in the program had made constructive criticism possible.[78]

But not all the criticisms of Head Start were coming from people trying to improve it; many came from people who wanted to limit or even end the program. John Hood, research director at a think tank in North Carolina, argued that claims that early intervention can reduce later problems such as dependency and delinquency rested on "several shaky foundations." In fact, Hood argued that the studies that showed success— the Perry Preschool studies—were not relevant, that brief outside interventions could not make an important difference, and that even if they could, government would not be an effective provider of such interventions. Hood even called Head Start's supporters "hucksters." He believed the money spent on Head Start should be converted into vouchers for poor children, who could then attend schools of their parents' choosing, claiming that this would offer "a much better prospect of ending the poverty cycle."[79] Hood's argument that the Perry Preschool results were not especially relevant to Head Start as it currently existed had some merit. His belief that outside interventions could not make a difference was set on rockier ground: that they could if done well was something Perry had shown rather convincingly. The underlying basis of his argument was philosophical: the federal government did not do things well. (Interestingly, he wanted federal government money put into vouchers in the belief that these would make a difference for poor children that Head Start could not. This was a widely held belief among conservatives during the 1990s, but there was even less evidence for vouchers in 1993 than there was evidence supporting Head Start. For more on vouchers and evaluation evidence, see the conclusion.)

Newsweek summed up the rising tide of attacks against Head Start in April 1993. "Not too long ago, everybody loved Head Start," the article began. But an upcoming federal study had found major flaws in the program, it reported, and some conservatives wanted the program ended. The program's problems were not a secret during the 1980s, but during the Reagan-Bush years Head Start's supporters had kept quiet, in an effort to keep the program running. President Clinton's arrival had made it safe for supporters to criticize the program in the process of trying to improve its quality and overall funding, since Clinton himself was a strong supporter. Conservative critics, however, felt that if they could show that Head Start, the most widely supported antipoverty program run by the federal government, was a failure, it would be a major blow against all such efforts by the federal government.[80]

Just as these debates over Head Start were heating up, the Perry Preschool program returned to the limelight. An update of its findings followed the children through almost a decade of adult life, to the age of twenty-seven. In addition to briefly recapping the earlier findings, the new study showed a number of important differences between the program group and the control group at age twenty-seven. The group that had attended the preschool had significantly higher monthly earnings, with 29 percent of its members earning $2,000 or more per month, compared with just 7 percent of the control group. The preschool group was significantly more likely to own their own home (36 percent versus 13 percent), and had had significantly fewer arrests, including fewer arrests for crimes involving dealing or manufacturing drugs. The cost-benefit analysis was now based on a full decade in the workforce, rather than just two years, and it showed that "over the lifetimes of the participants, the preschool program returns to the public an estimated $7.16 for every dollar invested."[81] Thus, with more evidence at hand, the predicted cost savings had gone up slightly, from $7.01 when the subjects had been nineteen. The earlier cost-benefit analysis was proving to be accurate: adults who had attended the Perry Preschool program more than two decades earlier were making more money and costing society less than the control group that had gone without preschool of any kind.

As they had in the past, the authors of the Perry Preschool study cautioned against taking their findings as proof that Head Start worked. Instead, they argued, their work showed that high-quality preschool programs had important results, and they called for Head Start to be fully funded so that it could expand to reach all eligible three- and four-year-olds. They once again emphasized the importance of high-quality preschools, and tacitly acknowledged that the quality of Head Start programs varied. Their results did not show that Head Start worked but rather "defined the full potential of Head Start and similar programs."[82] While many in the media nonetheless rushed to say that Perry showed Head Start worked, some observers were more hesitant, and conservative critics of Head Start were quick to argue that Perry was irrelevant to the federal preschool program.

But in the mid-1990s, research evidence that was directly relevant to Head Start's success did appear. Steve Barnett reviewed twenty-two studies of preschool programs that had followed children until at least third grade, to see whether preschool effects faded out, as many believed. Perry was one of the twenty-two studies, but also included were eleven studies of Head Start programs. Barnett, who had worked on the Perry cost-benefit analysis, found the studies to be "remarkably consistent in at least two respects." The first was that children's IQs were temporarily increased, but that this increase did indeed fade out fairly quickly after children moved into kindergarten and elementary school. The second, however, was the finding that despite this fade-out of IQ gain, many preschool programs improved such later outcomes as placement in special education, promotion from grade to grade, and graduation. Barnett saw several possible explanations for this, one being that IQ was a "poor measure of intelligence."[83] Some scholars have argued that fade-out occurs because the disadvantaged children who attend preschool later attend schools that are, to put it simply, not very good: schools that have limited resources, are unsafe, and where expectations and achievement are generally low.[84]

As noted earlier, the Clinton administration was willing to admit to, and try to address, some of Head Start's weaknesses. In January 1994 the bipartisan Advisory Committee on Head Start Quality and Expansion issued a report arguing that, overall, Head Start was a success, but also acknowledging that Head Start centers varied dramatically in quality. The committee pointed out that the world in which Head Start functioned had changed dramatically since 1965. The needs of families and children in poverty had grown more striking, as had the problems of urban America more generally. With that in mind, the report recommended that more effort should be put into providing high quality in all Head Start programs, by raising teacher salaries and improving management training. It also stated that services should be expanded to include more children, including much younger children, and to be more responsive to the needs of Head Start families. The panel called for the expansion of Head Start, which currently served only 40 percent of eligible children, but warned against increasing enrollment without improving quality. Finally, it said that local Head Start programs should be encouraged to develop more partnerships with other programs and institutions dealing with early-childhood issues. Secretary of Health and Human Services Donna Shalala saw the report as a blueprint that recognized the program's strengths, recommended adjustments to modern circumstances, and would help Head Start improve in the future. "This proposed legislation reflects agreement on both sides of the aisle that we need a new Head Start program—not just bigger, but also better. The emphasis here is on quality in every Head Start center," said Secretary Shalala.[85]

In April 1994 the Senate approved a major expansion of Head Start, and the following month President Clinton signed the bill into law. At the same time, however, Congress was trying to decide how much money to actually appropriate for various programs in the midst of drastic cutbacks and deficits. The Head Start legislation introduced standards to improve quality, set aside funds to expand service to children below three years of age, and allowed planners to schedule full-day, year-round classes. (The legislation was based on the Advisory Committee's recommendations; over the next three years, seventy-seven Head Start grantees lost their federal funding because they did not comply with the program's standards.) How much of this would actually be funded was uncertain, though given the rigid budget ceilings created in 1993, it was clear that the program would not receive the full appropriation. The House of Representatives later gave President Clinton only a small portion of the money he asked for to fund his domestic initiatives, including just 30 percent of the increase he had sought for Head Start.[86]

In the summer of 1994 Head Start began expanding, but the expansion was far from smooth. Demand was so high that approximately half of eligible children were turned away in the fall. In addition, many children who were accepted had to attend classes in crowded classrooms and rundown buildings. Hiring quality staff at low salaries was a problem, and turnover remained high. Average teacher salaries had risen to $16,000, but that was hardly a competitive salary for well-trained teachers, and many Head Start teachers still lacked retirement benefits and health insurance. At the same time, the reauthorization bill put pressure on local programs to improve: by September 30, 1996, all classroom teachers were required to have a Child Development Associate credential or another appropriate qualification. By the end of that year, Head Start was serving almost 750,000 children.[87]

In 1997, at the request of Congress, the Government Accounting Office (GAO) reviewed the extensive literature on Head Start and found that only 22 of the more than 600 studies it examined met the GAO's (not very strict) criteria as reliable. The GAO search found that the research on Head Start was inadequate; no conclusions could be drawn about the national program's success in either the educational or the health arena. Most of the studies suffered from methodological flaws, and many of the 22 studies the GAO considered worthwhile lacked good comparison groups, making even their results highly questionable. Even more interesting, the GAO reviewed the Department of Health and Human Services' plans for future research on Head Start, and found that it was focused on new programs. There were no plans to learn more about whether Head Start actually had the kind of impact it hoped to have nationwide. When questioned about this, HHS officials replied that Head Start's effectiveness had been proven by early research, but the GAO disagreed.[88] HHS officials could argue as they did because Head Start supporters *know* that the program works, just as its (relatively rare) conservative critics *know* that it does not work. There is little support on either side for doing the kind of extensive, long-term research that would show exactly what the program's impact is on a national scale. For both sides, it is a matter of politics and philosophical opinion, not factual evidence. As we have seen, there is considerable evidence that strong preschool programs do have a long-term positive impact on their students. So it is reasonable to assume that the best Head Start programs have positive effects. What influence most Head Start centers actually have on the children who attend them, however, remains an open question, and seems likely to stay that way.

President Clinton was probably the strongest supporter of Head Start to occupy the White House since its founder, Lyndon Johnson. Even so, like George Bush before him, Clinton always promised more than he was able to deliver for the program. In his first major address to Congress in 1993, Clinton proposed making Head Start available to all eligible children. In

February 1997, in his *fifth* State of the Union address, Clinton proposed expanding Head Start enrollment to 1 million children by 2002, not mentioning that he and Congress had not met his earlier goals, though they had increased the program's funding. He also failed to mention that his new proposal of enrolling 1 million children would account for just half of eligible children in 2002.[89]

In early 1998, Congress took a close look at Head Start as it prepared legislation to reauthorize the program for four more years. Legislators expressed interest in improving salaries for teachers (then averaging $17,800 per teacher) and for aides (averaging $12,000 to $13,000). They sought ways for parents who moved from welfare to work to continue participating in Head Start. Finally, legislators said they wanted more research showing that the program prepared children to start kindergarten "ready to learn." The program was serving 830,000 children at a cost of $4.4 billion annually. Two Republican leaders stated that Head Start reauthorization legislation would require a long-term study of program effectiveness. In October 1998, President Clinton signed legislation directing a larger portion of federal Head Start money be used to improve quality rather than expand enrollment. Sixty percent of new money would go to improving quality.[90] This marked a dramatic change from the expand-first thinking of the late 1980s, and an even more marked change from the neglect of the Reagan years.

In the late 1990s, state governments also continued to develop and expand preschool programs. At least thirty states had some form of preschool program, whereas before 1980 only ten states did. Some states have adopted Head Start guidelines in creating their own programs, while others try to work closely with the federal program; still other state preschool programs have no real relationship with Head Start. Some states allow children from families above the poverty line to attend their preschools, and some have more highly qualified and better-paid teachers. Some spend more than Head Start's annual average of $4,000 per child, while others spend much less.[91] In other words, state preschool programs for disadvantaged children probably vary in quality even more than do Head Start programs across the nation.

Head Start's strong grassroots support helped it survive and even expand in the 1990s, while other social programs for the disadvantaged, such as Aid to Families with Dependent Children, were dismantled. Some of its support comes from people who have direct contact with Head Start, but much of the middle class's perception of the program stems from what the media or politicians tell them. Media coverage has generally been pro–Head Start, although, as we have seen, the coverage has not always been accurate, especially when discussing evidence about Head Start's impact. But there is another danger in getting information from the media, which is that many journalists seem to have an extremely short memory. An article in the *Orange County Register* in August 1998 began, "In the more than 30 years since President Johnson's 'War on Poverty,' perhaps no social program has had a halo as bright as that of Head Start. Yet for the first time, the early learning program that primarily prepares low-income 3- and 4-year-olds for school has become the target of partisan controversy." In fact, Head Start's halo had been dimmed several times, most notably by the Westinghouse report in 1969. And it had been the target of conservative attacks in the early 1980s, and even harsher ones in the mid-1990s, just a few years before the *Register* article was published.[92] (Politicians get the story wrong as well, of course. As a candidate for president in the 2000 campaign, then-governor of Texas George W. Bush proposed to move Head Start into the Department of Education, stating that it "was originally intended as a literacy program," which was not the case.)[93]

Over the years, the public and political perception of Head Start has shifted from a program designed to permanently increase children's IQ to a program that would address many of the nation's urban problems in a cost-effective manner. In effect, Head Start has gone from one impossible task to another. Meanwhile, actual Head Start programs continue doing what the original Head Start Planning Committee expected in 1965: providing an array of health and social services that help children, encouraging parental involvement, and offering an educational boost that *may* have some long-term positive results. On that final score, however, we don't really know the truth, and judging by the attitude of many government officials, we are in no hurry to find out.

American society has never had a very good idea of how to best help poor people, in part because large segments of our society have generally opposed government aid to the poor. But contrary to conservative images of a past in which private charity supposedly sufficed, there has never been anywhere near enough money in charitable circles to help all the people who need help. Thus the task falls to the government, which is itself made up of individuals with a wide variety of views about how, and even whether, to help the poor. This is one of the fundamental problems faced by Head Start. Its advantage, however, is that it deals directly with poor *children.* Unlike poor adult men, who have historically been viewed as undeserving of help, and poor single mothers, who have come under severe attack in recent decades, poor children are the ultimate innocents, the quintessential "deserving poor."

This fact is related to Head Start's survival since 1965, but attitudes toward the poor also help explain why Head Start has never come anywhere near providing all eligible children with one year of preschool, much less two or more, as many supporters of the program have argued it should. Head Start is not simply another educational program. It is also a program for the poor, and the way such programs are treated in the United States is different in important ways from how schools have generally been viewed. Given its creation in Lyndon Johnson's War on Poverty, this should be obvious, but it is not. Favorable media coverage and political support usually focus on Head Start as an *educational* program for poor children. But it has faced several serious attacks and never come anywhere close to "full funding" because it is an educational program for poor children *and their families.*

What role has evaluation evidence about Head Start's actual impact on children played? First, it is essential to realize that both support for and attacks on Head Start have been driven by ideological beliefs far more than by evidence. Supporters of the program often claim that it has been shown to be successful; this is especially true among politicians, who may or may not know that the evidence is actually mixed. Critics occasionally point to one study or another to show that Head Start doesn't work, but most such attacks would be voiced regardless of evaluation evidence, and critics studiously ignore evidence that suggests Head Start helps children. The first serious hit Head Start took was due to the Westinghouse study in 1969. But both of the major attacks on Head Start since then, in 1981 and 1993, were fueled by a distrust of liberal government programs and opposition to federal aid to the poor, not by any new evidence that the program wasn't working.

There are hundreds of studies of Head Start and other preschool programs besides those mentioned in this chapter, and most of them are modest in scope. The GAO's 1997 summary of the findings of twenty-two of the best of these studies showed how uncertain the evidence actually is regarding Head Start. Most focus on cognitive issues, leaving health and nutrition, where the program's impact may be strongest, unexamined. And even among these "choice" evaluations, most have severe methodological weaknesses and follow children for only a few years. The GAO's almost inevitable conclusion was that we simply don't know what Head Start is achieving. The main reason the Perry Preschool evaluation has gotten extensive attention from politicians, the media, and social scientists alike is simply that it follows children for a long time and has a rigorous design, including a proper control group. We know that Perry had a significant impact on its children. What we don't know is whether that says much about Head Start, although the body of evidence on Head Start certainly gives us some reason to think that the best Head Start programs do make a difference for the children who attend them.

Even so, we still don't have a definitive answer to the deceptively simple question, Is Head Start a success or a failure? We have fairly good evaluation evidence showing that whatever increases do occur in IQ scores do not last. And there are some reasonably compelling studies that indicate Head Start graduates are less likely to be placed in special education classes or to drop out than they would have been without Head Start; in other words, some of the results that Perry brought about also occur for Head Start graduates.[94] But as to its overall, long-term impact, there is no clear-cut answer. For that matter, there is no agreed-upon answer as to what "working" would mean for Head Start. One of the nice things about the 1960s' hope that IQs could be permanently lifted was that it was a goal everyone thought desirable. The same could probably be said for some of the health services provided by Head Start, such as immunizations and dental care. Many local Head Start administrators consider the program to be "working" when parents become involved, succeed as teacher's aides, and move on to better jobs, or when children receive immunizations and other health care. Critics of the program might reasonably argue that preschool education needs to stand or fall on the basis of what it does for children's achievement in school, and that job training and health care are different programs altogether. Even focusing the discussion on how Head Start graduates do in school in later years, there would be little agreement on what constitutes success or failure. Some would see decreasing the need for special-education placements and increasing the likelihood of high school graduation as significant triumphs, while others might not. There are no simple answers on this front.

What about the things we do know about a preschool program in one

Michigan city three decades ago? Even after recognizing that the Perry Preschool findings do not apply to the Head Start program as it currently exists, Perry's results can be taken as having several very different policy implications. Critics of Head Start who question Perry's meaning for Head Start argue that there is no real reason to think Head Start is having much impact on its children. And in fact the Perry results are not particularly relevant to whether current Head Start programs are achieving similar results. But there's another way to look at it: the Perry Preschool program provides evidence that quality preschool programs can work and can have important long-term results. Improving Head Start, by giving it a boost up to the level of the better private preschool programs with more qualified teachers and better staff-child ratios, might therefore be a worthwhile endeavor.

Does the lack of clear-cut evidence that Head Start has a consistent, long-term educational impact on its graduates mean we should abandon Head Start? Suppose we were discussing the current success of the medical profession in treating cancer. Some forms of cancer still have appallingly high fatality rates; in other words, medicine is currently a failure at treating those kinds of cancer. But it would be absurd to suggest that we should abandon medicine because it has not yet cured those particular illnesses. Admittedly, there is little reason to think Head Start has had as much success in helping poor children as medicine has had in curing illness. But there is reason—beyond anecdotal evidence, including the Perry results and some Head Start studies—to think it does some good, and that if the government continues to focus on improving the quality of Head Start programs, it will do more good.

This matters for a very simple reason. Given how little we know about helping poor families, the evidence in favor of Head Start does not look quite as weak as it might otherwise appear. From a knowledge standpoint, we don't know what the long-term impact of Head Start is and, unfortunately, we don't seem very interested in finding out. Head Start has been kept alive, and it has also been kept a limited program that serves only a moderate percentage of eligible children, by politics, not knowledge. It continues to enjoy widespread support, but only enough to let it move forward incrementally. President Clinton's last budget agreement with Congress before leaving office included an increase of $1 billion for Head Start, bringing the program's funding up to $6.2 billion; an impressive figure, to be sure, but still far short of what would be required to serve every eligible child. President George W. Bush, seeking bipartisan issues after a contentious election, made it clear immediately after taking office that education would be one of his first priorities. His main goals for Head Start, however, seemed to involve moving it to the Department of Education and focusing it more strongly on literacy, not improving overall quality or expanding the program to include all eligible children.[95] Both of Bush's proposals may be good ideas, but they are not necessarily what the program, and the children likely to be helped by it, most need. Whether or not Head Start is making a significant difference for its children now, it probably will make a difference if we focus on improving its quality. Until we find better ways of helping poor children do well in school, this seems to be a reasonable thing to do. If we are truly concerned with educating disadvantaged children, one significant step would be to make sure there are places for all in high-quality preschool classrooms.

2

Is Bilingual Education
a Good Idea?

Bilingual education need not be regarded as the tool in a conspiracy to force Spanish on this country as a second national language . . . But bilingual education has created a bureaucracy that, like many government institutions, is intensely committed to maintaining its power and control and strongly resistant to change. Twenty years of experience have demonstrated the fundamental fact that bilingual education just doesn't work.
— ROSALIE PEDALINO PORTER, 1990

Does bilingual education really work? Politicians and journalists remain obsessed with this unrewarding question, which practitioners feel they answered long ago. Three decades of experience in the classroom, refinements in curriculum and methodology, and gains in student achievement have made believers out of countless parents, teachers, administrators, and school board members . . . [T]here is no question that it has helped to dismantle language barriers for a generation of students.
— JAMES CRAWFORD, 1995

Bilingual education is one of the most complicated, and one of the most controversial, issues in education. In media coverage of the issue, schools where members of the student body speak dozens of different languages are often referred to as "Towers of Babel."[1] And so they can seem. In transitional bilingual education (TBE) classes for Spanish-speaking children, students are taught most subjects at least partly in Spanish, and they also take English as a Second Language (ESL) classes. A Korean TBE class would be taught partly or mostly in Korean, and so on, possibly for as many as eight or ten more languages in a school district. At the same time, those schools would have ESL classes in which children who speak languages less common in the United States are taught English. Children in one ESL class might speak a dozen different languages in their respective homes, such as Mandarin, Russian, and Khmer. They spend the rest of their day learning subjects such as math and history in classes taught in the English they are trying—perhaps with little success—to learn. In general, bilingual classes are small, often by government regulation. For most of the past three decades, for example, Massachusetts required an eighteen-to-one student-teacher ratio for bilingual classes.[2] All of these approaches are geared toward teaching English to children who come to school speaking another language. Many of these "language-minority" (LM) children are immigrants, while others are the children of immigrants. There are millions of LM children in America's public schools, and the numbers continue to grow. Helping these children learn English so that they can succeed in school, and in adult life and work, is a tremendously important issue for American society as well as for the children themselves, their families, and their communities.

But how to do so is, to say the least, complicated. The bilingual-education debate itself might be called a Tower of Babel. People on both sides of the issue often talk past one another; they have so little trust in their opponents' good intentions that they cannot even hear the other side's arguments. Both sides believe they are right; worse, they think their opponents are ignorant, or even evil. The argument is heated because bilingual education is, and has been for thirty years, about far more than education. For many of its proponents, it is *the* central issue of Latino civil rights, fully as important as integration was to African Americans in the 1950s and 1960s. Thus to question or criticize bilingual education is not merely to oppose an educational approach; it seems an attack on Latino culture and Latino civil rights. Advocates of bilingual education are certain it works and tend to see its critics as opposing it for racist, rather than pedagogical, reasons.[3] To many of its opponents, however, bilingual education is seen as an attempt to resist assimilation into American society; some even view it as an attempt by immigrants to maintain a separate culture at the nation's expense. Opponents also sometimes see supporters of bilingual education as part of a vast bureaucracy that is far more concerned with its own power and prestige than with children's education.

There are a variety of ways in which children for whom English is not their native language have been taught in public schools in the United States. At one end of the spectrum are "submersion" programs, where children are placed in regular classes taught in English, and are expected to learn English along with all the other topics they are being taught—in a language they do not initially understand. Submersion classes were widespread prior to the 1960s, and that is the way most immigrant children have historically learned English (or, in all too many instances, failed to learn English very well). "Sheltered immersion" classes use English almost exclusively; children are allowed to ask questions in their native tongue, but teachers answer in English. Also common are ESL courses, in which children are pulled out of their normal class to learn English.

In contrast to these English-based methods of teaching LM children, there are several different kinds of bilingual education that rely, to a varying extent, on teaching children at least partly in their native language. TBE classes teach children all subjects in their native language while also teaching them English. The idea is that this will allow the children to keep up with other students in all school subjects while gradually learning English. The students' English skills will grow until they are fluent, at which point they will be mainstreamed into classes taught in English. TBE classes have become the most commonly used form of bilingual education. It is important to note, however, that many courses labeled "transitional bilingual" are actually taught largely in English right from the start. Bilingual courses can try to mainstream children within two or three years, or they can keep children for five or six years or longer. If a major effort is made to maintain the child's culture and language, the programs are known as "maintenance" bilingual programs. Finally, "two-way" or "dual-immersion" classes contain both English-speaking children and LM children, with the goal of developing full fluency in two languages for all the students. Aside from these two-way classes and some maintenance classes—both of which are fairly rare—bilingual education courses do not try to keep children fluent in two languages as they grow older. The idea is to use both languages until the child is fluent in English and can be placed in mainstream classes; after that, nothing is done by schools to support the student's native language.[4]

What does the evaluation evidence say about bilingual education? That depends on whom you listen to; advocates of bilingual education say their case is proven, and so do opponents. This is partly due to the heavily ideological nature of the debate; it is more of a fight than a debate, and often more like a street brawl than a boxing match. Advocates and opponents are able to convince themselves that the evidence is on their side because most evaluations of bilingual programs have been performed with such poor methodology that their results can be easily attacked if one does not agree with them. Studies that one disagrees with are ignored as flawed (with reason), while studies that support one's view are taken as sound (usually with little reason). These evaluation problems do not stem from incompetence on the part of evaluators. There are a number of sizable hurdles to performing good evaluations of bilingual education owing to its complexity, varied goals, and the variety of programs offered under the same title, such as "transitional bilingual."

The more closely you examine bilingual education, in fact, the more complex it becomes. Which children need special help, and how do you identify them? What is an appropriate cutoff between a child who speaks English well enough to be in mainstream classes and a child who does not? How do you assess what each child's exact needs are? What kind of program would serve the child best? For that matter, who determines whether "best" means helping individual children to speak English as quickly as possible, or improving their use of their native language, or making sure they keep up in other subjects while they learn English gradually, or meeting some other goal? If you want to do all these things, how do you prioritize between them? And when are children ready to be placed in mainstream classes? Finally, not all schools with a large number of LM children face the same situation.[5] A school with a large number of children from working-class families that speak Spanish faces a very different situation from a school with children from dozens of different native-language backgrounds, from families ranging from poor to upper middle class. What might work well in one setting might not work at all in the other. This, in short, is the complex world of bilingual education.

A Brief History of Native-Language Instruction in the United States

Long before the American Revolution, a wide variety of different languages were used in North America by Native American tribes. The arrival of immigrants added to the number of languages in use, as it still does at the dawn of the twenty-first century. But no later effort to channel immigrants from Europe or elsewhere into the use of English, and into "American culture," matched the persistence or harshness of attacks on Native American culture and language. These attacks may have reached their peak in the late nineteenth century, when the federal government began separating Native American children from their families and tribes and educating them in boarding schools, where children were punished harshly for any use of their tribal language, even if they knew no English. This was part of a widespread and tragically long-lasting effort to eradicate Native American cultures completely. While these attacks have greatly diminished in recent decades, their effects persist. Dozens of Native American languages, now spoken by tribal elders but not being transmitted to children, are vanishing.[6]

In the mid-nineteenth century, even as Native Americans were under increasing attack (both cultural and physical), a variety of immigrant groups from Europe tried to maintain their language and culture through schooling. They sometimes did this by establishing their own schools, but they also used the public schools. In communities dominated by one immigrant group, according to historian Carl F. Kaestle, "a variety of bilingual schemes existed." These community schools offered courses in other languages, depending on what immigrant group or groups lived in the area, their political power, and what they expected of schools. In almost all such schools, teaching children English remained a fundamental goal, though in some communities dominated by German immigrants, instruction was given predominantly or even completely in German; this was especially likely to be true in the early grades. In the late nineteenth century, a number of states had laws specifically allowing for bilingual education.[7]

In some places, the presence of bilingual education in public schools was hotly contested as part of a broader conflict over who would control a variety of school issues such as hiring and funding. In Herman, Wisconsin, a Lutheran minister who did not speak English was hired as a teacher; other residents who wanted the school to teach in English succeeded in ousting him. In San Francisco conflict raged throughout the 1870s over the appropriate language of instruction for some immigrant groups. A Republican majority took control of the school board in 1873 and temporarily ended the practice of teaching some immigrant children in French and German, but the language programs were back in business a year later at the insistence of the immigrant community. Three years later the governor of California refused to sign a bill banning bilingual education. And segregated schools taught in other languages did not come about just because of some immigrant groups' desire for them. In 1885 San Francisco established a

Chinese-language school, and the city later segregated several other groups the same way, at least somewhat due to a desire on the part of white residents to keep the immigrant groups out of the schools their own children attended.[8]

As immigration increased in the early twentieth century, anti-immigrant sentiments grew as well, fueled in part by the changing nature of immigration. Growing percentages of immigrants were from southern or eastern Europe, and these Italians, Poles, Russians, and others were seen by native-born Americans as being "more foreign," "more different" than earlier immigrants had been. One of the most noticeable differences was that, unlike earlier immigrants from England and Ireland, many members of this immigration spoke little or no English; another was that many were Jewish or Catholic. In 1906 Congress first required some ability in English for naturalization. The federal government passed anti-immigrant legislation before and after World War I, as did state governments, sometimes targeting foreign-language instruction in schools. In the two decades preceding America's entrance into the war, more than a dozen states passed legislation requiring that subjects such as math be taught in English. This trend shifted to specifically target German in the mid- and late 1910s, as the anti-German stance of World War I led to cancellation of German-language classes in schools across the nation. By 1923 most states had passed laws that all teaching in public schools had to be done in English.[9]

Over the next few decades some schools in the remaining states continued to allow teaching in children's native languages. For example, it was not until 1950 that Louisiana insisted that teaching had to be done in English rather than French. In the meantime, Spanish had become the second most common language in the United States. In the Southwest there was a long tradition of teaching children in Spanish, as well as a long tradition of opposition to the practice. In 1919 Texas had made it a crime to teach in any language but English (excepting the teaching of foreign languages in higher grades). Even when a state legislature did not ban the use of Spanish in schools, some school districts did. In some cases, children were even banned from speaking Spanish on school playgrounds. Several states still had laws in place in 1969 making the use of Spanish by a teacher in a classroom a criminal act.[10]

Thus the argument used by opponents of bilingual education in the 1980s and 1990s that "their grandparents" learned English in schools using a "sink or swim" approach is only partially accurate. In many places prior to World War I, and in some schools for decades afterward, children were taught in languages other than English. But the grandparents argument is wrong for other reasons as well. Prior to the 1930s, most students left school long before graduating from high school. One of the reasons that immigrant children in particular did not continue their schooling—though not the only reason—was that they often had trouble following classes taught only in English. Many immigrant children *did* learn English in schools; many others left school in part because they were unable to learn English well enough to keep up. In actuality, many first- and second-generation immigrant children learned just enough English in schools to get by; it was often *their* children who became fluent in English and succeeded in school. The movement from immigrants' speaking their native language to becoming fully fluent in English and successful in school has often been a two- or three-generation story. Moreover, the nature of work in American society changed to require a much higher level of education by the end of the twentieth century than it did at the start. High school degrees were a rarity in 1900, but they became the expected minimum in the job market of the 1960s and 1970s; first-generation students who drop out of school will have little chance in the modern economy. For that matter, so will most children whose high school diploma marks the end of their education.

Modern bilingual education in the United States can be traced to the Cuban community that blossomed in Miami in the early 1960s, after the Cuban revolution. A number of the new arrivals had been teachers in Cuba, and the state helped them become certified to teach in Florida. The Cuban community was educated and wanted to maintain its culture; doing so meant protecting its language. In 1961, Dade County's public schools went beyond offering ESL classes and began a precursor to bilingual education. Two years later Coral Way Elementary School began a bilingual program for Spanish-speaking children that was also open to English-speaking children. The program's goals were ambitious: to create fully bilingual students. The Spanish-speaking children received half their lessons in Spanish and half in English; so did the English-speaking children who enrolled. Both groups mixed at lunchtime and on the playground, as well as in classes that could be taught without extensive use of language, such as art and music. The early results were encouraging, and this mode of "two-way" bilingual education spread to a few other schools in Dade County. The Coral Way program's one failing seems to have been that English-speaking children did not become as fluent in Spanish as the schools had hoped.[11]

In the Miami area in the 1960s, local control meant extensive bilingual efforts by schools. In general, however, advocates of bilingual education have not trusted local control. This should hardly be surprising. Prior to 1968 and the federal government's increasing involvement, children coming to school with little or no English were, far more often than not, treated shabbily. Many were categorized as "mentally retarded" and placed in classes for "slow" students, which was the kiss of death in terms of any educational future. Some children picked up English quickly and did well in school, but even as adults, many remembered the traumas they underwent in the process and favored bilingual education. As a result, bilingual supporters had no desire to see control of programs for LM children in the hands of local school officials. Instead, they wanted government intervention to assure that LM students were treated with respect. As one California bilingual education official put it in 1982, "Local control is simply a buzzword for local oppression of minorities." In addition to these fears, supporters of bilingual education knew that school districts required money to pay for qualified teachers and bilingual teaching materials. In hard economic times of declining education funding, such as the late 1970s and early 1980s, the federal government was an especially crucial provider of such resources.[12]

From 1968 to 1974: Bilingual Education Becomes the Law

The African-American civil rights movement of the 1960s inspired other groups that faced systematic discrimination to organize and seek social change and better access to societal institutions. One of the civil rights movement's central goals had been to achieve better schooling for African-American children. In the 1960s and 1970s, Latino groups also sought to improve their children's education. Whereas African-American activists had sought desegregation above all else, Latinos focused on changing the treatment received by children who entered school knowing little or no English. As Christine Rossell and Keith Baker write, "Bilingual education became an organizing principle for politically active Hispanics who considered themselves uniquely excluded from the educational process by language and cultural problems not addressed in other programs."[13]

Their most significant achievement came with the 1968 renewal of

1965's Elementary and Secondary Education Act (ESEA), which included Title VII, also known as the Bilingual Education Act. Title VII was designed to target support to local schools' efforts to develop new ways of helping children with limited English proficiency. No one knew if bilingual education would actually work, and early efforts under the act were largely directed toward developing teaching materials and training teachers. (The money provided was small at first, but it grew rapidly in the 1970s.) The Bilingual Education Act did not require any particular amount of instruction in children's native tongues. Instead, it encouraged schools to develop new approaches and required that school districts receiving federal money make serious efforts to help their LM students.[14] The government's use of the phrase "limited English proficiency" reflected the assumption that the problem was a lack of something—skill in English—and partly as a result, bilingual education was all too often seen as a remedial program. The Bilingual Education Act was not the only major 1960s legislation that would play an important role in educating LM children over the next several decades. The Civil Rights Act of 1964 had included a ban on discrimination based on national origin, which meant it was the federal government's job to prevent discrimination, even when it occurred in public schools, which were traditionally under local control.

In 1970 Kinney Lau, a Chinese American, was a six-year-old in the first grade in San Francisco's public schools. Lau's class was being taught completely in English, with no special help targeted to him; it was a classic sink-or-swim situation. Edward Steinman, a young lawyer, learned about Lau, and that a number of Chinese-American children were in the same situation. The children were sinking more often than swimming. Soon Lau's name led a list of plaintiffs in a lawsuit that began working its way through the court system, with initially mixed results. Mexican-American parents brought a similar suit in New Mexico. James Crawford points out that the new legal approach claimed discrimination because "*equal treatment* for children of limited English proficiency—in other words, 'submersion' in mainstream classrooms—meant *unequal opportunities* to succeed." The evidence that there was a problem was extensive, particularly the high dropout rates of Latino children. In 1972 the New Mexico case resulted in a federal judge's mandate that the state's Latino children should be taught in and about their native language and culture. In the meantime, the Lau case had been making its way to a federal district court, then to an appeals court, both of which agreed with school officials that, because the same instruction was being offered to all children, the schools' practices were acceptable. It was unfortunate that some children struggled because they did not understand English, the court stated, but it was not the schools' responsibility to make special efforts on their behalf. Everything changed two years later when the U.S. Supreme Court unanimously overruled the lower courts. In *Lau v. Nichols* the Court found that providing children with nothing except submersion classes violated the Civil Rights Act. Justice William O. Douglas wrote, "There is no equality of treatment merely by providing students with the same facilities, textbooks, teachers, and curriculum; for students who do not understand English are effectively foreclosed from any meaningful education." The Court ruled that students who did not understand English had to be given some sort of special help. The Court's decision basically outlawed submersion, but beyond that it avoided specifying a method, instead leaving the choice of approach up to the school district. At the time, the case received almost no media attention.[15]

One possible approach was to use ESL courses, pulling children out of their regular classrooms for special English instruction. However, that approach had an obvious flaw. If children did not understand English, then how would they learn subjects, such as math or history, being taught in English? They might fall years behind in school while trying to learn the language. Another option was to provide instruction in children's native language for some period of time while also teaching them English. Among supporters of bilingual education, different options appealed to different people. The central question was whether bilingual courses should be "transitional," with children quickly placed in regular classes taught fully in English, or "maintenance-oriented," supporting children's native language and culture. The Bilingual Education Act did not choose between these options, and neither did the Supreme Court. It was left to the executive branch of the federal government to decide whether local control should remain intact, with government oversight to assure children were given help, or if a specific method should be endorsed and encouraged everywhere. The Department of Health, Education, and Welfare's Office of Education formed a panel to determine how to enforce *Lau v. Nichols*. After considerable debate, the panel developed the "Lau remedies," which called for bilingual education. Commissioner of Education Terrel Bell made the rulings public in August 1975. The remedies described how districts were to identify children needing help, appropriate ways to teach them, and when to move them to mainstream classrooms taught fully in English. Most tellingly, unless a district could show convincingly that its approach was successful, it had to provide bilingual education for its LM elementary school students. In fact, transitional bilingual education was the *least* intensive version of bilingual education allowed under the Lau remedies (short of a district's offering proof that another approach worked). Bicultural and multicultural approaches were also acceptable. The Lau remedies were not actually law, but because they were strictly enforced by the federal government, they shaped local policy and also influenced a number of state laws. Over the next few years, the Office for Civil Rights (OCR) used the Lau remedies in negotiating hundreds of agreements with local school districts nationwide.[16]

Thus bilingual education became federal policy as a civil rights issue, with no real evidence about how well it would work. One hope was that it would reduce the tremendously high Latino dropout rate. Another related belief was that teaching children in their parents' language would improve their self-esteem. Some supporters of bilingual education believed that first- and second-generation immigrant children who were immersed in English felt badly about themselves when they struggled in school. Teaching children in their native language showed respect for them and their parents. This argument has been advanced, by and large, by Spanish speakers, but it has affected the education of children from other backgrounds as well. A number of bilingual education's strongest advocates said they had vivid memories of being confused, frightened, or even punished and deliberately embarrassed by their teachers because they could not speak English. Media coverage of the debate over bilingual education, and of bilingual programs, often included descriptions of what adult supporters of bilingual education had had to go through as children.[17]

Another argument for bilingual education, one that developed after *Lau v. Nichols* and served as a major intellectual justification for it in the 1980s and 1990s, is the belief that reading is a transferable skill. Once a child has learned to read in one language, the theory goes, it is easier for that child to learn to read in another language. So students are first taught to read in the language that they already speak, and that their parents speak; later, learning to read English will be easier for them, since they will already be readers in their native tongue. An additional justification for bilingual education is that it allows children to learn other subjects, such as math, while they are making the transition—be it slow or fast—from speaking their native language to speaking two languages, including English. Another way of looking at it is that children are taught *how* to think in their native language. Once they have developed fundamental thinking skills, as well as the basic skills needed to read, write, and do math, they are better prepared to learn to speak, and then to read and write, in English.[18]

The Spread of Bilingual Education in the 1970s

Some states had already passed laws supportive of bilingual education before *Lau v. Nichols.* New Mexico passed a law in 1971 allowing schools to provide instruction in languages other than English. Massachusetts became the first state to require bilingual education in school districts with at least 20 language-minority students who speak the same language, and Illinois allocated state money for bilingual education. Other states followed suit with laws, funding, or both, especially after *Lau.* Colorado passed a comprehensive bill for bilingual-bicultural education that required schools to offer bilingual education to children whose parents wanted it, through third grade. Several other states passed variations on these laws in the mid- and late 1970s, including Michigan and Connecticut. In some places, governments had to be pushed. In New York City, Aspira, a Puerto Rican advocacy organization, sued on behalf of 150,000 Latino students and won a federal court ruling. As a result, previously voluntary bilingual classes were to become mandatory for Spanish-speaking children with limited English proficiency. The decree was applied to children from other language backgrounds as well, and the federal government's support for bilingual education was strengthened. The Bilingual Education Act was amended in 1974 and 1978 to require that children with little or no English attending schools receiving federal funds had to be taught in their native language, to whatever extent was required to help them progress in school. This change meant that the funding could no longer be used to support ESL programs or other methods based on using English. Children no longer had to be from impoverished homes or from homes that used another language more than English; all students who had limited proficiency in English were eligible. The definition of what constituted LEP was expanded, and children could be included so long as they still needed help in reading and writing.[19]

How many children were affected? In the fall of 1975 at least 200,000 children were apparently being taught in their native language rather than in English. In most cases this meant Spanish, though there were dozens of other languages being used as well. Some educators estimated that as many as 2.5 million schoolchildren would benefit from bilingual education.[20] But not everyone welcomed the spread of bilingual education. Some teachers and parents opposed the arrival of bilingual education, believing it to be expensive and potentially divisive. Bilingual education faced other problems across the nation, most notably a shortage of qualified bilingual teachers. This would be an ongoing problem that would only get worse over time. By 1982 the U.S. Department of Education estimated that schools needed 55,000 more teachers qualified to help LM children than they had. And no relief was in sight, since education schools were training only about 2,000 more bilingual teachers each year.[21]

The first large evaluation of bilingual programs was released in 1977. The American Institutes for Research (AIR) report looked at more than 7,000 students in Spanish-English bilingual programs. It found that Spanish-speaking children in bilingual classes did less well in English and the same in math as Spanish-speaking children not receiving bilingual education; overall, the report concluded that bilingual education programs did not seem to have any significant or consistent advantages over the submersion method. Bilingual advocates were stunned, but they soon began arguing that the research was deeply flawed and its results were unreliable. In fact, the AIR study did ignore a number of central issues about bilingual education, just as its critics said. For example, the bilingual programs it included varied wildly in quality, and the study mistakenly included a large number of children who were actually fluent in English.[22]

Even so, some of AIR's findings were very important because they showed how bilingual education was actually being implemented—which was to say, very poorly. The vast majority of bilingual program directors questioned told AIR that Spanish-speaking children were kept in bilingual classes even after their English was sufficient to have them placed in mainstream classes taught fully in English. Worse, almost half the bilingual teachers who were interviewed admitted that they were not fluent in the language they were supposed to be using in the classroom. In other words, bilingual programs were trying to keep children rather than mainstream them, perhaps to maintain the extra funding that came to schools for students in bilingual classes. At the same time, students were being taught by people who were not qualified to teach them, owing to the lack of qualified bilingual teachers.[23]

The 1980s: Bilingual Education Ebbs and Flows

In 1980 the recently established U.S. Department of Education made a push for more extensive use of bilingual education by trying to strengthen the Lau remedies. A number of education groups and school officials complained loudly, arguing that the federal government was intruding into decisions that should be left to local school districts. Congress soon blocked the implementation of the new rules, and the arrival of the Reagan administration in early 1981 guaranteed they would not go into effect. Incoming secretary (and former commissioner) of education Terrel Bell's first official act was to allow schools to help children learn English in whatever way the schools deemed most effective. This fit with the Reagan administration's general view of social programs, which was that they should be left to states and local communities. Bell did say that schools were still responsible for protecting civil rights and educating children effectively; they were simply not required to use bilingual education to do so if they viewed another method, such as ESL, as preferable. And federal money still went only to schools providing bilingual education, not to schools using English-based methods. Nonetheless, the Lau remedies were basically out of business. Like the federal government, at the start of the 1980s some states that had been strong supporters of bilingual education were having second thoughts. In Colorado, for example, legislators repealed 1975's Bilingual and Bicultural Act, replacing it with a more short-term program.[24]

Before the Reagan administration was even in place, however, the Department of Education had taken one step back, at least from the perspective of bilingual advocates. The department had allowed schools in Fairfax County, Virginia, to continue using ESL rather than insisting they teach children in their native languages. The Fairfax County Board of Supervisors, faced with a sudden influx of thousands of students speaking dozens of different languages and no likelihood of finding qualified bilingual teachers for many of them, had decided to challenge the proposed regulations. An agreement was reached without any recourse to the court system, in part because students in Fairfax County's schools seemed to be doing well on national achievement tests. The decision was called "an explosive ruling" by the *New York Times,* and bilingual advocates attacked it.[25] One of the reasons for the success of Fairfax County's approach was that it provided considerable support to its LM students, sometimes spending as much as several thousand extra dollars on each child's education.[26]

There is little doubt that ESL is a more practical method than bilingual education for school districts faced with the need to educate children whose families speak dozens of different languages. In 1980 an astounding 139 different languages were spoken among the 90,000 students in Chicago who came from non-English-speaking backgrounds. This kind of variety presented an impossible hurdle to any effort to teach all children in their native language. How was a school district supposed to find qualified bilingual teachers, not to mention textbooks and other teaching materials? An ESL class can avoid these problems and can teach children who come in speaking fourteen different languages in the same classroom, as one high school class in Queens was doing in the 1980–81 school year.[27] But the fact that ESL is a *practical* method for schools does not necessarily mean it is a *good* method for students. The other half of the equation is whether ESL classes prepare students to do well in later years of schooling and in society more generally; or, to be more precise, which students does it help, and under what conditions? In 1980 no one really knew whether ESL or bilingual education was more effective, or for that matter even if either of these methods was pedagogically superior to sink-or-swim submersion classes.

The AIR report was ambitious but deeply flawed; most other evaluation studies done in the 1970s were much smaller, and many of them also had serious flaws. To see what could be learned from those studies, Adriana de Kanter and Keith Baker were asked to prepare a federal report on the evidence in support of bilingual education. They looked at hundreds of studies and found most of them to be seriously flawed. Baker and de Kanter ruled out a number of qualitative studies that supporters of bilingual education had pointed to as "proof" of the approach's superiority. James Crawford points out that they excluded *all twelve* of the studies once cited by Rudolph Troike as showing that bilingual education could have a strong impact.[28]

Baker and de Kanter's review concluded that there was little reason to believe that transitional bilingual education was the best available method. Some studies showed it to be more effective than submersion, while other studies showed the reverse. Some of the studies they examined found sheltered immersion or ESL to be superior to both TBE and submersion. The authors concluded, on the basis of very little evidence, that structured immersion might be the best option, and called for more and better research into its effects. They also acknowledged the weakness of submersion classes by stating that for a program to be successful, it was probably necessary to have an adult in the room who spoke the native language of the students.[29]

Structured immersion is different from the submersion classes that many Spanish-speaking children had to endure prior to the 1970s, and that many European immigrants went through around the turn of the century. In some structured immersion classes, teachers know the children's native language (ideally teachers would be fluent in both languages, but in practice that is not very common). Classes are taught in English, but when students do not understand, teachers can use the students' native language to explain, and children can ask questions in their home language and be answered in the same. (Some versions allow children to ask questions in their native language but expect teachers to answer in English.) Thus the vast majority of time is spent using English, but children, in theory at least, will not feel lost, shunned, or isolated if they do not understand the English they are hearing. Some observers believe this method works well for students who already have a good education in their own language but might not be appropriate for children with little prior education—which describes many, though certainly not all, immigrants.[30]

Meanwhile, the number of children receiving bilingual education was growing steadily, as was the number of children who needed special help but did not receive it. Estimates of each group varied widely, depending on who was doing the counting. By 1980 the number of children believed by the Department of Education to need help due to LEP was 3.6 million; another estimate was only one-third as large, in the vicinity of 1 million children. More than two-thirds were Spanish speakers, but another seventy languages were being used in bilingual classes. In 1982, Secretary of Education Bell estimated that only about one-third of the nation's LEP students ages five to fourteen were receiving special help.[31] The federal government was paying only a small portion of the cost of educating even those LM children who were receiving special help. Some states stepped in and supplied large amounts of money to their schools' bilingual programs. For example, in the early 1980s Illinois provided almost ten times as much funding to its bilingual programs as came from the federal government.[32]

In the late 1970s and early 1980s, California had what was seen as one of the strongest bilingual education programs in the nation. How California addressed the issue was extremely important to observers, since the state had far more LM students than any other. The way students were to be taught was carefully mandated by a state law passed in 1976. Schools had to offer bilingual education any time there were ten or more students in a grade who spoke the same language. (Individualized learning programs had to be developed for children when there were fewer than ten.) Wherever possible, bilingual classes were supposed to include both LM children and English-speaking children, to avoid segregating the former. English-speaking students were to make up one-third of each bilingual class. The law also stated that no students were to be forced to attend bilingual classes, but in practice it was hardly surprising that some children who spoke English wound up in bilingual classes against their and their parents' wishes. Schools that were determined to meet the ratio placed the necessary number of English-speaking children in bilingual classes, and many parents were reluctant or unable to challenge schools' decisions.[33]

California was also willing to experiment with bilingual approaches besides TBE. In the early 1980s the California Department of Education sponsored a bilingual experiment that soon became known as the Eastman model, because it had been most successful at Los Angeles's Eastman Elementary School. Under the Eastman plan, Spanish-speaking children were taught a few subjects, such as art and physical education, in English, where they mixed with children who spoke English as their native tongue. They also attended ESL classes. At the same time, these students were taught more complex subjects, such as math and reading, in Spanish. According to the principal of Eastman, it generally took about four years for children to become fluent in English, at which point they were placed in mainstream classes taught completely in English. Children in this program did better on standardized tests than LM students in nearby schools, and they made a smoother transition to mainstream classes than did children coming from traditional bilingual classes. In 1986 seven other schools in Los Angeles adopted the Eastman model.[34]

California also tried two-way bilingual or dual-immersion classes that mixed children who were native English speakers with children from a different background, all of whom were then taught in *both* languages. As was discussed earlier, some Florida schools had begun using this approach in the 1960s. These were not, like most bilingual and ESL approaches, remedial classes that assumed children had a deficit needing correction. Instead, they were enrichment courses, where the goal was for children to become fluent in two languages, to become truly bilingual. The nation's most prominent two-way bilingual program had begun in 1971, when the

Oyster Elementary School in Washington, D.C., developed a fully bilingual K–6 program. The school hired a Spanish-speaking teacher and an English-speaking teacher for each classroom—a commitment of money few schools could hope to match. In the mid-1980s students at Oyster, 60 percent of whom were Hispanic, were testing far above their grade level and were becoming truly bilingual.[35]

Such two-way classes functioned differently at different schools. Several schools in California adopted the dual-immersion approach, but not in identical form to the Oyster version, nor to one another. In 1983 San Diego's John D. Spreckels School began using the approach. Students spent half their day learning in English and the other half learning in Spanish; Basic skills such as math might be taught in either language. Ralph A. Gates Elementary School in southern California began a dual-immersion program in the early 1990s, with half the students from English-speaking households and half from Spanish-speaking households. The proportion of language use was different at Gates from what it had been at Spreckels. Instruction in kindergarten and first grade was 90 percent in Spanish and 10 percent in English, with the proportion of teaching done in English rising by 10 percent a year thereafter. In 1986 New York state funded a pilot two-way bilingual program in a number of New York City public schools, in which children speaking English were paired in classrooms with children speaking Chinese, Spanish, or Greek. Like other two-way programs, the goal was to have all the children become fluent in two languages, one of them being English. Between 1987 and 1993 the number of two-way immersion programs in the nation rose from 30 to more than 160.[36]

Even as the kinds of bilingual education being used expanded, no one knew what worked. In 1985 Ann Willig published a meta-analysis of evaluations on bilingual education. Willig agreed with virtually everyone else who had tried to review the evaluation literature on bilingual education: it was badly flawed. She performed her meta-analysis on twenty-three of the twenty-eight reviews that Baker and de Kanter had chosen as the best available a few years earlier. The Baker–de Kanter review had been highly controversial, and Willig wanted to see what bringing a more sophisticated approach to the same evidence would reveal.[37]

What did she find? That bilingual education programs had "significant, positive effects" compared with submersion classes, and that these effects held true whether children were tested in English or Spanish. Transitional bilingual education led to children doing better in reading, in math, and in other subjects than did submersion. Tests given in Spanish also showed that children in TBE classes scored higher on attitudes toward school. Willig used statistical adjustments to control for methodological problems in the studies she included in her meta-analysis, however, and she admitted that those problems meant her results were "less than definitive."[38]

Willig's meta-analysis was hailed as a major victory by bilingual advocates. Her results were, in fact, more convincing than those of Baker and de Kanter's review. The techniques she used were more sophisticated, and so her conclusion is compelling: bilingual education helps children learn more effectively than submersion programs. But then, by the mid-1980s very few people who knew much about educating LM children thought all-out submersion classes of the sink-or-swim variety were a good idea. The question was not *whether* to help LM children but *how* to help them. The real debate was among late-exit bilingual, early-exit bilingual, ESL, and structured immersion. Willig was right that bilingual education worked better than submersion, which was a moral victory for bilingual supporters, but her work did not offer any useful guidance about the best way to help LM children learn English and otherwise do well in school.

Willig's results certainly did nothing to end opposition to bilingual education. The most vocal opponent of bilingual education in the mid-1980s could hardly have been more prominent. Secretary of Education William Bennett believed that giving LM children extensive instruction in their native language was inappropriate because it took away from the role of English as the "common language" of the United States. Bennett wanted the law changed to end what amounted to a mandate for bilingual education, so that local schools would be able to use federal money for other approaches. (Note that he did not advocate a return to complete submersion. Bennett repeatedly stated that there was no proof that TBE worked, but his real opposition to bilingual education seemed far more driven by his cultural beliefs than by any evidence, or lack of evidence, about bilingual education's effects.) Bilingual supporters saw Bennett's views as an "act of war" and feared that his proposed changes would allow school districts to end their bilingual programs. They claimed that his policies would lead to children falling behind in school and that the Latino dropout rate would shoot up. In the early and mid-1980s, Latino dropout rates remained appallingly high. Nearly half of Mexican-American and Puerto Rican students who started high school did not finish it.[39] The nation's chaotic mix of bilingual,

ESL, and immersion classes—and the many schools where LM children got no special help—had not helped high percentages of Latino children graduate from high school. One study found that most LM children were not in either bilingual or ESL classes, making Bennett's claim that bilingual education had failed to stem the Latino dropout rates particularly unfair.[40]

Bennett's attack on bilingual education helped spur a movement in some states to declare English the "official language." Supporters of these initiatives were driven partly by the (unrealistic) specter of a possible future Hispanic separatist movement. Ballot initiatives succeeded in some states, most notably California, and lost in others. The timing of California's English-as-official-language Proposition 63 in 1986 seemed especially dangerous to bilingual education because the state's bilingual education law was due to expire seven months later, in June 1987. In the summer of 1986 Democrats in California's government had tried to extend the law but failed. Governor Deukmejian vetoed a bill that would have extended the bilingual education law through 1992, and questioned whether it was a cost-effective approach. California's bilingual law was thus allowed to end in 1987, but this was far from a death knell for bilingual education in the state, since federal law and most local school officials still supported it. The California Department of Education and a number of prominent school officials announced that they would not change anything in their schools' approach, with or without a state law. The law's end thus had little actual impact on bilingual education as it existed. (For that matter, when the law had been in force it had left many schools untouched; a 1986 study found that only one-third of the state's LM children were actually in bilingual classes.)[41]

Secretary of Education Bennett's opposition to bilingual education was not shared across the entire federal government. In 1987 the U.S. General Accounting Office released a report on bilingual education. The GAO asked ten experts to read a number of reviews of bilingual education evaluations (which the GAO supplied to them), including those by Willig and by Baker and de Kanter (not all the "experts" actually knew much about the topic). They were to then judge whether various quotes from the Department of Education, again supplied by the GAO, were accurate when they claimed there was a lack of evidence showing that bilingual education worked, and that there was evidence that other methods were promising. Thus the GAO survey was far from scientific. For whatever it was worth, the majority of those polled believed research showed that TBE programs did have positive effects on students trying to learn English. The majority also believed that research showed there were other good reasons to teach children in their native language: it helped them learn other subjects, and there was no particular reason to have high hopes regarding ESL or structured immersion. The Department of Education was sent drafts of the report and responded that its claims had been misunderstood and that the GAO's report was faulty.[42]

At any rate, in 1988 the Department of Education's era of open hostility to bilingual education ended with the appointment of Lauro F. Cavazos as Bennett's successor. Cavazos pronounced himself a "very strong advocate" of bilingual education and spoke some Spanish at a press conference on his first day in office. By the summer of 1989 Cavazos, now serving under President George Bush, was shifting the department's policy to favor bilingual education.[43] At the same time, however, the federal government's support for bilingual education actually weakened. Prior to 1988, only 4 percent of Department of Education (DOE) funding was allowed to go to other approaches to teaching LEP students. The 1988 reauthorization of the Bilingual Education Act increased the amount of federal funds that could go to approaches that were not based on native-language instruction to 25 percent.[44] Many bilingual advocates saw this as a disaster, because they did not trust local school districts to provide bilingual education if they could receive federal funds for other approaches.

In 1988 the Los Angeles School Board approved a "master plan" that called for a shift in the nature and extent of its bilingual education. It increased the amount of bilingual education provided in high schools, and offered bonuses of up to $5,000 a year to attract qualified bilingual teachers. The plan was based on the Eastman model described earlier, which had been expanded to a few additional schools in 1986; students at those new schools, like students at Eastman, had improved their test scores since the program began. Under the 1988 master plan, students would be taught math, science, reading, and social studies in their native language. Unlike the basic California plan of the previous twelve years, in which bilingual classes were to contain 33 percent English-speaking students to avoid segregation, the approach deliberately segregated LEP children for the bulk of the school day. They would also take ESL courses to learn English. Finally, they would be taught art, physical education, and music in English, usually with English-speaking students as their classmates.[45]

Los Angeles's plan to expand bilingual education passed with very little opposition. However, efforts to change bilingual education in other places could become contentious in the late 1980s, especially if they were seen as weakening rather than strengthening the use of students' native languages in the classroom. When Andrew Jenkins, the new District of Columbia school superintendent, tried to reorganize Washington's bilingual education program, the Hispanic community rose in opposition. Jenkins saw his plan to replace a central bilingual office with three offices (for elementary, junior high, and high school) as expanding bilingual education. Hispanic community leaders disagreed, quite loudly, and some school board members wondered if the outcry had been created and managed by bilingual officials who feared for their jobs. Jenkins agreed to protesters' demands and gave a group of experts on bilingual education three months to develop a new plan.[46]

The 1990s: The Beginning of the End for Bilingual Education?

In early 1991 a long-anticipated study of bilingual education was published. The study, funded by the Department of Education and led by David Ramirez, compared the results of transitional bilingual education (which the study labeled "early-exit") with two other methods, structured immersion in English, and "late-exit" bilingual education. In 1986, data from the first year of the study reached the press, and showed that children in bilingual classes were doing better academically than were children in immersion classes. Most surprising to critics of bilingual education, the early results showed that children in "late-exit" bilingual classes were doing the best in English, even though they were in classrooms where the most Spanish was being spoken. As it turned out, however, the study's final results were murkier than the first-year data had led many observers to expect.[47]

The study was longitudinal, running from 1983 to 1989. It was designed to examine what characteristics early-exit classrooms shared, and to do the same for structured immersion classes and late-exit classes. The study sought to understand what differences existed between the three approaches in actual practice, not just in theory. It also examined the students in each kind of program. The goal was to combine this information with student achievement and to be able to say with some confidence that the observed differences in outcomes, whether large, moderate, or nonexistent, were the result of different programs, not of other factors such as students' socioeconomic backgrounds.[48]

Only programs for Spanish-speaking children were included, a decision that was not unusual in evaluations of bilingual education, given that two-thirds of the LM children in the United States are Spanish speakers. Four school districts in Texas and California were chosen that contained both immersion and early-exit programs (a fifth site with these two programs was added in the second year of the study). Three districts participated that had late-exit bilingual programs, from California, Florida, and New York (these districts did not have either immersion or early-exit programs). As a result, the late-exit programs could not be reliably compared with the immersion or early-exit programs. Each year of the study included between one and two thousand children.[49]

The most reliable results involved comparing immersion and early-exit transitional programs that existed within the same school. Immersion and early-exit programs were also compared, less reliably, when they were in the same school district but not the same school. Another analysis compared the late-exit programs to one another. Each of these analyses attempted to take factors outside the programs, such as family background, into account. Finally, the "academic growth" of students in each of the three program types was compared to national growth norms. Unfortunately, these data were not very useful, since they did not take any non-program issues into account, and they showed rates of growth rather than actual scores on English and math tests.[50]

What did the results show? Students in immersion classes had better language and reading skills in English than did children in early-exit classes at the end of first grade, but by the end of third grade the early-exit students had caught up. In the comparison of the three late-exit transitional bilingual classes, students in the classes that used more Spanish in later grades had higher math skills than did the children in the late-exit class that shifted abruptly to English. The study's authors concluded that the policy implications were, "If the concern is for the achievement of LEP students in the short run, i.e., through third grade, instructional services can be provided through either immersion strategy or early-exit programs." Some media coverage of the report claimed that it showed the "late-exit" bilingual programs to be the most effective approach, but in fact the study was not able to compare the late-exit programs directly with either early-exit or immersion.[51]

One of the main weaknesses of this study (shared with most evaluations of programs for LM children) is that it does not follow children after they have been mainstreamed. Did children from one kind of program adapt to mainstream classes taught fully in English better than did children from another program? That the groups had similar skills at the end of third grade is important, but they might take divergent paths once mainstreamed, and surely that is part of how programs for LM children must be judged. Even disinterested parties such as the National Research Council criticized the study on a number of fronts.[52]

Like the AIR study in the 1970s, this longitudinal study was important and interesting more because of the things it found out about what actually happened in classrooms than for its claims about student achievement. English was used by teachers almost all the time in immersion classes, as the immersion "model" called for; Spanish was used only about 1 percent of the time. Immersion classes were the most consistent of the three programs, staying closest to their program model. Early-exit transitional bilingual classrooms in the study also generally functioned as one expected. On average, teachers in early-exit classes in kindergarten and first grade used English more than 60 percent of the time and Spanish less than 40 percent of the time. The percentage of English use by early-exit teachers rose to approximately 75 percent in second and third grade, with Spanish use correspondingly diminishing, and in fourth grade Spanish was almost never used, as in immersion classrooms. Thus the progression, on average, went as expected in early-exit programs, from moderate use of Spanish in the earliest grades to almost exclusive use of English by fourth grade. Even so, there was quite a bit of variety. One of the early-exit programs used English so heavily that it looked to researchers more like an immersion program than a transitional bilingual program. Another of the early-exit programs used English less than 60 percent of the time, making it similar to a late-exit program. Teachers' use of English and Spanish in late-exit transitional bilingual classes did not fit quite so closely with the expected model. Teachers used Spanish predominantly in kindergarten (almost 90 percent of the time) and continued to use Spanish a great deal, gradually declining until it was used somewhat more than 40 percent of the time in fourth grade. According to the model, late-exit classes were supposed to continue using Spanish at about that rate in fifth and sixth grade, but the researchers found that Spanish use actually dropped to about 30 percent in fifth grade and just 16 percent in sixth grade.[53]

The study found a number of other interesting things, many of which were similar to the findings of earlier evaluations. Most teachers in immersion classes and in early-exit bilingual classes had limited Spanish skills that were "not sufficiently strong for effective instruction in Spanish." As a result, there were real questions about the quality of the early-exit classes in the study and, more important, about the quality of teaching in transitional bilingual classes in general. The researchers also learned that teachers in all three programs, and at all the grade levels in the study, spent twice as much time talking as did their students. Given the importance of actually *speaking* while learning a language—and the superiority of active learning to passive learning more generally—this was far from ideal.[54] The issue of which program's children were mainstreamed and when it happened was complicated. For example, a higher percentage of children were reclassified as proficient in English from the early-exit programs than from the immersion programs after both kindergarten and first grade. After four years, more early-exit children (three-quarters) were reclassified as fluent in English than immersion children (two-thirds); about half the late-exit students had been reclassified as fluent in English after four years. But most of the children who had been reclassified had *not* been moved into mainstream classes! The study's authors believed that teachers reclassified students whom they did not believe were actually ready for mainstream classes; apparently, the standard for being reclassified was lower than the perceived standard for attending mainstream courses taught completely in English.[55] One would think the two would be identical, but in practice they were not. Once again, a major evaluation of bilingual education had produced important information about the flaws of programs for LM students, but little real evidence of what kind of program worked well.

Courts continued to become involved as lawsuits were brought against school districts for not providing extensive bilingual education. In early 1993 the Seattle school district was sued for failing to meet the educational and linguistic needs of 18 LEP children; in all, 350 LEP students in the school district were not receiving any instruction in their native language, and others were receiving inadequate help, according to the lawsuit. The school district responded by suing the state of Washington, claiming that if its bilingual services were in fact inadequate, it was because the state was not providing enough help. In a related vein, a Denver group filed a class-action complaint with the Office for Civil Rights against Denver's public school system, alleging that it was not complying with a 1986 court order regarding bilingual education. According to the complaint, a number of teachers in bilingual classrooms spoke only English, student-teacher ratios in bilingual classes were above the fifteen-to-one cap mandated by the court, and bilingual teaching materials were inferior to mainstream ones.[56]

As Fairfax County, Virginia, had done in 1980, some school districts sought waivers from state or federal oversight in the 1990s. In 1995 the trustees of the Westminster School District in California narrowly passed a resolution criticizing the state government's requirements—which mandated that the district had to have eighty-nine bilingual teachers fluent in Spanish or Vietnamese—as impossible to meet. The resolution called for a return to local control in decisions about how to best educate LM students. Westminster received a temporary waiver from the state's bilingual regulations permitting it to replace bilingual classes with courses taught in English, with uncertified aides who spoke the students' native language present to help when needed. Delaine Eastin, California's superintendent of public instruction, was advocating greater flexibility for local school districts and closer oversight of student achievement, whatever method districts chose to employ. Two years later, student test scores seemed to show that the new method was working well in Westminster, though the results were hardly definitive.[57]

In July 1995 California's State Board of Education recognized the growing opposition to bilingual education, as well as the ongoing difficulty in finding bilingual teachers, by adopting a new policy that gave local districts more control over how they taught LM students. The policy emphasized results rather than method; districts had to be able to show that students were learning at a reasonable pace. If they were, then whatever the district was doing, it was acceptable to the state. It was left up to school districts to decide how to measure student progress. By early 1997, only three small school districts in Orange County had actually received waivers to teach LM children in English.[58]

In early 1996 conflict erupted between parents and school officials at Ninth Street Elementary School in Los Angeles. Latino parents were upset that their children were not learning English quickly enough. Sister Alice Callaghan, who ran an after-school program for the area children, had become increasingly concerned about how little English children seemed to know and use, and served as the leader of the parents' complaints. In February, unhappy with school officials' unsympathetic response, parents kept more than eighty children out of the school in a protest against bilingual education. Despite the widespread support for the boycott among parents, one school official called the opposition to bilingual education the "pet peeve of one person," Callaghan. It was clearly more than that. The boycott lasted more than a week, and ended only when school officials promised to begin teaching more than one hundred LM children in English at the start of the next school year.[59]

Just as California's mandate for bilingual education was weakening, a new study appeared that received extensive media attention and was hailed by many bilingual supporters. An op-ed article in the *Houston Chronicle* in April 1997, written by a congressman and a highly placed DOE official, called it "the largest evaluation of bilingual education" and treated its results as proof of bilingual education's efficacy.[60] In fact the study, conducted by Wayne Thomas and Virginia Collier of George Mason University, was not exactly an evaluation of bilingual programs. Instead, Collier and Thomas examined the school records of 700,000 students in "five large school districts," from 1982 to 1996. They also conducted interviews in each school district, and used a variety of statistical methods to analyze the school records.[61]

Collier and Thomas labeled their approach "noninterventionist" because it had not affected children by randomly placing them in one or another kind of classroom. They claimed to have examined a wide range of validity issues, far more than "many so-called 'scientific' studies" of bilingual education. Thomas and Collier also stated that they had examined only programs "that are well-implemented." They looked at more than 700,000 LM students' records, including children from more than 150 different language backgrounds; this inclusion of LM students from a wide variety of language backgrounds is another advantage of their approach. Spanish was spoken by 63 percent of their sample. The most important, and the most compelling, thing about the study is that it looked at the long-term academic success of LM students. Thomas and Collier argued against the usual evaluation practice, which was to see how long it took children to be mainstreamed or to look at their test results after two or three years of schooling. They argued that the real issue was how children who had been in TBE or ESL or other programs in elementary school were doing down the road, when they were in high school.[62]

Thomas and Collier found that LM students taught in English made "dramatic gains in the early grades," thereby leading to the assumption that they would continue to do well in school thereafter. But they found that this did not turn out to be true: children who had been in ESL classes "typically finish school with average scores between the 10th [and] 18th national percentiles"—*if* they finished high school. Students who had attended TBE classes did better, but still fell well below the national average in their achievement levels. Children who had attended "one of several forms of enrichment bilingual education" finished schooling at or above the fiftieth percentile. Two-way bilingual education had the strongest long-term impact, followed by other bilingual enrichment programs. Transitional bilingual education did less well, but it did better if combined with a cognitively challenging, content-based ESL course than if paired with a traditional ESL class. Students taught ESL via academic content did even more poorly, with those from ESL pullout classes doing the worst.[63]

To say these are striking findings is an understatement. If accurate, Thomas and Collier's work does not just show that the move away from TBE is a mistake. It shows that the only programs that really work—that help LM children catch up *in the long run*—are the most extensive and expensive, and the least common, forms of bilingual education. What was it about these bilingual programs that led to long-term academic success for LM children? Thomas and Collier found that three issues were strong predictors. The first was "cognitively complex on-grade-level academic instruction through students' first language" for at least five or six years, along with similarly challenging instruction in English part of each day. The second was "the use of current approaches" in teaching in two languages, including "discovery learning," "interactive classes," and "cooperative learning strategies." The third predictor of long-term success was a "supportive sociocultural context."[64]

Unfortunately, there are problems with the study. The study was based on 42,317 students who had been in schools in the study for at least four years. That is an impressive number, but remember that Thomas and Collier looked at more than 700,000 student records. Fewer than 10 percent of the student records they studied could be included, and there is no way to know what factors caused the 42,000 students to remain while more than 600,000 other students moved or were not included for other reasons. It could be that students who were doing well in ESL classes were more prone to moving than students who were doing well in bilingual enrichment classes, thereby skewing the results toward enrichment classes. Attrition almost undoubtedly affected the results, but how much, and in what direction, is unknown. Another problem is that Thomas and Collier could not have actually spent enough time in the *thousands* of classrooms that the students in their study attended to be able to accurately judge which classes were "socioculturally supportive" or "well implemented." A major way in which they judged the programs they examined to be "well implemented" was by looking only at school districts that "are very experienced in providing special services to language minority students."[65] But this assumption is questionable at best. So are their assumptions about which schools and programs provided "sociocultural support," which they based on interviews. Any number of problems could result: for example, they could have included only good bilingual programs, while including both good and weak ESL programs, which would skew their results in favor of bilingual classes.[66]

Despite these various problems, Thomas and Collier's work is striking. Their argument that LM children need to be challenged, and that being challenged in both languages for a number of years helps students do well when subjects become much more complex in high school, probably has merit. Their evidence, while far less rigorous than Thomas and Collier claim, is still probably better than any other evidence on the effects of bilingual education. Thomas and Collier also claim that "three large school systems" had performed their own studies, which confirmed their findings about the relative long-term effects of different approaches.[67] Thomas and Collier's results are important and need to be seriously considered by policymakers today, in the midst of the recent shift away from bilingual education.

In early 1998 Jay Greene completed a meta-analysis of evaluations of bilingual education. After examining more than seventy evaluations, Greene found that only eleven were methodologically sound enough to merit inclusion in his review. The Ramirez report from 1991 and the American Institutes for Research evaluation from 1977, both described earlier in this chapter, were among the eleven; five of the eleven were randomized experiments. Greene chose as one of his criteria that a study had to compare LM children who had received at least some of their instruction in their native tongue with LM children who had been taught solely in English. He was not concerned with the *amount* of instruction in the native tongue; like Willig's earlier meta-analysis, Greene's compares "bilingual education" construed broadly with "submersion."[68]

Greene's results were similar to Willig's: children who were taught at least partly in their native language did better on standardized tests than did children who were taught completely in English. The difference was not huge, but it was statistically significant. More intriguing, the five randomized experiments showed a noticeably greater advantage for native-language instruction. Greene's conclusion was straightforward: "An unbiased reading of the scholarly research suggests that bilingual education helps children who are learning English."[69] Like Willig's meta-analysis, Greene's shows that submersion is a bad idea, but it says nothing about what versions of bilingual education were most desirable. In fact, it says nothing about whether classes taught largely in English, in which children can ask questions in their native language, are better or worse than bilingual education. But it does seem to show that such an approach is better than out-and-out submersion, where only English can be spoken.

The retreat from bilingual approaches in California sped up shortly after the release of Thomas and Collier's report, even as Greene was performing his meta-analysis, more due to public and political ignorance of their work than in defiance of it. In July 1997 Ron Unz, a millionaire who had run for governor of California a few years earlier, announced that he was beginning a petition drive to place an initiative on the state ballot the following year that would drastically limit the use of bilingual education in California's schools. Unz claimed that the parental boycott against bilingual education at the Ninth Street School the previous year was his inspiration. His cosponsor was a teacher, Gloria Matta Tuchman, who taught a first-grade English-immersion class and had long opposed bilingual education. What would soon become Proposition 227 stated that bilingual classes would be replaced with English-immersion classes. Children were to be in those immersion classes for no more than one year, after which they would be mainstreamed into "normal" classes taught completely in English. But there was a loophole: parents could ask that their children be placed in bilingual courses.[70]

When the petition for the ballot initiative was first filed in November 1997, one poll showed that 80 percent of white voters supported it, while 84 percent of Latinos supported it. Unlike the Latino population as a whole, however, Latino activists usually opposed the initiative, often vehemently. In April 1998, two months before voting would take place and despite extensive publicity against the initiative in the Latino media, polls still showed 61 percent of likely Latino voters supporting the initiative.[71]

In March 1998 the state Board of Education changed its policy so that school districts that wanted to replace bilingual education for LM children with English-based instruction could do so without having to seek approval. In April the U.S. Department of Education denounced Prop 227 because it reduced local control (ignoring the federal government's own historical role in forcing bilingual education on hundreds of school districts through the Office for Civil Rights and requirements for federal funding). But the state's attempt to preempt the proposition, White House opposition, and an advertising campaign against Prop 227 all failed to weaken public support for it (though Latino support did drop dramatically). In June 1998 California voters went to the polls and passed Proposition 227 with 61 percent of the vote. The vocal opposition of Latino advocacy groups had not affected the overall outcome, though it had helped reduce Latino support to about 40 percent, only half of what it had been in early polls.[72]

Supporters of Proposition 227 expected their victory to signal an end to bilingual education in California, and opponents feared the same. But it quickly became apparent that many school districts intended to resist. By mid-July 1,500 Los Angeles bilingual teachers had pledged to continue teaching children in their native languages, and San Francisco school officials had announced that they would maintain their bilingual programs. School districts could try to take advantage of the provision that allowed bilingual programs to continue if enough parents at any individual school requested them. Some school districts sent waiver forms home with children for their parents to sign, along with letters encouraging them to do so. Two-thirds of the state's districts at least informed parents about the waiver process.[73] There were other options for school officials determined to continue providing bilingual education. Proposition 227 seemed to state clearly that children should be taught almost completely in English, using phrases such as "nearly all" and "overwhelmingly." But did that mean teaching classes 99 percent in English, or 95 percent English, or less? Could teachers use children's native language 1 percent of the time? Or 5 percent? In August 1998 the Los Angeles County Board of Education decided the new law meant children could be taught in their native language *49 percent* of the time, and several other southern California school districts decided that 40 percent would be acceptable. Some school districts in northern California joined a lawsuit seeking to have Proposition 227 struck down by the courts as unconstitutional; the lawsuit failed.[74]

The first month of school under Proposition 227 was chaotic for schools with sizable LM populations. A few principals and superintendents were happy to abandon bilingual education, and a few others were determined to stay with it regardless of what they were told by others to do. Most, however, were unsure how exactly they were supposed to teach LM students; what teachers were supposed to do, and what teaching materials and textbooks would be appropriate were just the most pressing of many unanswered questions.[75] Overall, the 1998–99 school year in California saw a wide array of approaches to teaching LM students. Some school districts experienced a relatively smooth transition to sheltered immersion, with parents apparently approving of the new approach. In other school districts, the majority of parents of LM students asked that their children be placed in bilingual education classes rather than sheltered immersion. Things were greatly complicated by the fact that in some immersion classes a large percentage of teaching was actually done in the children's native language. Even so, it was clear that the number of children being taught in bilingual classes was much smaller than in previous years. Soon the actual figures came in, showing that the percentage of California's LM students enrolled in bilingual education classes had dropped from 29 percent to 12 percent.[76]

By the middle of the 1998–99 school year, some newspapers were running stories about teachers who were surprised at how quickly children were picking up English in immersion classrooms. In the summer of 1999, test results from the end of the first year of diminished bilingual education were released. They showed that children in all grades in California had improved scores; test scores for English-speaking students and for LM students had both risen. California's schools were undergoing a host of reforms in the mid- and late 1990s, so there was no way to tell which reforms—or which combinations of reforms—had led to the improved scores. For that matter, it wasn't even clear that the improved scores were proof that students really knew more than in the past. It was the second year the test had been used, and scores usually go up in that situation because students are more comfortable with a test the second time around and teachers know what to teach to help their students do well on the test. Thus the rising test scores could have been due to smaller classes (see Chapter 3), or the new approach to literacy, or the somewhat changed nature of how LM children were taught, or some combination of those factors. Or they could have simply been the result of increased familiarity with the test itself.[77]

California is often seen as a trendsetter in educational issues, and there is some truth to this belief. Shortly after the passage of Proposition 227, a small group of Hispanic parents and teachers began a campaign to end bilingual education in Arizona, with help from Ron Unz. In November 2000 they succeeded, as Arizona voters approved that state's Proposition 203 with 63 percent of the vote, limiting LM children to one year in immersion courses. But it was not at all clear that this movement would sweep the nation. Even as Proposition 227 was being passed in California, New York and several other eastern states seemed to be strengthening their support for bilingual education. Connecticut placed a three-year limit on children's enrollment in bilingual education, but at the same time it encouraged school systems to consider developing two-way bilingual programs.[78]

Ongoing Issues

Despite the opposition that bilingual education has faced almost since its beginning, the biggest problems it faces have generally been practical. The ongoing shortage of qualified bilingual teachers has been the most daunting. In 1985 the *Washington Post* reported on the problems faced by Franklin Elementary School in Oakland, California. The school was supposed to be offering bilingual classes in six languages. Finding qualified personnel to teach Spanish bilingual classes was difficult, but finding a teacher qualified to teach Khmer (Cambodian) or Tigrinya (Ethiopian) made that seem simple in comparison. A teacher at Franklin was assigned to a group of first-, second-, and third-grade Ethiopian children, and was asked to promise in writing that she would *learn* Tigrinya. The class also included a number of children whose native language was English (mostly African Americans), since the state law required that at least one-third of the children in bilingual classes be native English speakers. In California in 1985 half of all "bilingual" teachers were actually teachers who had promised to become fluent in a second language but had not yet managed to do so. The promise was usually to learn Spanish, but sometimes, as at Franklin, it was to learn a language that is rare in the United States, such as Tigrinya or Hmong. The problem went the other way as well. Some bilingual teachers were fluent in Spanish, for example, but spoke little English; in California in the 1980s, they were asked to sign waivers stating that they would learn English. In 1991 California schools needed 467 teachers who could speak Cambodian; they had just 1. The state needed more than 22,000 trained bilingual teachers and had only about 8,000 with the proper credentials.[79]

The ebb-and-flow nature of immigration also creates problems for school districts. In just a few years a school district can go from having very few LM children to having a large proportion of students in need of language help, from a variety of linguistic, cultural, and class backgrounds. Furthermore, school districts with large LM populations saw them sky-rocket in the 1980s. In early 1988 Los Angeles had 160,000 LEP children, an increase of 30,000 over just three years before. Between them they spoke eighty-one different languages; the district had managed to offer bilingual programs in only seven of those languages. And many immigrants tend to be even more geographically mobile than native-born Americans, so students arrive and depart throughout the school year. A carefully worked-out bilingual plan may fall apart two months into the school year as new students arrive and others depart. Discovering what needs the new arrivals have, and then finding classroom space and qualified teachers for them, can prove impossible.[80]

The public dialogue is over whether or not bilingual education is the "best" approach. One of the central questions about how to help LM children is more fundamental: which children should be placed in special language programs? In the early 1980s, children from households that spoke something other than English, and who scored below the forty-third percentile in an English-proficiency test, could be placed in bilingual programs. Beginning in 1986 the Department of Education changed the test scores it considered indicative that a child had LEP and was in need of special help from those in the forty-third percentile to those in the twentieth. Thus in one fell swoop the number of children who would be counted by the federal government as having LEP dropped dramatically.[81] A few years later New York went in the opposite direction, changing its testing standard from the twenty-third percentile to the fortieth, thereby increasing the number of children expected to be enrolled in bilingual programs in the state by 33,000. Of course, *any* number chosen as a dividing line, where children scoring above it are "fluent" in English and children scoring below it are not, is arbitrary. If a number must be used to differentiate between LEP children and children whose English is sufficient for them to be in mainstream classes, scores in the twentieth percentile may be too low, but the forty-third is clearly too high. Children whose English is only a little below the national average are unlikely to develop better English skills by being in classes taught in another language. In practice, according to Rossell and Baker, "states generally use one or more of six methods to identify LEP students needing services." Twenty-two states have mandated that one or another method has to be used by its school districts, but even in those states, districts can often choose to use additional methods. These methods include tests, surveys of the language used at home, information received when enrolling students, observation by a teacher, interviews, and referrals by teachers or others.[82]

Sometimes these methods work well, but at times they fail rather badly. Problems with children being improperly placed in bilingual education classes were cited throughout the debate in the 1980s and 1990s. Media stories regularly mentioned parents unhappy with their child's placement. Some children were placed in bilingual education because they had low English test scores, when what they really needed was remedial help. It was not that they were fluent in another language but not in English, but rather that they were struggling with English for reasons that bilingual courses would not address. Children's names could play a role in these placements. A child with a Hispanic last name and a weak test score in English might be placed in a bilingual course, where a child with an Anglo last name and the same score might be designated as learning disabled. In New York City in the early 1990s, children with Hispanic surnames were automatically tested for skills in English (but not in Spanish), and were sometimes placed in bilingual classes even though their parents spoke fluent English. Those scoring below the fortieth percentile were placed in bilingual education, even if they knew little or no Spanish. Other children were placed in bilingual education courses because there was no space at their school in classes conducted completely in English.[83]

At the other end of a child's experience with classes designed to teach English, of course, is the question of how to decide when children are ready to be placed in mainstream classes. Many schools rely on a similar array of options to those used to designate children as having LEP: tests, observations, and so on. In the mid-1990s, a dozen states required schools to use tests they had approved. The rate at which children are mainstreamed has been used to criticize bilingual education. Reports in the 1990s in California showed that only a small percentage of LM children were moved into all-English classes each year. In 1994, for example, only 5.5 percent of the children who had been in bilingual programs were removed from them and placed in mainstream classes. In Los Angeles, the number was even lower, just 4.6 percent. In 1996 the Los Angeles Board of Education decided to give financial incentives to schools based on the number of children who passed tests allowing them to be mainstreamed.

Supporters of bilingual education argued, rightly, that long-term academic success was the appropriate measure to use in judging the success of bilingual programs, not how quickly children were moved out of bilingual education. Even so, the tiny fraction moving from bilingual education to mainstream classes every year meant that children were staying in bilingual education longer than had been expected, presumably at least in part because they were not developing good skills in English. What was not acknowledged, but should have been, was the fact that many of the school districts having trouble moving LM children into mainstream classes were actually teaching them in ESL or immersion classes. Bilingual education was not helping children become fluent in English very quickly, but neither were the state's other approaches.[84]

The kinds of factors used to decide when children should be placed in, and when they should exit, bilingual (or ESL or immersion) programs obviously influence how long children stay in these programs. But sometimes states mandate that children should be in programs only for a certain period of time, regardless of how the children are performing—as California now limits most LM children to one year in an immersion program. In late 1999, three years was becoming increasingly accepted by politicians as the maximum time it should take to prepare children to be mainstreamed into regular courses taught fully in English. The number was simply politically appealing; there was no particular research evidence to show that three years was the "best" or right number.[85] Given the widely varied skills children come to school with, and their different learning rates, there is no "right" number that would fit all LM children. At least not if it is their education, rather than politics, that concerns us.

Much of the bilingual education discussion is about the best ways to help young children, between four and six years of age, who arrive at public school knowing little or no English. But it is also important, and even more difficult, for schools to somehow address the problems of older children, because immigration is an ongoing process, and many families arrive in the United States with older children. Some of these children have received an excellent education in their country of origin, and need to be helped to learn English while they continue to learn other subjects. But many older children arrive in the United States with little or no formal schooling, and some come from uneducated families whose grasp of even their native language is less than what might be desirable. How can schools help them most effectively? This is, in some ways, a separate question from the ones involving children first entering school. One possibility is that LM teens entering high school should be placed in bilingual education classes if they have a limited educational background, and in ESL classes if they have a good educational background in their native language.[86]

Hispanics were the first major supporters of bilingual education in the United States, and Hispanic organizations remain its most prominent and vocal advocates. Given the high percentage of LM students who are Hispanic (73 percent in 1991–92, for example) and the fact that bilingual education plays an important role in many Hispanics' thinking about civil rights, this is hardly surprising. But whether an educational approach favored by many Hispanics is appropriate for every other immigrant group arriving in schools not speaking English is far from clear. As Rosalie Porter rightly points out, "Different groups have different objectives. Some groups are intent on rapid assimilation: others are more concerned with holding on to their language and traditions." Russian parents, for example, generally seem to want their children to learn English as quickly as possible; so do many Chinese parents. Haitian parents, however, have often welcomed the idea of classes that would teach their children Creole and about Haitian culture, in part because many of them expected to return to Haiti. It is also crucial to recognize that Spanish-speaking immigrants come from multiple nations and cultures; it is folly to assume all Latinos have the same interests, or the same view about how they do and do not want to adapt to the United States.[87] (Of course, not all members of any specific group want the same things educationally or linguistically; the patterns described above are generalizations and must be recognized as such.)

One of the most compelling reasons for the growing use of bilingual education in the late 1960s and 1970s was the high dropout rate for Latino students, which was widely believed—with good reason—to be related to children's frustration at not understanding their teachers. This argument played a role in the passage of the Bilingual Education Act of 1968 and in state legislation as well.[88] Dropout rates for Latino children have unfortunately remained very high, between two and three times the dropout rate of white children in both California and New York.[89] Whether this is because bilingual education has not been implemented widely or effectively enough, or because bilingual education does not address the real reasons for Latino school departure, is unclear.

Part of the complication in discovering how to best help children struggling with English overlaps with an even more widespread problem in education: how to help children from impoverished backgrounds. Most LM students come from families with limited financial means. They are therefore likely to attend schools where most, or virtually all, other students are also from working-class or impoverished backgrounds. Poverty and poor attendance at school, which is more common among student populations largely in poverty, are both risk factors in education; combined, they signal a rough road ahead for students.[90] The ongoing discussion about bilingual education is political, cultural, and methodological; it focuses on what being "American" should mean, on how different cultures should be treated, and on questions surrounding how children learn. But *classrooms* where many LM children learn, and the schools surrounding them, exist in a world where poverty is predominant and has real power, both in terms of affecting children and schools and in shaping the broader society's perceptions about bilingual education and children who do not yet speak English. This must not be forgotten.

Both sides of the debate over bilingual education argue from personal experience, assuming that what they have experienced or seen—or thought they saw—can be used to understand, critique, or support a nationwide program. Advocates have seen some students flourish in bilingual education, so they consider it "proven," even though those same children might have flourished without bilingual education. Opponents make the same kind of logical mistake, assuming their experience is representative of what is happening (and what is "wrong") everywhere else. Rosalie Porter, for example, continually refers to her personal experiences in arguing that bilingual education does not work and that a bilingual bureaucracy is wreaking havoc on schools and teachers. Personal experience is important, of course, but Porter, like many bilingual advocates, makes the mistake of assuming that what she sees is representative of what is happening in schools across the nation. The complicated nature of who favors and who opposes bilingual education is further revealed by the splits among various immigrant groups, and even within individual immigrant groups, between parents who want their children to be taught in their native language and those who want them taught in English.[91]

Each side is partially right in the criticisms it levels against its opponents. Some attacks on bilingual education do seem to be motivated by prejudice, and some supporters of bilingual education seem unable to step back and see that bilingual education may not be as desirable as they claim. Where both sides err equally is in their mutual claim that "the evidence is on their side." When advocates say that the evidence shows bilingual education works, they are, at the very least, overstating the case. When critics claim that research has proven that bilingual education does not work, they, too, are wrong. The body of evaluation evidence on bilingual education shows that many different kinds of programs are lumped into a few general categories, such as "transitional bilingual education," and that many of them are poorly structured, poorly supported by administration, or taught by unqualified teachers. What it does *not* do is present compelling evidence one way or the other on what kind of program will help children learn English and be successful students over the course of their educational career. What we know is that submersion classes where *only* English is spoken do not work; beyond that, the evidence is vague.

Willig's and Greene's meta-analyses, and the recent study by Thomas and Collier, are probably the most reliable pieces of evidence, yet it is not at all clear what their real implications are. Willig's work shows that bilingual education, *as it was practiced in the 1970s,* had a small or moderate advantage over submersion classes. This does little good for a school official or an elected legislator trying to decide between sheltered immersion, TBE, or a more extensive program such as two-way bilingual education. Greene's work shows that *some* use of children's native language is better than none at all, but does not distinguish between different bilingual approaches or compare them to sheltered immersion. Thomas and Collier's work is certainly intriguing, but it is difficult to tell how much it can be trusted. Questions about their methodology simply leave too many possibilities for error to take their claims at face value. (It is worth noting that by their arguments, the kind of success some children have experienced in excellent ESL programs could not have happened for more than a handful, nor could more than a few people in the past have succeeded after being placed in submersion classes—but many did.) Their focus on long-term success is something that all researchers in the education of LM children need to adopt, and their argument that challenging, interactive courses are crucial to children's success are undoubtedly on target. But because of their methods and their obvious political agenda, Thomas and Collier's results are ultimately less than completely convincing. The most plausible part of their findings may be the advantage of two-way bilingual education. In early 2000, Secretary of Education Richard W. Riley came out in favor of the approach, but not with any expectation that it would become one of the most common methods in use. Riley hoped that the nation's 260 or so dual-immersion classrooms would increase to 1,000 within a few years.[92]

In the heated 1990s debate about social issues such as illegal immigration and affirmative action, it was almost impossible to have a rational discussion about the strengths and weaknesses of bilingual education. Even if there had been clear-cut evidence about the results of different approaches to teaching LM children, it probably would have had little effect. Think about California's programs for LM children, which were widely praised prior to the upheavals of the late 1990s; James Crawford, for example, calls them "exemplary."[93] Many bilingual supporters may even look back on that period now with nostalgia. The fact is that in California's schools some bilingual programs were high quality, but most were not. Dropout rates for Hispanic children remained high, and test scores remained low. So what was so admirable about California's approach to bilingual education over the two decades preceding Proposition 227? The answer seems to be, simply, that the state mandated teaching in children's native language. It was the *fact* that bilingual education was the dominant mode that was admired, and the low quality of most programs and less than desirable results were acceptable. It is exactly this kind of thinking on the part of bilingual advocates that led many critics of the approach to talk about a "bilingual bureaucracy" that was more concerned with its own survival and growth than it was with how well children were doing in school.

Much of the battle over bilingual education has been described as a search for the "best" method of teaching English to students who do not speak English and doing so in a way that keeps them from falling behind in school in general. But the idea of a "best" method simplifies a number of issues that matter, including diversity among children, varying goals, and such practicalities as the availability of qualified teachers. The quality of the program may matter more than its approach; the best transitional bilingual classes probably work well for many children, and mediocre ones do not. The best ESL classes, paired with excellent teachers in mainstream classes, probably work well for many (though not all) children, while mediocre teaching and half-hearted ESL or immersion will fail to help children effectively. The biggest problem may be that we have had far more mediocre or bad programs, of all kinds, than excellent ones.

What is abundantly clear, it seems to me, is that there is no one-size-fits-all solution. Any specific method mandated for everyone, whether it be instruction in children's native languages or structured immersion in English, will help some students learn English and succeed in school while harming others; it will please some parents while outraging others. As

Birman and Ginsburg wrote in 1983, "The needs of [LM] students vary with a host of factors: socioeconomic status, language group, family reliance on a language other than English, and, more important, the child's own language proficiency."[94] We need to know more about what best helps LM children who arrive in school with little formal education, or who arrive as teenagers, and we need to think carefully about long-term academic impact as well as short-term development of English skills.

The lack of certainty about how to proceed does not, however, mean that a return to local control is necessarily an appropriate solution. The push for bilingual education grew out of a very real problem: children who did not speak English were being ignored in public schools nationwide. Now, thirty years later, in large part because of the work done by advocates for students of color and civil rights activists more generally, school officials are more likely to be sensitive to the needs of their students who do not understand English. But some school officials will not be so sensitive, or will have inaccurate notions of what is best for such children. Other school officials will want to help children but will lack the resources—money, qualified teachers, classroom space, or knowledge—to do so. Federal and state oversight, to make sure schools have these resources and to verify that schools are making serious, thoughtful efforts on the behalf of all their students, LM and otherwise, is still needed, and in fact needs to be strengthened. But strength should not imply rigidity. There is ample reason to think that the federal government's policy over much of the past twenty-five years, to virtually *insist* on bilingual education, was a mistake. But the insistence on school districts' making special efforts to educate LM children was not. There needs to be flexibility in the approaches school districts take, and also insistence on, and financial support for, extensive efforts to teach children to read and write English.

3

Does Class Size Matter?

The President has proposed to shrink class sizes in the early
grades by hiring 100,000 more teachers at federal expense . . .
There is precious little evidence that smaller classes help students—achievement may even go down if the new teachers are
mediocre—but don't try telling this to voters. Smaller classes
are a pollster's delight.
—CHESTER E. FINN, JR., AND MICHAEL J. PETRILLI,
1998

Compelling evidence that smaller classes help, at least in early
grades, and that the benefits derived from these smaller classes
persist leaves open the possibility that additional or different educational devices could lead to still further gains . . . The point is
that small classes can be used jointly with other teaching techniques which may add further gains.
—FREDERICK MOSTELLER, 1995

One of the most widely discussed reforms in American education in the
1990s was the idea of reducing class size, especially in the first few grades,
when children are learning to read. California has spent billions of dollars
to create small classes in the early grades in every elementary school, dropping from thirty children in many classrooms to just twenty students per
classroom, and at least eighteen other states have adopted some sort of policy to reduce class size. The federal government began a plan to hire
100,000 new teachers, directed specifically toward lowering class size for
young children in impoverished communities—but the arrival of a new
president in 2001 signaled the end of the federal commitment. In the late
1990s, incumbent politicians and challengers all across the country had an

opinion on class size, and most stated that they were the ones who would reduce it the most, or at the lowest cost. A Harris poll found that more people were concerned about education than about any other issue.[1] Why did class size become one of the most talked about issues in education, and one on which so many politicians, Democrats and Republicans alike, were willing to spend large amounts of money? And why does almost everyone believe that small classes are better for students?

Few things are more basic to education than the relationship between teacher and student. This relationship is shaped by many factors: the teacher's personality and training, the student's interest in the subject and general attitude toward education, and so on; the list can be made very long. But when observers walk into a classroom, one of the most obvious things they see is the number of students the teacher is responsible for educating. A second-grade classroom with fourteen students in it is, in some fundamental ways, different from a second-grade classroom with thirty-four students. (It is important to note that there are several different ways of counting class size. One is the student-teacher ratio, which looks at a school as a whole and usually includes counselors, librarians, and other individuals who do not actually teach in classrooms. A more accurate method is to count the number of children per class, which will always be higher than the student-teacher ratio, sometimes by as many as six or seven students per class, but actually reflects the number of children in classrooms.)[2]

Most parents and teachers firmly believe that reducing class size will lead to improved student achievement. The path by which they generally expect smaller classes to lead to more successful students is fairly straight: teachers would be able to give more individual attention to every child; this would lead to more creative and more effective instruction, and to quicker recognition when a student needs extra help; these things, in turn would help students learn more. These effects would be enhanced by other advantages of smaller classes, such as improved teacher morale and fewer discipline problems in classes.[3] For many people, both in education and in the general public, this seems to be nothing more than common sense.

But is common sense correct? Does compelling evidence exist that children learn more in a small class than in a large one? In fact, expert opinion has changed dramatically over the years. In the 1960s and 1970s, most researchers believed that class size did not matter. In the 1980s, several scholars argued that smaller classes were clearly better, but not everyone accepted their work. In the 1990s, the weight of evidence swung strongly toward smaller classes, but there are still doubters. Is the evidence ambiguous, or do politics shape how the skeptics interpret the evidence? Furthermore, even supporters of reducing class size recognize that it is an expensive reform, and one that can be difficult to implement. So questions remain: will reducing class size improve student achievement? And if so, under what circumstances will it help children, and how much will it help them? After decades of debate, hundreds of studies, and with numerous states investing large sums of money in reducing class size, do we actually know if it's a good idea?

Class Size across the Century

The average size of public school classes has decreased since public school systems were first established nationwide in the middle and late nineteenth century; the reductions in class size have sometimes been dramatic. In 1846 Boston's student-teacher ratio was 58.8 to 1, but by 1870 it was down to 39.9 to 1. In 1900, average class size in the nation's public schools was probably somewhere between 35 and 40 students per class, but those numbers masked tremendous variety from place to place. Even within individual communities there was usually a wide range of class sizes. For example, in Seattle in the 1910s classes averaged 35 students in kindergarten through eighth grade, but Seattle's high school classes averaged just 20 students, which was well below the size in most cities.[4]

In the early twentieth century, the effect of class size on student learning was just one of many educational issues that was widely debated. Class size was both a practical issue, shaped by the high cost of hiring more teachers and finding more classrooms, and a pedagogical matter, believed by some to have an important influence on how well children learn. In the 1920s some school boards concerned with saving money in the face of rapidly growing enrollments saw increasing class size as a reasonable way to cut costs, and presumed large classes would not harm students. At the same time, teachers wanted smaller classes to ease their workload and because they believed children would learn more effectively.

Dramatic changes in the economy have often affected class size. During the first five years of the Great Depression, from 1929 to 1934, the student-teacher ratio in elementary schools remained constant at 33 to 1, but in high schools it rose from 21 to 1 to 25 to 1. This occurred because school finances were strained and because high school enrollments grew when more and more teenagers had difficulty finding work. After the Depression ended, the student-teacher ratio for elementary schools remained at 33 to 1, while high school ratios dropped below 20 to 1 in the mid-1940s, and fell to 17 to 1 in 1950. Classes were generally a good bit larger than student-teacher ratios implied, since the ratios included counselors and other personnel who did not actually teach in classrooms. And there was considerable variety from class to class, school to school, city to city, and state to state. In addition, other aspects of schooling also influenced class size. Most urban classes probably had more students than the average in one-room rural schools, but some one-room schools were quite large.[5]

The median size of classes continued to vary from state to state across the twentieth century. In 1970, for example, the student-teacher ratio (which, again, underestimates average class size by at least three or four students) in Utah was 27 to 1, in Georgia 25 to 1, and in California 24 to 1. In the same year Vermont's student-teacher ratio was just 18 to 1, and six other states had ratios under 20 to 1. These numbers show real regional differences, but they also mask both local variation and differences between primary and high school levels. Over time, however, the size of classes at all levels was declining. By 1960 the median number of children in elementary school classes was down to 30, and by 1986 it had fallen to 24. The median size of high school classes declined gradually for decades and then fell rapidly between 1981 and 1986, from 27 to 22. During roughly the same period, however, the mean number of students per class rose from 23 in 1976 to 26 in 1986. This occurred because the percentage of classes with more than 35 students almost doubled, thereby shifting the average (mean) upwards.[6]

Teachers are especially sensitive to class size. The number of teacher strikes rose during the late 1960s and peaked in 1975–76. Wages were usually the main issue in these disputes, but in the late 1970s large classes were also one of the main reasons teachers gave for striking. School boards were becoming less willing to negotiate a variety of professional issues, including class size. This frustrated many teachers, because large classes meant more student work to grade and less time to interact with individual students, and it could also lead to an increase in disciplinary problems. Class size would continue to be one of the most often heard complaints of striking teachers.[7]

The Glass-Smith Meta-Analysis of Class-Size Studies

In the late 1970s, Gene Glass and Mary Lee Smith conducted a review of research on the effects of class size on student learning and related issues. They published the results in several articles that received wide attention in the research community, and then in a 1982 book coauthored with Leonard Cahen and Nikola Filby. In the book, Glass, Cahen, Smith, and Filby reiterate their findings and respond to several criticisms the earlier publications of their research had received. They begin by pointing out that, prior to their work, scholars had generally disagreed with the idea that smaller classes help students learn better. As they put it, "By 1960, scholars and experimenters considered the question of the benefits of small classes to be dead, more dead than Latin."[8]

Glass, Smith, and their colleagues did not perform their own experiment on class size. They argued that there was no lack of information, since "literally hundreds of empirical studies" on the effects of class size had already been performed. Instead they wanted a deeper understanding of what those existing studies had to say. After reviewing 300 studies conducted over the course of the century, they found 77, from a dozen different nations, that examined the relationship between class size and student achievement. The methodological quality of the studies varied enormously, but each made a comparison between classes of different sizes. (After all, "small" and "large" classes are relative ideas, not absolutes. One study might compare "small" classes of 30 with "large" classes of 45, while another might compare "small" classes of 24 with "large" classes of 32. In the 1990s a third-grade class with 24 children would have been considered small in many parts of New York City but large in many nearby Connecticut communities.) Roughly half of the studies examined elementary schools, half secondary schools. And the 77 studies actually yielded 725 comparisons between classes of different size, because many of the studies contained multiple comparisons.[9]

Using meta-analytic techniques, they combined the 725 comparisons from their 77 studies. Some of the results were straightforward, such as the finding that 60 percent of the comparisons favored smaller classes; other findings were more complex. They did not find that the effects of small classes were different between elementary school and high school, or that they affected any specific subject, such as reading, more than other subjects. One of their most interesting findings was that studies in which children were taught in small classes for more than 100 hours were more likely to show an advantage for small classes than were studies in which class time was less than 100 hours, which seems to fit well with common sense. In addition, studies that used random assignment of students were especially likely to show an advantage for smaller classes (81 percent favored smaller classes). Probably the most compelling findings came when Glass and Smith and their colleagues examined the "best" studies—experimental comparisons—in which children were taught for more than 100 hours. To explain their results from these best studies, they proposed that the reader imagine a child in a class of thirty-five whose test scores are average, exactly in the fiftieth percentile. The authors claimed that that same child, if placed in a class of twenty-five, would have slightly improved scores. And the improvement would become more dramatic as class size dropped further: in a class of twenty that same "average" child would score in the sixtieth percentile, and the student's test scores would approach the seventieth percentile as class size approached twelve children. There was nothing equivocal about their conclusion: "The relationship of class size to pupil achievement is remarkably strong. Large reductions in school class size promise learning benefits of a magnitude commonly believed not within the power of educators to achieve."[10]

Smith, Glass, and their colleagues also examined the relationship between class size and students' and teachers' attitudes toward school and toward each other. In trying to examine these issues, they found approximately 130 studies that had looked at student and teacher reactions in one form or another. (Unlike the studies of student achievement, which stretched over the century, the bulk of these studies were from the 1960s and 1970s.) Here too the results were fairly clear. As class size decreased, student attitudes toward learning and school improved, and teacher attitudes toward their students and teacher morale improved even more dramatically.[11] This finding also fits with what many parents and teachers believe is obvious.

Having found that smaller classes are better, Glass, Cahen, Smith, and Filby set out to explain *why* achievement and attitudes improve in smaller classes. After all, their meta-analysis provided what they believed to be compelling evidence about results but said nothing directly about what it was in the smaller classes that led to improvements in student learning and attitudes. Using their own fieldwork and evidence from some of the studies they had examined, Glass and his colleagues speculated on the links be-tween small class size and the observed results. They proposed that smaller classes provide opportunities for improved instructional techniques; that is, the fewer students a teacher has to deal with, the greater the attention he or she can give to each student in the class. Smaller classes do not *guarantee* better teaching, they simply make it easier.[12]

Not everyone accepted these findings as definitive. The Glass-Smith class-size meta-analysis as it was first published in the late 1970s was criticized on several fronts. (In their 1982 book they addressed many of these criticisms.) Educational Research Services (ERS), which had ear-lier published its own review of class size, argued that Glass and Smith had relied on too few studies and had made overly broad conclusions. ERS maintained that changing class size within a range of thirty-five to twenty-five students would have very little impact on children's achieve-ment (which was actually not that different from the Glass-Smith findings, which showed the real impact coming as classes shrank below twenty). Smaller classes might have a slight impact in the early grades for low-achieving or disadvantaged children, but ERS maintained they would have little effect if teaching methods did not change to take advantage of the op-portunities smaller classes created.[13]

There was some coverage of the meta-analysis, and of subsequent criti-cisms of it, in the media. For example, the *New York Times* treated the work of Glass and Smith with respect but also reported on ERS's response. The *Times* concluded that more research on the specific effects of class size was needed, but that the experience of large cities such as New York supported Glass and Smith's argument that smaller classes in the early grades made better teaching possible.[14] While not perfect, their work on class size re-mains the best summation and review of class-size studies that were con-ducted before 1980. The main lesson taken by supporters of reducing class size was that it does help improve student achievement. The main lesson taken by opponents of reducing class size was that to make a meaningful difference, classes had to drop all the way down to fifteen or so students, which critics argue, with some justification, is prohibitively expensive. By the mid-1980s, the findings of Glass and Smith were being widely debated; the one thing everyone could agree on was that they had revived discussion about class size. Academics were divided on the topic, with many finding the meta-analysis compelling, and the earlier consensus that class size mat-tered little or not at all had been shattered.

Class Size in the 1980s

Glass and Smith's claims that dramatically reducing class size would have a powerful impact on student achievement had little influence on most public school systems in the early 1980s. Even if all school districts had known about and believed the arguments of the meta-analysis, most were in no financial shape to attempt such an expensive reform. Adjusting for inflation, spending on public elementary and secondary schools fell 7 percent between 1977 and 1982. Federal spending was dropping at the same time, and although it accounted for less than 10 percent of total school funding, this decrease hit urban schools especially hard, since federal spending tended to be targeted toward disadvantaged children and urban schools. In oil-rich states such as Oklahoma and Texas, state funding, which paid for nearly half of school budgets in 1981–82, remained strong. But in states where the economy suffered, so did school financing. Some states placed limits on school spending. California's Proposition 13, passed overwhelmingly by voters in 1978, amended the state constitution to limit property taxes, thereby also effectively limiting local spending on schools. A number of other states quickly followed suit. At the same time, the cost of textbooks and of gasoline for buses were skyrocketing. As a result of this financial crunch, teachers were being laid off, class sizes were increasing, and some schools were even closing.[15]

Virginia was one of many states concerned with the quality of its public schools in the mid-1970s, and class size was a central issue. The state developed standards in 1976 declaring that by September 1977, no first-, second-, or third-grade class should have more than twenty-eight students. If there were more than twenty-eight students in a class, either an instructional aide was to be added or another class formed. School officials in Fairfax County supported the idea of small classes but wanted more flexibility under the law. They pointed out that to meet the law's requirements, they would actually have to keep classes to twenty-six children, so that if one or two children transferred in during the school year, officials would not have to form new classes and split children away from their teachers. As a result, Fairfax officials, along with a number of other education groups in Virginia, urged the state's General Assembly to change the law from a twenty-eight-student maximum to an average number per class of twenty-eight. Supporters of the law opposed this change, pointing out that under the proposed wording, classes could have thirty-five or more children.[16]

Large urban areas had more dramatic class-size problems. In 1980 the average class size in New York City's elementary schools seems to have been about thirty, but there were hundreds of classes approaching or exceeding forty children. In late 1984 the city put more than $12 million into an attempt to lower average class sizes in the first grade to twenty-five, but with limited success. The *New York Times* indicated that only six of the city's thirty-two districts had reached the goal, and they had apparently done so at the expense of other programs. To find the money for the change, some school districts had even increased class sizes in later grades. Most of the districts had reached an average of twenty-seven or twenty-eight students in first-grade classes, down from twenty-nine the previous year. Schools chancellor Nathan Quinones indicated that a lack of classroom space and higher than expected enrollments were among the reasons for the program's limited effect. Quinones eventually announced that the city's schools had met their class-size goals across grade levels, though those goals were relatively modest: a maximum of twenty-five in kindergarten, a first-grade average of twenty-five, and an average of twenty-nine for grades two through eight. Classes in several areas, such as physical education, art, and music, were not included in the limits.[17]

Schools in older industrial regions were probably hit the worst by economic downturns, as might be expected. Cities such as St. Louis and Detroit had suffered a decline well before the recession of the late 1970s. Elementary schools in St. Louis lost art programs, music programs, and physical education in late 1982. Federal aid had dropped by $12 million, local tax revenue had decreased, and voters had rejected a tax increase that would have aided public schools. At the same time, enrollments were rising faster than school officials had expected, apparently driven in part by recession-hit families removing their children from private schools they could no longer afford and sending them to public schools instead. Average class size in St. Louis schools rose from twenty-five students the previous year to an astounding thirty-five children per class.[18]

In the wake of the 1983 report *A Nation at Risk*, a number of states considered reducing class size as one possible way to improve school performance and student achievement. A 1986 resolution of the National Education Association (NEA) called for smaller classes as a means of improving education, owing to the greater opportunity for individualized attention; the NEA called for an average class size of fifteen children.[19] But few states actually did anything systematic about reducing class size in the 1980s. It was, after all, an expensive educational reform, and one that would be especially difficult to implement in an era of tax cuts, rising costs, and government retrenchment.

The student-teacher ratio continued to vary dramatically from state to state. In 1986, five states were below 15 to 1, led by Connecticut's 13.7 to 1. In the same year, seven states had ratios of more than 20 to 1, topped by Utah's 23.4 to 1 and California's 23 to 1. Of course, within every state there was also wide variation from school to school and district to district. And since student-teacher ratios include special education teachers, guidance counselors, and other personnel who don't teach, actual class sizes averaged three or four students more than the ratios would indicate. The average class size in Connecticut in 1986 was actually probably about seventeen students, in California and Utah perhaps twenty-six students. In the mid- to late 1980s, the average class size in American schools as a whole was believed to be about twenty-four children.[20]

Throughout the 1980s, proponents of small classes faced a number of problems, the greatest being the high cost of smaller classes and the lack of sufficient classroom space in many school districts. The National Education Association pointed out another problem at its 1987 annual gathering. A survey the NEA had conducted of many of the nation's larger school districts revealed a shortage of qualified teachers. Almost half the responding districts said they would use temporary or substitute teachers to address an expected flood of vacant teaching positions. Just how extensive the teacher shortage would be (if it existed at all) was questioned by other groups; the U.S. Bureau of Labor Statistics reported in 1986 that no major teacher shortages were expected over the next decade.[21] Even if the bureau were right and the NEA wrong, however, any serious widespread attempts to reduce class size were almost certain to require more qualified teachers than teacher training programs usually produced.[22]

The most interesting effort of the early 1980s to examine smaller classes was made in Indiana, where a demonstration project called Prime Time reduced the class size in twenty-four kindergarten, first-, and second-grade classrooms to fourteen children. Prime Time was not a carefully controlled study, but its results were considered promising. Children in the smaller classes did better on standard achievement tests than children in larger classes. Disciplinary problems were reduced in the smaller classes, and teachers reported they were being more effective in their work. Indiana Governor Robert Orr and the state legislature agreed on a number of education bills for the 1984–85 school year, with the most significant being a class-size reduction bill that greatly expanded the program. The bill reduced class size in the state's first-grade classes, at a cost of $19 million. In later years the program would expand to kindergarten and the second and third grades, with the cost steadily rising as a result. The money ($18,000 for each new first-grade teacher) would go to schools to hire additional teachers and thereby shrink classes; schools without enough space to do this would receive money to hire teacher's aides.[23]

In August 1984, a month before Prime Time was to take effect, 285 of Indiana's 303 eligible school districts were preparing to reduce class size in first grade. Thirteen were undecided, and only 5 school districts had decided not to join the program. Governor Orr saw the class-size reduction program as "a real opportunity, perhaps the first real opportunity in recent history, to make a long-range difference in the education of our children." Orr also announced that Prime Time would be funded as long as he was governor. Along with being an interesting implementation of smaller classes, Indiana's effort was an important step in studying their impact. As Jeremy Finn notes, it showed "the feasibility of a statewide class-size initiative and the need to conduct an intervention of this type over a number of years." But it did not provide much reliable information about the effects of class size to outside observers. There was no real control group, which meant that any results that came out of the smaller classes could be questioned. And as it turned out, the results were not impressive. For example, a comparison of the test scores of third graders who had been in the smaller classes for three years (as of 1987) with third graders from the previous year who had not been in Prime Time classes showed little difference. The authors of that study concluded that in Indiana's case "the long-term effects of a state-sponsored reduced class-size program are negligible."[24] But the program was popular—teachers, parents, and politicians all believed it made a difference—so findings that showed Prime Time had little effect had, as it turned out, little effect on Prime Time.

By the early 1990s, most schools participating in Prime Time were using the option of adding teacher's aides rather than the "pure" version of actually reducing classes to eighteen students with one teacher. It was unclear which approach worked better. A 1991 study showed that a group of first- and second-grade students in so-called pure classes did better on a standardized test than did children in classes with aides. But the same study found that second- and third-grade students in classes with aides did better on the standardized tests than did a similar group in pure classes. To call these results ambiguous is stating the obvious.[25] Overall, there was relatively little research done on Prime Time in its first ten years of existence, and no clear-cut evidence that either version really made a significant difference in student achievement. It was entirely possible that Indiana's children would have had basically the same test scores had they all been in classes of twenty-five, with Prime Time never having existed. It was equally possible that both versions of the initiative had made a huge difference, and that without them student scores would have been considerably lower. There was no way to be certain.

Even so, an article in the *Indianapolis Star* in late 1995 argued that Prime Time was probably Robert Orr's "most enduring legacy" as governor. Almost all of the state's school districts were still participating in the program, which cost the state about $75 million a year. The article's author, Andrea Neal, pointed to the results of Tennessee's Project STAR (described later in this chapter) as showing that Prime Time's reliance on teacher's aides was a mistake. As we will see, the STAR results showed that a class of thirteen to seventeen students provided considerably greater benefits than did a class of twenty-two to twenty-five with a teacher's aide. Furthermore, Neal pointed out that Tennessee had made its classes smaller than had Indiana, reaching an average of fifteen students rather than Indiana's goal of eighteen to twenty in the early grades.[26] One of the most immediate effects of Prime Time was that its positive results—that teachers, students, and parents all liked the program—encouraged other states to pass class-size reduction plans. By late 1985 at least fifteen states were trying to reduce class size in at least some of their elementary schools.[27]

What did the federal government have to say about the effects of changing class size? In 1988 the Department of Education published "Class Size and Public Policy: Politics and Panaceas." Authored by Tommy Tomlinson, a researcher at the DOE, the report argues that there is no real evidence to support the belief that reducing class size would lead to improved student achievement, unless classes were reduced to fifteen children, which he considered unlikely and prohibitively expensive. To support his argument that reducing class size was not a promising reform, Tomlinson points out that while average class size fell between the mid-1960s and late 1970s, achievement-test scores also fell (instead of rising) during that period. Tomlinson takes this as evidence that reducing class size does not increase student achievement; his logic is that if class size mattered, then gradually declining class sizes should have led to better test scores. Tomlinson admits that states with smaller classes generally have higher student averages on college entrance exams, and that states with large class sizes do less well on average on those same tests. But he claims the relationship is irrelevant, writing "that cultural influences are strong, perhaps determining, is plain to see." Tomlinson then turns to an international comparison, and points out that in 1982 Japan scored first in a comparison of eighth-grade mathematics scores, even though its average class size was forty-one, while the United States was well down in the rankings despite an average class size of just twenty-six. He claims this is further evidence that class size does not matter.[28]

In fact, however, the logic of these arguments is extremely weak. Children's learning is affected by any number of factors, some that shape schools and some outside of schools, such as parental income and education. Numerous other changes were occurring in the 1960s and 1970s in both education and the broader society that may have accounted for declining test scores, all of which the report ignores. Tomlinson does not argue that the differences between test scores of different nations might be the result of different cultures, because they fit his argument as they are. Yet he does use cultural differences to explain away the connection between class size and the average college entrance scores of students from different states in the United States, where the apparent relationship contradicts his argument. But are the differences between Connecticut and Georgia, for example, greater than the differences between the United States and Japan? That argument seems absurd. Yet in both cases where class size does not seem to matter, the historical trend within the United States and the international comparisons, Tomlinson treats class size and test scores as if they are the only pertinent factors and that one must be directly connected to the other. Class size is just one of many factors that *may* affect student achievement. None of the simplistic arguments Tomlinson uses to argue against class size as having an impact holds up under even moderate scrutiny.

In fact, the report itself is an excellent example of the highly political nature of debates over class size. Evidence arguing that class size matters was ignored or belittled, while relationships that seem to show class size to have little or no effect on student achievement were treated as powerful, no matter how flawed the actual logic. The main goal of the report seemed to be to oppose reducing class size because of the high cost it would entail. Instead of spending money on smaller classes, the report stated that money should be channeled into improving teacher quality and training, even though no evidence was presented that the quality of teaching matters.[29] Of course, it seems the most basic common sense that the quality of teaching does matter but then supporters of reducing class size, particularly parents, see their proposals as being firmly based in common sense.

Despite the report's logical flaws and surprisingly simplistic view of education, Tomlinson's argument that class size is a very expensive reform is valid. Even if one believes reducing class size makes a real difference, the question remains whether that difference is worth what it costs. So does the question of whether other reforms might achieve greater results at a lower cost. Since the report came from the Department of Education, it received considerable media coverage, but not everyone accepted its arguments. The *New York Times* covered the report but spent more time citing critics of Tomlinson's arguments and supporters of reducing class size than it did detailing the report's claims. An editorial in the *Washington Post* criticized the report on several fronts, with statements such as "even more misleading are the comparisons of class size with SAT averages, which vary enormously with the proportion of students who are college bound."[30] The report was influential, however, since it came from the Department of Education. The arguments Tomlinson made against reducing class size have been echoed by opponents of smaller classes ever since.

Tennessee's Project STAR

The most ambitious experiment ever performed on the effects of different class sizes, and one of the most impressive educational experiments ever done on any topic, took place in Tennessee in the 1980s. The experiment was, in part, the result of lengthy advocacy for class size reduction by Helen Bain, past president of the National Education Association and a professor at Tennessee State University. Over the course of several years Bain convinced some state legislators of the potential importance of smaller classes. While they were unwilling to fund small classes throughout the state, they did decide to provide funding for an extensive experiment on the effects of reducing class size. (Bain wanted smaller classes statewide, not an experiment, as she was already certain they would make a difference.) Bain's influence in the legislature was enhanced because she had the backing of the state teacher's union. Another fortuitous factor was that Steve Cobb, an influential member of the state House of Representatives in the early 1980s, had a Ph.D. in sociology and understood the potential power of program evaluation and randomized experiments. Project Student/Teacher Achievement Ratio, dubbed Project STAR, received more than $10 million in funding for teachers and aides. STAR involved more than 7,000 students across seventy-nine schools and forty-two school districts. Roughly one-third of the children were African American, and almost half were eligible for free or reduced-price lunches. The experiment was designed to build on the findings of the studies described earlier in this chapter, including Indiana's Prime Time and the Glass-Smith meta-analysis.[31]

In each participating school, students were randomly placed in one of three types of kindergarten classes. Small ("treatment" or "experimental") classes ranged from thirteen to seventeen students, with an average of fifteen. Regular ("control") classes had between twenty-two and twenty-six students. A third placement option, "regular with aide," was a class with twenty-two to twenty-five students and a full-time teacher aide as well as a regular teacher. Children were to remain in the type of class they were initially assigned to for four years, through the end of third grade. Teachers were randomly assigned to classes in a separate process. Teachers were not provided with any special training regarding teaching in a small class (although there was limited training provided before the third year to a sample of the teachers). The teachers were, on average, highly trained and experienced. Each school in Project STAR had classes of all three types, to control for local variables such as the quality of school leadership, the community, the textbooks used, and so on. Some randomized experiments in education are flawed because they do not examine or control for crucial factors such as variation among teachers, but STAR was developed and conducted with a deep understanding of the numerous factors that influence education. Because the STAR experiment was rooted in the results of earlier studies, it focused on the primary grades and lowered class size to around fifteen children, where the Glass and Smith meta-analysis showed that the impact was likely to be powerful. STAR was also designed to compare the effects on children of different racial and economic backgrounds, and to compare urban and rural settings.[32]

Implementation of Project STAR was not perfect. School practicalities overrode the evaluators' hopes. After kindergarten, half the children in regular classes were reassigned to classes with aides, and half the children from classes with aides were shifted to regular classes. Because of this, the comparison between regular classes and classes with aides was weakened.

(Children who arrived at schools during the course of the experiment were randomly assigned to a class.) And due to parental complaints there was even some movement between small and regular classes over the four years of the experiment, though children were supposed to remain in their initial placement from start to finish. In fact, many of the early reports from Project STAR assumed they had done so. As it turned out, however, almost 8 percent of the children assigned to small classes in kindergarten were *not* in small classes in first grade. Nevertheless, a detailed analysis of the data by Barbara Nye, Larry Hedges, and Spyros Konstantopoulos found that the results of STAR still held up remarkably well even when these problems were taken into account. Nye and her colleagues actually determined that "problems in the implementation of the experiment probably led to underestimates of the effects of small classes."[33]

Project STAR ran for four years, as planned, until the students finished the third grade. At the end of each school year, all participating students were given standardized achievement tests; all except kindergarten children also took curriculum-based Tennessee tests. Although no single experiment could answer every important question about the various possibilities associated with changing class size, there was nothing ambiguous about the results of Project STAR. It showed smaller classes had a clear and significant effect on how well children performed on standardized tests. Children in the smaller classes did notably better than both children in regular classes and children in classes with aides. The gains in kindergarten and first grade were the most impressive. Perhaps the simplest way to describe the results for children in smaller classes is that the boost amounted to at least a 1.5-month advantage in reading and a 2.5-month advantage in mathematics. Children in classes with an aide scored higher than children in regular classes, but the difference was small. Perhaps most important, given concerns about public schools in some poor urban communities with large minority populations, children of color (which in Tennessee generally meant African American) benefited the most from the smaller classes, in terms of test scores. In most of the comparisons, smaller classes had *twice as great an impact* on the test scores of children of color as they had on white children.[34]

At the start of fourth grade all the children were placed in regular classrooms, where they became part of a follow-up study to determine the long-term effects of being in small classes in the first four years of school. After all, if children who return to normal classrooms lose the advantages they showed earlier, then how much good does reducing class size really do? (Remember the apparent cognitive effects of Head Start, which fade out quickly, as described in Chapter 1.) The Lasting Benefits Study, run by researchers at Tennessee State University, followed nearly 5,000 students to see whether the gains last after children return to regular classes. After fifth grade, children in the experimental group were still doing markedly better than children from the control group. The gap between the groups had decreased only slightly, and children from the smaller classes continued to score higher on reading, language, and math tests. In 1994 the results for children in sixth grade showed that the benefits of smaller classes continued. Barbara Nye, research director for the Lasting Benefits Study, described the results as giving students in the experimental group a "six-month advantage" over children who had attended regular-size classes through grade three. At the end of eighth grade, children who had been in the smaller classes still performed better on tests than their counterparts. These results held true for reading, math, and science, and were all statistically significant; while the advantage they enjoyed over children from the regular classes had diminished somewhat, it was still more than two-thirds of what it had been at the end of third grade. Initial analysis of the data showed that small classes in kindergarten and first grade had a large effect, and that small second- and third-grade classes maintained the advantage the children had gained. But remember that it was later found that some children had switched from small classes to regular classes, or from regular to small classes, despite STAR's design, which mandated that children should maintain their assignment for all four years. Other children entered in midstream and were randomly assigned after STAR had begun, and thus spent one, two, or three years in the program, rather than the intended four years. When Nye, Hedges, and Konstantopoulos performed a more sophisticated analysis taking this unintended movement into account, they were able to examine the effects of having different numbers of years in small classes. They found that the effect of small classes grew stronger as children spent more years in them. Students who spent four years in small classes gained approximately twice as much as did children who spent just one year. In high school, the children who had been in small classes continued to do better on a variety of standardized tests than did the children from the regular classes. They were also less likely to drop out of school, more likely to graduate from high school on time, and more likely to take advanced courses, earn high grades, and go on to college. The longer the

children from small classes are followed, the more impressive their outcomes seem.[35]

Given the strength of the early results, which as we have seen held up
well over time, it is not surprising that some members of the Tennessee
government wanted to act on them. But what exactly were they to do? The
pilot program had been in seventy-nine schools. In December 1989, there
were just over 260,000 Tennessee children in kindergarten through third
grade. According to the state's assistant education commissioner, there
were 10,481 teachers at those grade levels. To reduce the class size for all
children in those grades from twenty-five to fifteen would mean finding almost 7,000 more teachers, at a cost to the state of almost $180 million a
year, and local communities would have to spend another $47 million per
year. In addition, schools would need to develop nearly 7,000 new classrooms, at a cost of approximately $270 million. Some members of the leg-
islature were in favor of phasing in smaller class sizes gradually; one state
representative proposed legislation several times that would reduce class
size, but the measures all died in committee because of their high cost.
Raising state spending for education is especially complicated in states like
Tennessee, where there is no state income tax.[36]

But Tennessee did act on Project STAR's results. Instead of trying to institute small classes across the entire state, the legislature created Project
Challenge. Challenge focused on the state's seventeen poorest school districts, as measured by per capita income and the percentage of students in
the subsidized lunch program. Beginning in 1990, every primary school in
each of the chosen districts had some classes reduced to fifteen students. By
1992, all classes from kindergarten through third grade were in the target
range. By 1993, second-grade reading scores in the Challenge districts had,
on average, risen in rank from ninety-ninth (in 1990) among the state's
138 school districts to seventy-eighth. Even more impressive, mean math
scores had risen from eighty-fifth place in 1990 to fifty-seventh in 1993,
which put them well above the state average. Early results from Project
Challenge seemed to show convincingly that Project STAR's findings could
be made into effective educational policy.[37]

In 1992 the Tennessee legislature passed the Education Improvement
Act, which called for lowering class sizes. Because the legislature approved
only $115 million in funding (less than a quarter of the $564 million requested), smaller classes would not become mandatory until four years after the program became fully funded. The state sales tax was increased by a

half cent to raise the money. The prior limit on student-teacher ratios was twenty-five to one in kindergarten through third grade, and it gradually grew in higher grades, culminating in a limit of thirty-five to one for grades 7–12. The new law would lower those ratios by five, dropping the K–3 ratio to twenty to one, grades 4–6 to twenty-five to one, and grades 7–12 to thirty to one. Beginning in the 1993–94 academic year, schools that were unable to meet the new requirements would have to apply for a waiver, which would be based on whether they were perceived as having made a good-faith effort.[38]

A 1997 audit showed that 125 of Tennessee's 139 school districts had either met or were making progress toward meeting the twenty to one student-teacher ratio for K–3. Increases in per-pupil spending, which rose from $3,491 in 1991–92 to $4,405 in 1995–96, had made this possible. The bulk of the increase had come in the state's share of spending, which had increased 68 percent, to $2,302 per pupil, while local spending had risen 17 percent, to $1,896. But there was still a long way to go. In the fall of 1998 the state's school districts had just three years left in which to meet the class-size mandates, and many were struggling to build the necessary classrooms and hire more teachers.[39] The program was popular. In Tennessee's fall elections, according to *The Tennessean,* politicians were "clamoring to take credit for the dramatic reduction in class size in public schools."[40]

While Project STAR itself was rarely criticized, not everyone agreed that its results were definitive, or what the exact policy implications of its findings should be. Opponents of reducing class size sometimes gave STAR a brief nod, but they did not change their mind because of its results. A handful of education experts continued to be quoted in the media as opposing class size reduction after STAR's release. Their basic argument was usually either that studies were inconclusive about the effects of lowering class size, or that smaller classes might work but did not make enough difference to be worth the considerable expense. Tommy Tomlinson was quoted in the *St. Petersburg (Fla.) Times* in March 1993 that the main benefit from class size reduction was to the teachers. More to the point, Tomlinson argued that reducing class size was not cost effective. Chester Finn, who had been Tomlinson's superior in 1988, stated that "politicians across the spectrum are almost universally wrong on this issue" when they favor reducing class size.[41] Eric Hanushek, a University of Rochester economist (his work on school funding is described at length in Chapter 5), also questioned the value of smaller classes. In 1995, *Current* published an article by Hanushek entitled "Money and Education: Making America's Schools Work." One of his targets was the movement toward smaller classes. Like Tomlinson, Hanushek made the impressive-sounding but irrelevant point that class sizes had been on a gradual decline since 1890, while test scores had been declining over recent decades. He then claimed that "econometric and experimental evidence shows vividly that across-the-board reductions in class size are unlikely to yield discernible gains in overall student achievement." In more recent work, Hanushek has continued to question various details of STAR, and to hold up his own studies of the effects of school funding as proof that smaller classes have little impact.[42] The evidence clearly does not support Hanushek's argument, though his opinion that smaller classes will not help student achievement continues to be quoted widely.

Despite the impressive results of Project STAR, there are numerous unanswered questions about class size. What are the effects of reducing classes from thirty to twenty students, as California has done? STAR, after all, reduced class sizes from twenty-four to fifteen; according to the meta-analysis by Glass and Smith, going from thirty to twenty is a much less significant reduction. And will such a reduction help children from the hundred different cultural, ethnic, and racial backgrounds in California's schools the way it helped native-born African-American and white children in Tennessee? Will small classes in only the first grade have the same long-lasting impact that small K–3 classes had in Tennessee, or do children need four years? Or three years? The most recent results of the Lasting Benefits Study indicate that the number of years spent in small classes does have a long-term impact, but just how much and for whom is not totally clear. Would five or six years be dramatically better than four, or not at all better?

California

Proposition 13, which was passed in 1978 and severely limited property taxes, was the beginning of the California public schools' plummet down the national ranks of school quality by almost every measure. Californians may have been happy about lower taxes, but they have not been happy about the declining schools that resulted. Proposition 13 and its immediate effects on efforts to create greater funding equity between different school districts are described in Chapter 5; because it limited funding for public schools, it inevitably touched on class-size issues. By early 1982 the state had the second worst student-teacher ratio in the nation. In 1983 the California legislature and Governor George Deukmejian managed to agree on an education reform bill designed to turn the state school system's fortunes around. The law led to increased funding, academic reforms, longer school days, and a variety of other improvements, but it only slightly reversed the disasters of the preceding decade. California's classes were, on average, still the nation's largest. At the same time, Deukmejian had vetoed bills that would have reduced class size and helped fund school construction. The California Teachers Association (CTA), which represented more than three-fourths of the state's teachers, had made reducing class size its first priority and was placing ads about the issue in newspapers. Opposition to the idea centered on a very basic and daunting fact: reducing the average class size by just one student in a state with California's massive population would cost an estimated $400 million, and getting class sizes down to the national average would cost $3 *billion* every year. And that was without adding in the cost of enough new schools and classrooms to hold those smaller classes, which would also be enormous.[43]

Local districts that wanted to reduce class size tried or considered a variety of approaches. Some overcrowded schools in California made use of their buildings for twelve months instead of nine. In the early 1980s a number of schools in southeast Los Angeles converted to year-round schedules. In mid-1986 some school officials in San Diego were considering a year-round calendar that would require many students to be in session during the summer. But year-round schooling faced opposition from parents in most places where it was considered, in part because they wanted all the children in the family to have the same vacation period; year-round schooling also created problems for single or divorced parents. By the late 1980s, most of the Westside schools in Los Angeles had considered and rejected year-round schooling, choosing instead to deal with overcrowding by buying portable classrooms and letting class sizes grow. Other schools targeted money from various sources to create smaller classes in specific areas. Some school districts created combined classes, mixing children from different grades, as a way to even out classes and keep class size at least somewhat under control. In many locales, however, there was little or nothing that could be done to keep class size under thirty. Some high schools held more than twice as many students as their campuses had been designed for. Under such conditions, thirty students may have been a relatively small class.[44]

For the next decade, California's politicians and educators bickered over how much money should come from the state and how it should be targeted, and class size continued to be an issue that received a great deal of discussion but relatively little actual state help. Public schools faced a "fundamental political dilemma," as one columnist put it, in that the political process was dominated by an aging bloc of white voters with decreasing numbers of school-age children. At the same time, schools were serving a growing number of children of color coming from numerous cultural backgrounds and speaking literally more than a hundred different languages. In the face of often stagnant or even falling revenues and rapidly growing student populations, local schools continued to make do as best they could. Throughout the late 1980s and early 1990s, class sizes in California public schools remained among the highest in the nation. Teachers regularly complained, to little apparent effect. In the fall of 1987, the California Teachers Association spent a million dollars on television, radio, and newspaper ads built around the theme "Don't Crowd Our Kids." But the problems faced by the state's public schools deepened when California's economy suffered more setbacks in the severe recession of the late 1980s and early 1990s than did most of the nation, *and* the state then lagged in its recovery. State funding for local schools was badly hurt as a result.[45] But the greatest problem facing schools with growing enrollments was a lack of space. School construction in California was traditionally paid for by a combination of local property taxes and state aid, but the passage of Proposition 13 in 1978 had greatly limited the former, and the latter was strained throughout the 1980s.[46] Portable classrooms became a common sight at many schools, particularly urban ones, all too often covering large portions of school playgrounds.

In the midst of these dark economic times for California's public schools, there was a silver lining. In the fall 1988 elections, state superintendent of public instruction Bill Honig and the CTA sponsored a ballot initiative, Proposition 98, to guarantee that a fixed portion (at least 39 percent) of the state's budget would go to education (meaning public schools and community colleges). Although voters had rejected the same initiative in June, in November they passed it by a small margin. It meant more money for the schools, every year. Perhaps its most important aspect, not especially noted in 1988, was that once the state's economy improved, Proposition 98 could mean a *great deal more* money for California's schools. Prop. 98 included a list of things for which the money should be spent, including reducing class sizes to twenty and raising teacher salaries, but without specifying priorities for the allocation. Exactly how the money would be spent within schools, of course, would be fought over by various interests. Since the CTA had helped sponsor the initiative, it seemed likely its members would expect a considerable amount of the new revenue it provided to go to higher teacher salaries. Other people had different ideas, however. Governor Deukmejian had opposed Prop. 98, but after its passage he announced that the money should go to reducing class size. The superintendent of the Santa Ana Unified School District, which had 40,000 students, called Deukmejian's desire to reduce class size "admirable" but pointed out that his district's need was for more classroom space.[47]

The Los Angeles Times estimated that the state was "at least $5 billion behind in its school construction program." Marlene Davis, superintendent of the Filmore Unified School District, called proposals for class size reduction "ridiculous" because there was no space in which to put additional classes. Democratic gubernatorial candidate Dianne Feinstein argued for a twofold approach to reducing class size, without any major state commitment. She supported year-round schooling, which in effect made more classrooms available. Feinstein also wanted to change the nature of local school bond votes, from requiring a two-thirds majority to a simple majority, to make it easier for communities to approve funds for much-needed new school construction.[48]

In 1992–93 California's estimated average class size of thirty-one placed it second worst in the nation, behind only Utah. Utah's population was overwhelmingly native-born to English-speaking parents, but many of the children entering California's schools spoke little or no English, increasing their need for one-on-one attention from teachers if they were to succeed in school.[49] Another problem faced by urban schools in disadvantaged communities was the difficulty of keeping experienced teachers. Shirley Weber, president of San Diego's school board, claimed in 1991 that every year 50 to 60 percent of the teachers in the district's schools were new. Weber argued that class sizes in her district should be reduced to twenty from their current range of thirty to thirty-five, in part as an incentive for experienced teachers to remain. In early 1994 Weber and the San Diego school board narrowly approved a class-size reduction proposal "after a lengthy and often emotional hearing." The goal was to hire 124 new first- and second-grade teachers, and reduce class size in those grades to twenty-five. There was no money for additional classrooms, however.[50]

In 1996, after years of debate about class size in California's schools, an actual program to shrink classes came from a surprising source, and it received little attention when first suggested. Since becoming California's school chief, Delaine Eastin had been arguing for smaller classes in the early grades. As California's economy improved in 1995 and 1996, tax receipts began to rise dramatically. Because of Proposition 98, a hefty percentage of the new budget surplus had to be targeted to education, but to exactly what aspect of education was undecided. Many Republicans favored school vouchers, but after a proposal for vouchers (which Republican Governor Pete Wilson supported) was defeated, Wilson decided to ensure that local districts throughout California used the money for class size reduction. In May 1996 Wilson's budget revision for the upcoming school year included an incentive that would pay schools $500 per child for any first and second graders in classes of twenty or fewer students. Because the actual costs of such a reduction would be quite a bit higher than $500 per child, and because local schools continued to be strapped for money, most educators refused to take the proposal very seriously. When Wilson suggested expanding the program to the third grade as well, the idea received more attention. His plan initially included $460 million in financial incentives for districts that reduced class size. In late June Wilson called for adding another $218 million for third grade, and even announced he would not agree to an overall state budget deal without it. (Additional money was available because Wilson's attempt to cut personal and corporate income taxes had been defeated.) The program was not a mandate, however, as school systems could decide for themselves whether to apply for funding for first grade only, for first and second grades, for all three grades, or even not to apply at all.[51]

Wilson's support for reducing class size in the early grades came only after his failures with tax cuts and school vouchers, but once behind the idea, he made it his own and stuck with it. Ironically, one of Wilson's motivations was to keep the $1.8 billion in additional money available for education from going to increases in teacher salaries, in keeping with his ongoing feud with the California Teachers Association. So Wilson opposed the CTA by advocating the very idea, class size reduction, that the CTA had long supported. Of course, there also seemed to be good educational reasons to focus on reducing class sizes in the first and second grades, particularly the importance the first years of school play in determining whether students learn to read well. The stated reason behind reducing class size was fairly fundamental: Wilson wanted to improve children's scores on reading and math tests and believed smaller classes, in combination with a changed curriculum, would be a good way to do so. During the 1980s California had taken a literature-based approach to teaching reading and had seen test scores drop dramatically. A few months before the class size program was introduced, the state had shifted toward a system more heavily based in phonics instruction. Smaller class sizes were expected to go hand in hand with the new approach to improve student achievement in first and second grade. The spokesman for Wilson's Office of Child Development and Education stated that "class-size reduction is not a panacea. It's not a cure-all." What smaller classes provided was the opportunity for teachers to give more individual attention to children. Teachers had to change the way they taught to get the maximum impact from smaller classes, by stressing more interactive teaching and hands-on learning. It is worth noting that although Wilson's advisers were apparently aware of Project STAR's results in Tennessee, the program they proposed did not fit perfectly with STAR's findings, since the target class size of twenty was actually between STAR's experimental classes of fifteen and its regular classes of twenty-four. However, it did focus on grades K–3, just as STAR had. The CTA and others correctly noted that reducing class size would be difficult, or even impossible, without funding for additional classroom space as well as for additional teachers. Wilson's budget included $140 million for deferred maintenance for schools, which had to be matched by local districts. While that was almost three times the amount Wilson had proposed for building repairs a few months before, it was only a drop in the bucket compared to what would be needed to provide enough classroom space to reduce class sizes across the state.[52]

Conflict between Democrats and Republicans over the class size bill delayed its passage. A compromise bill was passed in early July, containing most of what Wilson had wanted. Schools that shrank their first- and second-grade classes and wanted to do even more could choose between reducing class sizes in kindergarten and in third grade. Schools would receive $650 for each child placed in a class of twenty or fewer students. The cost for additional teachers would run between $775 and $800 per child, meaning local districts had to make up the difference of $125 to $150 per child. The state would also provide $25,000 toward each new portable classroom (up to $200 million in total expenditures by the state), well short of their actual cost of $40,000. There were also expenses entailed in preparing them for student use; as a result, local districts would have to provide more than half the total cost of the new classrooms.[53]

The class-size reduction program was to go into effect when school began at the end of the summer, leaving school officials just two months to prepare for the start of the school year. To receive state funding, schools had to apply for money for new classrooms by October 1, 1996, for money for new teachers by November 1, and actually have small classes in place by February 16, 1997. Some school officials were excited, others extremely cautious. Pressure from parents statewide, as well as the widespread belief that smaller classes were better for both teachers and children, meant that most schools treated the program as a mandate even though it was a voluntary program. Schools around the state began to convert libraries, gymnasiums, cafeterias, computer labs, offices, and science labs into classrooms. Some schools discontinued preschool programs to free up space and make smaller classes possible. But the most common method of creating more space was to buy portable classrooms and park them on playgrounds or parking lots. Portables were already a common sight at many California schools, and with the new incentive they became omnipresent in some communities. Some schools had already covered all their available space and had no room for more portables. To make matters worse, orders for new portable classrooms exceeded the number manufacturers normally made in a year, so waiting lists quickly developed. Another method many schools turned to in the effort to "create space" was placing forty students in a room with two teachers, thereby creating a twenty to one student-teacher ratio, if not an actual class of twenty children. This was expected to be the most feasible and common method of reducing classes in Los Angeles. In general, crowded inner-city schools were the least able to find the space needed to reduce class size. In Los Angeles County alone, fifty-seven schools lacked space for all the new portables they needed, and as a result were unable to fully implement smaller classes in the first year of the program.[54]

The need for more classroom space was matched by the need for more teachers. The California legislature tried to address this problem with a new law that made it possible for college graduates who passed an examination given by the state to teach their own classes. They would also have to take education courses at night and attend teachers' workshops, thereby making progress toward becoming fully certified. Suburban schools were attractive workplaces in the eyes of many teachers, and such districts were able to hire some of their extra teachers from other schools, instead of having to rely completely on hiring new teachers. This meant that urban schools were more likely than suburban schools to *lose* some of their better teachers just as they were trying to increase their total number of teachers, so they had to rely even more heavily on new teachers than they would have otherwise. School officials from Orange County's school districts met in August 1996 and agreed to not steal teachers from one another, but in general districts throughout the state competed for experienced teachers and newly accredited teachers; some went out of state to hire teachers from elsewhere.[55]

Many schools had at least some smaller classes in place when the school year started in August or September 1996, while others struggled to be ready by the February 1997 deadline. In overcrowded Orange County schools, almost every district began the school year with at least some small first-grade classes, as did some schools in seven of the ten largest districts in Los Angeles County. Los Angeles Unified School District received $16 million from the state for portable classrooms, but the classrooms cost $57 million. The district had to make up the $41 million difference from other parts of its budget. All in all, affluent districts had an easier time affording new classroom space, and also had an easier time bringing in qualified teachers; urban districts faced considerably greater problems, particularly in finding qualified bilingual and special education teachers.[56] By December 1996, only forty-four districts in California had chosen not to take part in the class-size reduction program, and they were almost all small rural districts. Astoundingly, more than 18,000 new teachers had been hired in the state by February 1997. More than 30 percent had just received their teaching credentials, and another 21 percent had emergency credentials. In school districts with more than 20,000 students, 28 percent of the new teachers were working on emergency credentials. Remember that the program was for first and second grades, with an option for either kindergarten or third grade. This meant that children in all four grades were technically eligible for smaller classes, but schools had to choose between kindergarten and third grade (if they chose either), they could not receive state funds to reduce class sizes in both. This meant that only 75 percent of all "eligible" children (all K–3 students) could actually have been in small classes if every school had opted for the maximum of three grades. In fact, an impressive 51 percent of eligible children were in classes of twenty or fewer students by February 1997. Just over 950,000 students out of California's 1.9 million children in grades K–3 participated in the program's first year, a huge shift by any standard. First graders were the most likely to be in small classes (88 percent were), followed by second graders (57 percent), third graders (18 percent), and kindergarten children (14 percent).[57] Given the inexperienced teacher corps and the less than ideal classroom spaces in new portables and former gymnasiums and cafeterias, it was impossible to say with certainty what the effects of the program would be. So many things were different from Project STAR that there was no way to know if its findings would hold true in California. What was clear was that local districts had risen aggressively to take the opportunity the state government had offered.

A handful of changes were made in the class-size reduction program in its second year. Beginning in the 1997–98 school year, schools that wanted to reduce class sizes in kindergarten and third grade could receive state money for both. Also, the state would pay schools $800 for each child in a class of twenty or fewer, thereby coming much closer to paying the full cost of a teacher's salary. In crowded districts that had used up every possible foot of classroom space the year before, the shift toward smaller classes inevitably slowed, but it did not stop. A daunting 62 percent of the new teachers hired by Los Angeles Unified in the fall of 1997 were working with emergency credentials, bringing the total number of teachers doing so to 5,400, more than double the number in the district two years earlier. Early estimates were that approximately 10 percent of teachers in California in 1997–98 lacked formal credentials; the number turned out to be considerably higher.[58] There is ample reason to think teacher quality plays a considerable role in how children learn. It would be unrealistic to assume that all fully credentialed teachers are good teachers, or that all teachers working on emergency credentials are not good teachers. But to whatever extent the typical experienced teacher is better than the typical new teacher with little or no training and experience, children in classrooms with the latter suffered.[59]

Remember that in the first year, 51 percent of children in eligible grades had been in small classes, led by 88 percent of first graders and 57 percent of second graders. In the second year of the program, an astounding 84 percent of eligible children were in classes of twenty or fewer children, led by 99 percent of first graders and 96 percent of second graders. Fewer than 20 percent of kindergarten and third-grade children had enjoyed small classes in the first year of the program, but in the 1997–98 school year, 69 percent of kindergarten children and 67 percent of third graders were in small classes.[60] In April 1997, voters approved a $2.4 billion school repair bond, of which $900 million was to be used for new school construction. The money was long overdue. Conservative estimates placed the state's need for deferred school maintenance at $2.6 billion. Nearly 20 percent of students were in portable classrooms, and additional children attended classes that were held in cafeterias, auditoriums, or other inappropriate environments. In 1998 California's Department of Education estimated the state would need an astounding 456 new schools within five years to house the growing enrollments. More than half of California's schools were at least thirty years old, and the cost to repair them and build the needed new schools was expected to be $20 billion over five years—if the money could be raised and the schools built, that is. One promising note was that local communities had become more willing to pass bonds for school funding. In 1992 the bond passage rate had been just 39 percent, but by 1997 it had risen to 63 percent.[61]

Describing small classes as popular would be an understatement. In late 1997 the class-size reduction program helped to drive Governor Wilson's approval ratings to their highest point. An article in *Newsweek* in August 1998 began by quoting the principal of an elementary school in Los Angeles as saying that smaller classes were having a direct effect on learning. "When you walk into a classroom, you can taste it, feel it and see it," Pam Marton said, apparently feeling that smaller classes were worth the changes her school had had to make: the cafeteria, the auditorium, the library, a bathroom, and much of the playground had been converted into classroom space. Some school districts were already reporting sizable gains in test scores.[62] Governor Wilson and others sponsored a petition drive to place a new proposition, Proposition 8, on the November 1998 ballot. Prop. 8 called for making small classes in kindergarten through third grade a permanent part of future state budgets. In November 1998 voters defeated Prop. 8, but they passed Proposition 1A, which approved the sale of $6.7 billion in state bonds to fund renovation of existing schools and construction of new schools.[63]

Will California's students benefit in the long run from smaller classes, as much as Project STAR would indicate? There are a number of uncertainties. First, STAR showed results when class sizes were lowered from roughly twenty-four students to roughly fifteen; California has reduced average class sizes in the early grades from thirty to twenty. While these two different reductions in class size may lead to the same kind of impact on student achievement, they also may not. Remember that the meta-analysis of class size by Glass and Smith showed that smaller classes really begin to make a notable difference when they are below twenty, and especially when they reach fifteen. Of equal importance, Project STAR made use of randomly selected teachers who were largely experienced, whereas California is heavily reliant on new teachers, many of them without any formal credentials. Inner-city and rural schools most in need of high-quality teachers have been the most likely to wind up with teachers with limited training and experience. STAR's findings showed that low-income children benefited the most from small classes, but if low-income children in California receive inferior teaching, they may actually gain *less* from small classes than middle-class children.

When California's program began there was no apparatus in place to perform a thorough evaluation of its effects on students. Parents, teachers, administrators, and politicians nonetheless agreed that the program was a success, and newspapers were full of statements to that effect. For example, in April 1997 the *Los Angeles Times* described a first-grade teacher in Capistrano whose eighteen students were all reading at grade level; actually, fourteen of them were reading at the second-grade level. She said she was "thrilled with the results" of having smaller classes.[64] In June 1998 state superintendent of public instruction Delaine Eastin finally announced a four-year study to evaluate the impact of reduced class size. A consortium of research institutions would conduct it.[65]

Early statewide evaluation results were encouraging in some ways, discouraging in others, and due to the reduce-everywhere nature of the program, they could not be very rigorous. More children in small second- and third-grade classes scored at or above average on a national achievement test than did children in larger second- and third-grade classes. But the schools that had managed to reduce class size were different in numerous ways than those that had not, so there was no real way to know what role class size actually played in the superior scores. The assumption that schools with the most disadvantaged populations were the least able to hire qualified teachers was borne out. And the nature of student test results raised the possibility that the statewide class size program was actually *widening* the achievement gap between middle-class and low-income students. If so, it was a particularly damning commentary on how California was implementing smaller classes, given Project STAR's evidence that smaller classes could dramatically *reduce* the achievement gap between children from well-off and impoverished families.[66]

Around the Nation in the 1990s

Like the economic slump of the late 1970s and early 1980s, the downturn of the late 1980s and early 1990s affected school funding. One of the most obvious results in many locations, as in California, was overcrowded schools. At the same time, class size had been a part of the ongoing discussion about school reform since 1983. Parents and teachers formed a continual support group for smaller classes, but their political power was generally quite limited, particularly on issues where the general public's resistance to higher taxes comes into play, as it does in any discussion of reducing class size on a large scale. Even so, a number of cities and states made efforts to reduce class sizes in their schools, while others found themselves struggling to stay where they were in the face of escalating enrollments. Many of these efforts to reduce class size were at least partially inspired by Project STAR's results.[67] Following is a sampling of such efforts from around the nation, moving roughly eastward from California.

In 1989 the Nevada legislature began a gradual effort to reduce class sizes in the early grades. The goal was fifteen children in K–3 classes, with the reduction beginning in first grade; once all first-grade classes were down to the target size, reduction would begin in the second grade, then in the third grade. In 1997 Governor Bob Miller, who had been a major force behind the reform since its inception, was still trying to get funding to make the lower class size mandatory in third-grade classes.[68] Unlike the rush to smaller classes in California, Nevada's changeover was gradual at every step. By early 1999, third-grade classes in Nevada had been reduced to an average size of nineteen children. Even with much more time to plan than California schools had had, the lack of classroom space was a major obstacle in Nevada. In 1991, 90 percent of Nevada's smaller classes were being team taught in groups of thirty-two students and two teachers, for a student-teacher ratio of sixteen to one. By 1997 the percentage of "small" classes that actually consisted of thirty-two students being taught by two teachers was down to 45 percent. Nevada's government did not fund any thorough evaluation of the effects of smaller classes on children's achievement. Three relatively modest studies showed mixed effects.[69] Part of the problem here is that there is no reason to think one class of thirty-two children and two teachers will have the same positive effect on children's achievement scores as would two separate classes of sixteen children each. There is little evidence on the effects of team teaching, and the STAR finding that classes with teacher's aides were far less effective than smaller classes with just one teacher would indicate that the two methods are not, in fact, very similar.

In the mid-1990s Wisconsin began a pilot, five-year class-size reduction program targeted at disadvantaged children. Called SAGE, for Student Achievement Guarantee in Education, the program provided $2,000 per student to school districts with high percentages of low-income students if they reduced class sizes in kindergarten and first grade to fifteen children. The program took effect in September 1996, but it was not a mandated program, nor was that amount of money guaranteed to all eligible districts that chose to participate. The legislature had provided a set amount of money; if more districts than expected joined the program, then the actual amount of money received by each would decrease accordingly. Most SAGE classrooms had one teacher and fifteen or fewer students, but other arrangements were also used to reach a fifteen to one ratio, such as two teachers and thirty (or fewer) students. A study of SAGE was released in December 1997 showing that first graders in small classes were scoring higher than were children in a comparison group, after statistical adjustments for family income, race, and several other factors. The results were statistically significant in mathematics and language arts (though not in reading), and African-American males benefited the most, in keeping with the findings from Project STAR. By the fall of 1998, there were seventy-eight SAGE schools, at a cost to the state of just under $15 million per year. Later evaluation results also showed positive, and statistically significant, results.[70]

The recession of the early 1990s hit southern schools as savagely as it did urban schools. In Georgia in 1991, just as tight budgets were leading to overcrowded classrooms, the number of state monitors overseeing whether schools were complying with state limits on class size was reduced from sixteen to one. The only way state education officials would know if classes were oversized was if parents or teachers called and told them. In the fall, the DeKalb County school board approved allowing local school systems to increase class size to help deal with budget cuts. Under pressure from parents, however, the board reversed itself regarding kindergarten and first grade—although the maximum numbers were still very high: twenty-eight students for kindergarten and thirty-three for first grade.[71] In the summer of 1995, state schools superintendent Linda Schrenko proposed a plan to free up more than $400 million in state funds as block grants, which would allow local districts to decide whether to use the money for reducing class size or for special programs for at-risk children. At a lengthy hearing on the plan, however, representatives from a variety of school districts across Georgia argued that they did not have adequate classroom space to make reducing class sizes feasible.[72]

Debates over class size played an important role in Virginia politics in the 1990s, especially in the 1993 and 1997 races for governor. In the 1993 campaign, Democratic gubernatorial candidate Mary Sue Terry proposed spending $100 million to reduce class sizes from twenty-five to eighteen in the first three grades, targeted specifically at the state's poorest areas. Her Republican opponent, George F. Allen, accused Terry of wanting to throw money at the state's educational problems. Allen won the election, but in early 1994 the state's General Assembly passed a $103 million program to reduce the disparity between funding for schools in wealthy and poor communities. Much of the money would go to creating smaller classes in less affluent communities, as Terry had proposed. Allen agreed to the plan with some modifications, and the budget he proposed in December 1995 contained funding to continue it.[73] Four years later, in the next race for governor, Republican James Gilmore defeated Democrat Don Beyer. Beyer had promised to improve education by raising teachers' salaries, and he supported continuation of Virginia's class-size reduction plan, which targeted schools where at least 16 percent of the students qualified for federally subsidized meals. Gilmore had advocated giving teachers simple cost-of-living raises and using the savings to reduce class size more broadly. Gilmore's approach proved more popular, and was credited by *U.S. News and World Report* as playing a "key role" in his victory. At the same time, neither candidate was willing to commit additional state aid to school construction, even though there was expected to be a $4 billion shortfall on construction and improvements over the next five years. In 1996, the Virginia Department of Education concluded that almost two-thirds of the state's public schools needed replacement or major renovation, and almost half were using portable classrooms. In 1998 the General Assembly continued to provide money for class size reduction, but allowed some of it to be used in other ways if local districts so chose. Democrats also successfully voted to provide $110 million toward school construction, arguing that money for additional teachers made little sense if there was nowhere for them to teach.[74]

In New York City, large classes have been an ongoing problem. In the first few weeks of school in the fall of 1991, more than 2,000 teachers in New York City filed grievances over the size of their classes. There was supposed to be a cap of thirty-four on high school classes, but that held little meaning in districts that simply could not afford to meet it; some overcrowded classes had as many as fifty students. For years, classes in New York City's first, second, and third grades had been capped at twenty-five. But budget cuts during the early and mid-1990s continually threatened increases to twenty-seven or more children. In July 1995 the city's Board of Education voted to give local districts the power to choose between increasing class sizes and shortening the school week by one or two class periods, if budget limitations became severe. Schools in working-class communities often had average class sizes of more than thirty.[75] When schools opened in September 1996 some were drastically overcrowded. One Brooklyn elementary school built for 660 children held 1,200, including a first-grade class with forty-six students, some of whom sat on mats on the floor. Another class at the same school was held in a bathroom, owing to lack of space. The media were full of stories about gyms being used as classrooms, and of elementary classes with between thirty and forty students. In April 1997 the *New York Times* claimed that a report released two months earlier by Mayor Rudolph Giuliani, which concluded that the school system had met its target goal of a maximum of twenty-five children in kindergarten through third-grade classes, was inaccurate. When the *Times* talked to school officials who had provided City Hall with class size data, the officials admitted their numbers were simply guesses.[76]

In 1997 the New York State Legislature decided to tackle New York City's overcrowded elementary school classrooms. The legislature planned to furnish $286 million over three years to reduce class sizes in New York City's K–3 classes to twenty children, beginning with the 1999–2000 school year. Since more than half of the city's schools were overcrowded, space would clearly be one problem. Another would be finding qualified teachers, since there was already a shortage. Nearly one-third of the teachers in District Seven in the South Bronx were uncertified, which was a larger percentage than in Los Angeles *after* two years of California's class-size reduction program. There was also doubt that the money the state was providing was sufficient to reach the stated goals. Public Advocate Mark Green sent Mayor Giuliani a letter claiming it would cost an additional $300 to $500 million to actually reach the target level of twenty children. Early in the 1998–99 school year—almost a full year before the program would begin—the city's Board of Education announced that since the funding was not enough to lower classes across the entire city, it would focus on reducing class sizes in low-performing schools.[77]

Just north of New York City, Connecticut towns have also had regular discussions about class size during the 1990s. But their perceived problems would be seen as desirable in many other communities, and are often solved with an ease that would make most school officials and parents elsewhere envious. For example, when two elementary schools in Glastonbury had average class sizes of twenty-four in 1993–94, two new teachers were hired in the summer with the expectation that in the following school year class size would drop to an average of nineteen. Similarly, East Windsor's Broad Brook Elementary School began the 1994–95 school year with second-grade classes averaging twenty-five students. The school board promptly decided to hire another teacher, dropping the average class size to twenty-one children. When several first-grade classes at Plainville's Toffolon Elementary School held twenty-three children in September 1995, school officials offered parents the option of shifting their children to nearby schools where first-grade class sizes were under twenty.[78] The message is neither surprising nor terribly useful to urban schools or state legislatures: small, affluent communities can provide small classes with relative ease if they consider doing so a high priority, and they often do.

The Federal Government

In 1998, ten years after Tommy Tomlinson's Department of Education paper arguing against the importance of class size, another Department of Education paper was released on the issue. Professor Jeremy D. Finn, who had played a role in analyzing the data from Project STAR, was the author; not surprisingly, Finn's findings differed greatly from Tomlinson's. Finn began by summarizing the findings of a number of overviews of the class size research, and then discussed Indiana's Prime Time and Tennessee's Project STAR. He found that Project STAR and the Lasting Benefits Study that traced its children in later years provided "compelling evidence that small classes in the primary grades are academically superior to regular-size classes." Finn recognized that the major difficulty in reducing class size across the nation was the tremendous financial cost, and he tried to compare the cost-effectiveness of smaller classes to other reforms. But he was left with the central problem that American society has never decided what it is willing to pay for a "good" education for all children, or even what such an education would entail. Finn argued that smaller classes promote greater student engagement in learning and better conditions for teachers to encourage students. In addition, he said, such factors were "likely to be especially profound for minority students and for other students at risk of educational failure." Finn concluded by calling for more research to determine how smaller classes interact with other factors to help students learn more effectively.[79]

President Bill Clinton chose his 1998 State of the Union speech to unveil a new education agenda containing a number of proposals, including federal funding for smaller classes and for school repair and construction, and incentives to ban social promotion (see Chapter 4). Clinton's plan for class size reduction was ambitious: to hire 100,000 new teachers to dramatically reduce the size of classes in the earliest grades. One can only guess what role the evidence from Project STAR played, though Clinton undoubtedly knew of the program. That California governor Pete Wilson's approval ratings had soared after his class size efforts had also presumably caught Clinton's eye. Perhaps paying attention to the tremendous difficulties the lack of classroom space had caused in California, President Clinton also proposed spending billions of dollars to pay interest on school district bonds, which would make it somewhat easier for local communities to pay for new schools or renovations on deteriorating schools.[80] Under Clinton's plan the federal government would provide $1.2 billion in the 1999–2000 school year for the hiring of an estimated 37,500 new teachers to reduce class sizes. Eighty percent of the money would be distributed on the basis of student poverty, and 20 percent on the basis of school enrollment. This could be seen as in keeping with Project STAR's findings that low-income children benefited the most from small classes. It also stayed within the federal government's traditional role, focusing largely on programs for disadvantaged children. Local districts would have to provide $400 million in matching funds; the districts with the highest poverty levels would have to come up with 10 percent in matching funds, while districts with somewhat lower poverty rates would be required to provide matching funds ranging from 10 percent to 50 percent. The long-term goal was to reduce the average class size in the first, second, and third grades to eighteen students per teacher. Any school district with class sizes in those grades averaging above eighteen children had to use at least 85 percent of the money to hire new teachers, and the remainder could be used for teacher training and testing. Districts that already had small classes could use the money to reduce class sizes even further, or to expand the program to other grades, or for teacher training.[81]

Lack of classroom space and the deteriorating condition of many school buildings are problems across the nation, and as we have seen they pose a special problem in attempts to reduce class size. In 1995 the U.S. General Accounting Office estimated that it would cost $112 *billion* to restore all the nation's public schools to "good overall condition." Building new schools to meet growing enrollments and equipping schools with modern educational technology would drive the overall cost of updating the nation's schools to more than $200 billion. A national survey in early 1998 showed that 74 percent of voters supported federal assistance to help states and local communities build and modernize their schools. President Clinton's proposed education package included $22 billion for construction and school modernization. Despite widespread public support for such an idea, however, in April 1998 the Senate rejected the proposed funding for school construction. Clinton did receive $1.1 billion for the hiring of about 30,000 new teachers for the 1999–2000 school year, which the *Los Angeles Times* called "his biggest victory" in the budget. The White House called it a down payment toward its eventual goal of reducing class sizes in first, second, and third grades to eighteen.[82]

President Clinton's proposal for a national effort to shrink class size was met by many of the same claims that surfaced earlier, in other places, that class size did not particularly matter. Chester E. Finn, Jr., now president of the Thomas B. Fordham Foundation and an ardent supporter of school vouchers, coauthored an editorial that called Clinton's initiative "a warm Labrador puppy of a policy notion, petted by teachers and parents alike, but destined to bite when it grows up." Finn and coauthor Michael Petrilli claimed there was "precious little evidence that smaller classes help students." They quoted Eric Hanushek's work, and repeated the simplistic claim that since class sizes had shrunk over time and test scores had worsened, small classes did no good. They ignored the STAR study.[83]

California's program was extremely popular in large part because it included *all* children in the early grades, thereby gaining the strong support of the middle class. Clinton's program targeted chiefly low-income children, which made sense in light of Project STAR's findings, but as a result it had less political support. The federal commitment to smaller classes would have to be renewed every year, which was far from guaranteed. While reducing class size seemed to be Clinton's top education priority, some members of his own party believed an emphasis on teacher quality made more sense, and recognized that hiring large numbers of new teachers could also mean hiring thousands of poorly qualified teachers. And a number of educators were openly nervous that the funding rug would be pulled out from under them after they began to make dramatic changes. The executive director of the Indiana Association of School Superintendents asked in the *Indianapolis Star*, "Is it a political commitment that will change as politics change?"[84] With the shape of Congress changing every two years, and the presidency contested every four years, the survival of the federal program was far from certain.

One of the lessons to be learned from Tennessee's Project STAR has nothing to do with class size and everything to do with how evaluations do or don't make their way into policy. If a study of this quality and magnitude had been conducted by researchers from Harvard University on schools in Massachusetts or by Stanford University in California, early reports of its results would have drawn tremendous interest. Instead, it was a number of years before the media or educational policymakers began to pay attention to Tennessee's findings. But sometimes quality wins out. Project STAR has been highly influential, helping to shape federal policy and playing a role in the widespread movement toward smaller classes on the part of state governments. If some of the attempts to reduce class size have not fit STAR's results very well, that has as much to do with political compromises and the difficulty of drawing exact policy conclusions from evaluations as it has to do with misunderstanding the study's results.

The question of the exact effects caused by reducing class size is hardly settled. There are more things we do not know than things we do know, and matters are greatly complicated by the simple fact that class size interacts with a number of other factors in shaping educational outcomes. How many years of small classes do children need to show the long-term benefits found in Tennessee's Project STAR? What is the difference between classes of twenty children (as in California), eighteen children (as in the federal initiative), and fifteen children (the average in Project STAR)? STAR found benefits for classes averaging fifteen children compared with classes averaging twenty-four children. Does that mean California's classes are not small enough to have an impact? We simply do not know. Another fundamental and unanswered question is, How does teaching quality interact with class size? Is a class of thirty children with a high-quality teacher preferable to one with twenty children and an inexperienced teacher? In addition there are issues in California that the evidence from Project STAR does not address, and many of them are pertinent for other places such as New York City and Florida. Will children in different regions benefit less from small classes than did children in Tennessee? Or more? Or will that depend on other factors?

One thing we do know is that, all factors being equal (which they rarely are), small classes of fifteen children do improve student achievement, and the effects last through high school. Critics who still argue that class size doesn't matter are, quite simply, ignoring the evidence. When they claim that the evidence "shows" small classes don't matter, they are either ignoring the *quality* of the evidence—the best studies generally show the strongest effects—or they are relying on irrelevant arguments such as international comparisons. We do not know all that we would like to know about the effects of small classes in different settings, but we do know this: class size matters.

But does class size matter enough to become the centerpiece of school reform, costing billions of dollars? That is another question altogether. An editorial in the *Sacramento Bee* stated that Project STAR showed achievement gains that "were not great," and that diminished somewhat as students went though school.[85] This raises a fundamental issue: what constitutes a large gain in achievement? If the improved test scores found by Project STAR had come from something simple and inexpensive, such as a new line of textbooks, virtually everyone would be astounded by the size of the increase in student achievement, and even more amazed that it lasted through high school. Instead, the improvements were the result of a very expensive reform. Whether an observer sees the gains found in STAR as large or small may depend on how that observer views public education and society's duty to children. If any gain for children is viewed as valuable, small classes may be worth even a great expense. If education is seen as already costing too much, and suffering from too much intervention from state and federal government—clearly required to reduce class size on a broad scale—then the gains may not be worth the cost. Evaluations seek to provide objective knowledge, but that knowledge rarely leads to anything resembling clear-cut policy decisions. The "value" of providing children with an education of this or that quality is highly subjective, and outside the realm of evaluation.

Virtually everyone wants to improve education; they disagree on how to do so and how much to spend. Is creating small classes the best way to improve student achievement, or could other methods that are less expensive achieve more? One of the factors in deciding whether a program is cost effective is the long-run cost it reduces or increases. If smaller classes in the early grades reduce children's later likelihood of dropping out of school, or of being placed in expensive special education classes, then class size reduction may be far less expensive than it seems on the surface. It is also important to remember that educational reforms are generally not such that we have to select just *one* choice from the menu. It may well be that one of the great potential advantages of small classes is that they make other reforms more effective or easier to implement. Officials in California assume that small classes and the state's new approach to reading instruction will go hand in hand. If student achievement in the early grades does improve dramatically, it may be because of that combination, not because of either the change in class size or the new curriculum taken alone.

There are two fundamental problems with California's approach, both of which could have been predicted in advance (and critics of the rush to small classes did point them out). The first is that it gives little regard to quality of teaching, which will probably weaken the impact of the program. The second (and related) problem in California is that more affluent school districts are better able to reduce class sizes in all the grades for which funding is available. This is a good thing for the students at those schools, or at least everyone involved believes it is, and there is solid research evidence to support that view. But one of the most compelling findings of Project STAR is that children from low-income families benefit more from smaller classes than do other groups. In essence, providing small classes for disadvantaged children gets more bang for the buck than providing them for middle-class children, and it does so where we need success the most. Of course, the program would not be so politically popular if it were not universal. The trouble is, the way small classes have been implemented, those who need them most and would benefit most are likely to have the least experienced teachers. This is not a new problem, but one that has been exacerbated by the specific nature of class size reduction in California.

The way smaller classes have been created, particularly in California, and the results of Project STAR and other evaluations, lead to several policy conclusions. The most important is that movement toward smaller classes should not occur at such a rapid pace that they are implemented poorly. California has done an impressive job, and one that is probably benefiting middle-class children. But the state has done less well by low-income children. Many of them are not in smaller classes for all four years, K–3, and many have substandard teachers. And the dependence on portable classrooms that is commonplace in urban schools may be an even greater problem than it first appears. A report released by an environmental group in May 1999 stated that the 2 million children attending classes in portable classrooms in California were in danger of exposure to high levels of carcinogenic building materials. As a result, their risk of developing cancer over the course of their lifetime might be dramatically increased.[86] Who knows what other unforeseen problems may result from the state's rush to create smaller classes. Whatever they may be, it seems likely that disadvantaged children will be the most affected by them.

Whether smaller class sizes should be provided for all children, or should be provided first and foremost to low-income children, is a political question more than an educational one. (So, for that matter, is the question of whether to provide smaller classes at all.) If they are to have the kind of impact that teachers, parents, and politicians all expect, small classes need to be implemented more carefully and with much more thought than went into California's plan, and many states are doing this. In particular, more must be done to protect the quality of teaching in schools with low-income student populations. With that care, small classes can play a critical role in any package of reforms that seeks to effectively address problems in America's public schools. Without it, small classes may help "lift every boat," but they will not lift them all at the same rate. Project STAR shows small classes can help narrow the achievement gap between middle-class children and low-income children by helping both groups, but helping the latter group more. Careless, widespread implementation may actually cause the reverse and increase the gap in what our schools provide for children from different backgrounds. That would be a shameful legacy from an idea with so much promise.

4

Is Social Promotion
a Problem?

Social promotion makes a mockery of the diploma, erodes public
confidence in the schools, and creates huge challenges for teachers
who inherit students who aren't ready for grade-level work. Worst
of all, it sends students the perverse message that real achievement
isn't important, and that the institution doesn't actually believe
that with greater effort they can master the tasks before them.
—EDITORIAL, *SACRAMENTO BEE*, 1997

The rising hum to end social promotion in schools, sounded by
state legislators, various metro school districts and even President
Clinton, harmonizes with other calls to get tough on problems
plaguing public schools. Alas, it also shows a growing denial of the
true causes of schools' and students' failure: children unprepared
for school for complicated social reasons; incompetent parents
and teachers; disrespect for teachers and learning; and cheap
funding, just for starters.
—EDITORIAL, *ATLANTA JOURNAL AND CONSTITUTION*,
1999

Social promotion is the practice of automatically promoting students to
the next grade, whether or not they have attained the skills they were supposed to achieve in their current grade. The social promotion of children
became increasingly common in public schools in the 1930s and 1940s,
and it has been widespread in most school systems ever since. Many children who fall far behind in school nonetheless move from grade to grade
with their higher-achieving classmates. There are a number of good reasons to promote children from one grade to the next even if they are falling

behind in school. For one thing, it keeps children with their age group, preventing classrooms where ten-year-olds and thirteen-year-olds sit side by side—a situation that teachers, parents, and children themselves all prefer to avoid. In addition, it saves school systems money, since a student who takes twelve years to receive a high school diploma costs schools, and taxpayers, less than a student who takes thirteen or fourteen years. Many people also believe that it avoids embarrassing children and damaging their self-esteem, since children who "flunk" are immediately labeled as failures in the eyes of other children (and many adults). Last, but definitely not least, *which* children have been held back has historically been related to race, ethnicity, and poverty; poor minority children have been far more likely to be retained in grade than middle-class children, and not just because of differences in achievement. Promoting all students in lockstep prevents discrimination, at least in this one area.

There are also a number of sound arguments against the practice of social promotion. If students do not have the necessary skills to understand what is being taught, teachers will be more likely to "dumb down" their curriculum, thereby shortchanging students who are at the appropriate level and ready to advance. Furthermore, some critics argue that there is little incentive for students to work hard if they know they will be promoted regardless of how much they know. The end result of social promotion, according to these critics, is high school graduates who can barely read, and who are not prepared to attend college or hold a decent job. Children who are promoted without having earned it are often viewed with sympathy, as "victims of 'social promotion.'" The practice is seen as "a dirty trick played on students." In 1998 California Governor Pete Wilson called the practice a "tragedy" as he signed legislation designed to stop social promotion in that state's public schools.[1]

Some critics of social promotion look at the meaning of diplomas rather than at the children who receive them, and at schools as institutions rather than at students as individuals. These critics are angry, not sympathetic. Social promotion "makes a mockery of the diploma," they say, and amounts to "educational malpractice." These critics of social promotion see it as degrading the value of a high school diploma; because some youths who receive diplomas are "functional illiterates," employers and colleges cannot assume diploma-holders have the skills they should. They believe schools without regularly enforced standards for graduation are not being held accountable for the poorly trained graduates they produce.[2]

Teachers, principals, and parents are failing, but when children are passed through the system this failure is covered up, and it eventually appears as the children's fault when they become barely literate adults. In this version of the story, no one is held accountable as schools fail to teach many of their students.[3]

Given this withering critique, it is hardly surprising that "end social promotion" became one of the loudest cries of politicians talking about education in the late 1990s. Politicians across the spectrum sounded the charge at the local, state, and national levels; it was one of the most bipartisan educational issues around. They did so for two very basic, and closely related, reasons: the idea was popular, and the necessary reform seemed clear-cut. In the mid- and late 1990s a number of school districts ended social promotion. The most famous effort was in Chicago, but many other districts also took actions to halt the practice. Several states, including Wisconsin, Texas, and California, passed laws intended to end social promotion, and President Bill Clinton called for the entire country to stop the practice. What effect these efforts will have on the actual occurrence of social promotion is far from clear; states and cities have been passing regulations against social promotion since the 1970s. And the movement ignores the first question that needs to be asked: Are these efforts a good idea? The closer one looks at the question of promoting children from grade to grade regardless of their achievement, the more complicated the issue becomes. What seems a simple, straightforward reform is in fact closely related to some of the most fundamental problems in American education.

How often are children promoted without the necessary skills to have at least a fighting chance at their new grade level? Does being held back a grade increase students' academic skills in the long run? Is the threat of "flunking" supposed to motivate students, and if so, does it? Or does being retained in a grade increase the likelihood that a child will drop out of school? What do we really know about how widespread social promotion is, and about what retention does to students? What does the evidence say about the effects of holding children back?

Social Promotion before 1970

In the early nineteenth century, the majority of American schools were one-room, "ungraded" classrooms that held children of many ages and widely different skill levels. School reformer Henry Barnard began calling for graded schools in 1838, arguing that they would be more humane and efficient. The shift toward graded schools was well under way in cities by the middle of the century. Early graded schools were divided into several levels, such as primary, grammar, and high school. (The movement toward a more finely graded school system was part of a broader movement, the increasing centralization of the control of schools.)[4] Exams and promotion decisions went hand in hand in many school systems. For example, in the late 1800s the schools in Somerville, Massachusetts, developed a standardized set of tests. A minimum average score of 70 (out of 100) was required for grammar school students to advance from one grade to the next. The idea was to create standards that would lead teachers across the system to teach a similar curriculum, and to take teachers' judgments out of the promotion decision. By giving a series of tests and taking the average score, district officials felt they would get an accurate image of how each student was doing, and could use that to make promotion decisions.[5]

During the last two decades of the nineteenth century, some school administrators became concerned that a sizable number of students were too old for the grade they were in. In other words, supposing that second graders were supposed to be seven years of age, it turned out that a number of eight- and even nine-year-olds were also in second grade. In 1904 the superintendent of New York City's schools began printing tables showing that more than one-third of elementary school students were "over age" for their grade. These statistics caused quite a stir. According to historian David Tyack, other educators assumed the unfortunate situation was unique to New York until they examined their own schools and found that many of their children were also older than was to be expected for their grade. Critics began arguing that children who were being held back were expensive for school systems. Leonard Ayres, the most famous of these critics, calculated that 13 percent of New York City's school budget was spent on teaching children who were repeating a grade. He also found that children in some immigrant groups were far more likely to be held back than others. Ayres argued that school systems would be much more efficient if they reduced retention.[6]

Note that Ayres's idea of efficiency was less concerned with what students learned than with how many children were channeled through school for a given amount of money. As the children of immigrants entered schools in rapidly growing numbers in the 1910s and 1920s, this concept of educational efficiency became widespread. Nonetheless, some groups continued to be held back in grade more often than other groups. Italian children and African-American children in Providence's public schools were held back at higher rates than were children from other groups in the 1910s and 1920s, for example.[7] While such discrepancies could have occurred because some groups tried harder in school than others, it seems certain that discrimination also played a role. The issue of overage children was related to other changes in how children were placed within schools. It was raised in the 1910s by Lewis Terman, probably the single most important figure in the development and spread of IQ tests in the United States, as a reason for schools to use his tests. Terman argued that in the near future, schools would use IQ tests on all children who either had already fallen behind or were about to fall behind in school; Terman believed this would provide "scientific" knowledge about which children were truly "retarded."[8] This way of thinking played a role in the development of education "streams" that tracked children into college-preparatory, vocational, and other classes.

The percentage of children held back varied wildly from one district to another. In 1914 Stanford University researchers examined data from 100 school districts and found that the percentage of children who were older than was typical for their grade (and therefore presumed to have been held back) ranged from 5 percent to 63 percent. Over the next few decades the practice of social promotion gradually spread throughout the entire nation. By the late 1930s most superintendents were in favor of social promotion. By the 1950s, retention had been on the decline for four decades. But the spread of social promotion did not occur without criticism. For example, in 1950 *Life* magazine published an essay attacking schools on a variety of fronts, including social promotion.[9] Despite occasional attacks, however, social promotion had become the normal practice in American education by midcentury. Its hold on schools would be long and strong, but it would not go completely unchallenged.

Uneven Opposition in the 1970s and 1980s

In the mid-1970s a movement against social promotion began, as school districts in many parts of the country either considered or implemented minimum competency requirements for high school diplomas. New York, California, and other states, as well as many local school districts, required that students demonstrate basic skills before receiving their diploma. They did this in response to a growing lack of faith in the meaning of high school diplomas, which many people believed no longer represented much of anything. Many of the plans followed recommendations made by a national organization of high school principals in 1975. The standards were generally not very high: functional literacy, basic math skills, and a basic knowledge of American history and the nature of democratic government. What that actually boiled down to was an eighth- or ninth-grade education.[10] Some cities took an aggressive approach to the issue of social promotion and the perceived widespread lack of skills among students. Kalamazoo, Michigan, used tests in all grades to see which students were at or above established national norms for their grade, and to identify children who were falling behind and needed remedial help. Even so, whether students were promoted to the next grade was left up to teachers. One school official reported that this approach had shown that many students had catching up to do, and had helped them to do so. In 1972 Kalamazoo's average third-grade student had been three months behind national norms, but by 1975 the average third grader was two months ahead of those same norms.[11] Duval County, Florida, ended social promotion in the mid-1970s and then developed tests for elementary and secondary students throughout the county. Between 1976 and 1980 the county's tests scores rose dramatically in response to these and other changes.[12]

Greensville County, Virginia, received widespread attention when it ended social promotion in the 1973–74 school year. Superintendent Sam Owen disagreed with the widespread belief that it was psychologically damaging to a child to be held back. He believed it was far worse to give a child a diploma without the accompanying knowledge. For his decision to stop social promotion cold, Owen faced considerable opposition from the community. African Americans made up two-thirds of the county's public school students, and some parents saw Owen's policy as discriminatory. In the first year of his program, Owen allowed parents whose children faced being held back to choose whether they would advance or not, and about 500 of the 1,300 children Owen wanted to retain were instead promoted to the next grade.[13] No such option was given the next year, when more than a quarter of the county's school children were held back. Teachers emphasized the basics and were told to give students honest evaluations of how they were doing. Students were tested extensively in the fall and again in the spring, and test scores were used in combination with teacher evaluations to determine whether or not children advanced. By May 1977 the *Washington Post* was calling the results of Greensville County's program "impressive." The dropout rate was down, and so were discipline problems. Many of the children being retained were advancing after half a year rather than a full year, after being placed in "in-between" grades. Standardized test scores at various grades had gone up over the four years since social promotion was halted, and in some cases had gone from far below the national average to above it. Not surprisingly, this weakened opposition to Owen's retention policy.[14]

By the early 1980s, however, things were no longer looking up in Greensville County schools, especially for Superintendent Owen. Under his strict policy against social promotion the number of high school graduates had declined, and the number of students who were "over age" for their grade had grown dramatically. Parents of overage children complained, and so did the parents of children who were advancing normally, because they were unhappy at having markedly older students in classes with their children. The percentage of African-American children being held back was higher than the percentage of white children being retained, which led to charges that the retention policy was discriminating against children of color. The National Association for the Advancement of Colored People (NAACP) charged that standardized tests discriminated against African Americans, making their use in decisions about promotion and retention unacceptable. The Greensville school board eventually agreed to drop the tests in an out-of-court settlement with the NAACP. By late 1981 there had also been considerable turnover on the school board, and Owen and the board were in continual conflict. On December 31, 1981, Owen resigned. Because of parental opposition and charges of discrimination, and negative consequences such as lower graduation rates, one of the nation's first and best-known attempts to end social promotion thus ended in flames.[15]

Other cities, including Baltimore and Philadelphia, and states such as North Carolina and Georgia, also moved against social promotion. One of the most prominent efforts began in April 1980 when the District of Columbia's school board ended social promotion in grades one to three, effective the following school year. The policy would expand to all elementary grades over the next few years, and eventually to high school. The same board had banned social promotion in 1977, but teachers had continued to automatically promote children, the most obvious case being the regular practice of sending children to junior high school once they were thirteen years old. In the intervening years, parents and educators in the Anacostia schools within Washington, D.C., had acted against social promotion, and now the entire city was prepared to follow suit. The district's plan was highly detailed, even including specific checklists for teachers about what children had to learn to be promoted. Parents would be informed at the start of each year what their children were expected to learn, and checklists would actually be attached to report cards, showing parents which items their children had or had not learned. Promotions were scheduled for every semester rather than every year, and children who were weak in only one or two areas would be placed in transitional grades.[16]

In the middle of the first year of D.C.'s program, officials feared they were approaching a disaster, because more than 10,000 children in the first, second, and third grades were behind where they needed to be to earn promotion. By the end of the school year, however, many students had made up ground and were expected to be promoted. As it turned out, fewer than 4,000 students were retained. That was a relatively small number compared to what had been feared a few months before, though still a huge number of children retained compared to previous years. In the first year that the policy was applied to fourth, fifth, and sixth graders, at midyear 27 percent of D.C. elementary students were held back, including an astounding 44 percent of fifth graders. But across the early 1980s student test scores rose. When the retention policy went into effect for seventh graders, school officials feared a high failure rate would again ensue. But the seventh-grade class, which had by then been held to high standards for years, passed at about the same rate as the previous year's class had done under an easier curriculum.[17]

Another approach to fighting social promotion occurred in 1980, when New York City set up "promotion gates" at the end of the fourth and seventh grades. Children had to meet performance standards to advance at these points. Students more than a year below grade level in reading and at least two years below grade level in mathematics would be retained. As it turned out, roughly one-fourth of all students at those two grade levels were indeed held back. The Board of Education added $63 million to the next year's school budget to put the plan into effect and provide students who were retained with extra help. Students who had to repeat would be grouped together to help teachers focus on their needs. The classes would be small, with fifteen to twenty students each. The New York Times called the plan, somewhat grandiosely, "an assault on the cycle of inner-city academic failure the like of which has seldom if ever been attempted in an urban school district."[18]

In practice, however, New York City's plan quickly ran into some of the complex problems any rigid attempt to end social promotion is likely to create. By March 1983, several thousand students who were in seventh grade for the *third straight year* faced the likelihood of being held back once again. Not surprisingly, these students were seen as being at extremely high risk of dropping out before much longer. When Anthony Alvarado replaced Frank Macchiarola as schools chancellor, Alvarado announced that in the future, seventh graders who failed to earn advancement would be held back only once (fourth graders who failed could still be held back twice). At the same time, Alvarado claimed that he too intended to hold students to high standards, but he did not consider keeping struggling students in the seventh grade year after year the best way to do so. As it turned out, budget cuts soon made any real attempt to end social promotion in the city's schools a moot issue and the program was gradually deemphasized.[19] The end of New York's program was not necessarily a bad thing, as an evaluation by Ernest House and others showed that it had not managed to improve the performance of retained students. The city had hired teachers and trained them to teach repeaters in small classes of eighteen students. But within a few years it was clear to the evaluators that the retained students had not advanced academically any further than had similar low-achieving students in earlier years who had been regularly promoted. And in the long run the dropout rate for retained children was much higher than it had been for the comparison group.[20]

Thus attempts to end social promotion often ended after a few years, owing to opposition from parents, limited funding, or failure to improve student achievement. The opposition to ending social promotion rested on a number of arguments. Most critics of the push for educational standards agreed with the basic goal of making sure children learned what they were supposed to learn, and that high school diplomas should show a certain level of achievement and knowledge; how could they not? But these opponents pointed out a variety of problems that could result from trying to impose standards and halting social promotion, and some of their arguments were important. For example, they argued that standardized tests were seriously flawed as a way to judge what children knew. Heavy dependence on standardized tests could also lead teachers to teach to the test rather than focusing on the broader body of knowledge children needed to develop. Another problem in an era of strapped education budgets was that the remedial programs needed to help students were very expensive, and without extensive remedial programs, widespread use of retention would simply turn into a path to higher dropout rates.[21] It was also far from obvious whether being held back helped students "catch up" in school. Students in Greensville County who were held back may have done better than they would have if promoted, but students in New York City who were held back continued to perform very poorly.

Some arguments made by critics opposed to ending social promotion were less compelling. The National Education Association argued against state-specified objectives, saying they would lead to a monolithic curriculum controlled by the state, which would supposedly make it impossible to tailor instruction to individual children's needs. Critics noted that high school diplomas had become rites of passage, and that denying a youth that diploma would cut him or her off from higher education and many job opportunities.[22] But the basic idea behind standards and the opposition to social promotion was to require actual high school–level skills before awarding a diploma. It is hard to see how this was unfair, since students without those skills would be unable to handle college courses or hold a job that required such skills. It was also not immediately clear why the NEA saw any level of state government interference as automatically dictatorial. Requiring that students know basic algebra and be able to read and write at a high school freshman level before receiving a diploma hardly precluded teachers' using a variety of instructional methods.

A central ongoing question in the debate over automatic promotions was who should ultimately decide whether a child was promoted or retained. Teachers regularly complained that children they had recommended for retention were instead promoted. Administrators often overruled teachers' decisions because a child's parents insisted their child be advanced. Relying on test scores avoided these problems and set relatively clear districtwide standards. Whether these standards were reasonable or fair was another question altogether. Because there is reason to believe that test scores are biased, they provide ammunition for opponents of strict policies against social promotion, as was the case in Greensville County.

The movement against social promotion in the 1980s presumed that very few children were being held back and many students were being promoted without earning it. But in the late 1980s Lorrie A. Shepard and

Mary Lee Smith examined data from thirteen states and the District of Columbia, and they found that this assumption was unfounded. Shepard and Smith estimated that between 5 percent and 7 percent of children in public schools were held back every year. If one took that figure and stretched it out over a number of years, just as children's school careers stretch over time, the picture changed: by ninth grade, between one-third and one-half of all students had been held back at least once (or had dropped out of school). The idea that social promotion was rampant was not supported by the facts, according to Shepard and Smith. It is also important to note that the 1980s saw a considerable increase in the number of kindergarten students asked to repeat that year before moving on to first grade.[23]

Of course, even if 40 percent or more of all school children were being held back once (and it is possible that the Shepard and Smith estimates were too high), that does not mean that social promotion was not happening. Even with high numbers of retentions, it was entirely possible that many other children were being passed despite not actually performing anywhere near the expected level for the grade they were in. Many children who have been held back once may still not be able to handle schoolwork in their courses. And many other children who have never been retained may also be performing well below their grade level. But the belief that everyone was simply being pushed ahead in the late 1980s, and that virtually no children were being retained, was simply wrong. Children were held back far more often than critics assumed, although many other students were being promoted without earning it, just as critics claimed. This brings us back to some basic questions: If many children fall behind, what is more to their benefit, being retained or promoted? In the 1980s, what did the evaluation evidence say about the effects of promoting children versus retaining them? Which is more likely to lead to success in school? Does either policy have a dramatic effect on the likelihood that children will drop out of school? What difference, really, did social promotion and retention make for student achievement?

The Evidence in the 1980s

In the early 1980s, C. Thomas Holmes and Kenneth M. Matthews performed a meta-analysis on forty-four studies that looked at the effects of retaining children in a grade. Each of the studies compared a group of retained students to a group of promoted students, though how well the comparison groups were formed varied. There were more than 11,000 students in the forty-four combined studies, with more than 4,000 who had been retained and nearly 7,000 who had been promoted. The students were in elementary school or junior high school; Holmes and Matthews did not look at studies of retention in high school. Most of the studies had been conducted between 1960 and 1975.[24]

Holmes and Matthews found that virtually all the studies showed that children who had been retained in a grade did even worse in school in later years than would have been expected, not better, as many opponents of social promotion predicted. More important than the results of the studies individually, Holmes and Matthews used meta-analytic techniques to combine all the studies and then analyzed them in a number of different ways. One method combined all the effect sizes found within the studies; because some studies were large and others small, this gave more weight to the large studies. Holmes and Matthews then reexamined the data, giving equal weight to each study, to see if the largest studies had biased their results. Finally, they examined only the studies that had matched retained and promoted children on some relatively sound measure such as achievement test scores or IQ scores, since there was reason to believe the results of these evaluations were more trustworthy than evaluations with less carefully designed comparison groups. Each method led Holmes and Matthews to the same basic conclusion: retaining children led to their doing *worse* in school than apparently similar children who were promoted.[25] While this did not mean retention *caused* students' decreased performance, it did show convincingly that retention did not lead to improved performance.

In 1989 Holmes performed another meta-analysis, this time examining sixty-three studies of the effects of being held back on student achievement. Once again, Holmes looked only at studies with a comparison group. The vast majority of the studies (fifty-four of the sixty-three) showed that children who were retained then did *less* well in school than did children who had been promoted. Once again, the overall finding of the studies was that children did less well if held back than if promoted. Holmes also examined nine studies that had found some positive effects for children who were retained. He found that those studies had all been conducted in what their authors described as suburban settings, and the students had been almost exclusively middle-class and white. In the schools studied, children who were falling behind had been identified early and given special help, and decisions to retain them were made in consultation with their parents. Students who were held back were placed in small classes, and often spent part of the day in classes with their age group. Children in the comparison groups who had been promoted did not receive extra help after being promoted. Also, the advantages gained by children who had been retained "tended to diminish" in later years. As a result, it was not at all clear that these "pro-retention" evaluations said much about what happened in urban schools, or in settings where retained children did not receive extra help. Holmes also examined the effects shown in the twenty-five most rigorous studies (those with the most carefully constructed comparison groups). The results were the same: children who were promoted actually did *better* in school than similar children who were retained in a grade. Holmes's conclusion was clear-cut: "The weight of empirical evidence argues against grade retention."[26]

By the late 1980s, then, there was a fairly sound evidence base *against* the idea that holding children back would improve their school performance in later years. In fact, retention seemed to weaken later achievement, with results that were below an already low level. What else did the evaluation evidence say about the effects of retention versus those of social promotion? One of the most important questions concerned the effects of retention on children's likelihood of dropping out of school. Earlier studies had shown that children who were held back twice were almost certain to drop out. Of course, it could be that being held back and dropping out stem from the same root causes, such as lack of success in school, lack of innate ability, lack of family support, and so on. However, that does not seem to be the case. James B. Grissom and Lorrie A. Shepard examined research on dropouts and found that retention actually had *more* impact on the likelihood of a child's dropping out than did low achievement. In addition, three large studies conducted in the late 1980s, each controlled for student achievement and for background factors associated with dropping out, found that children who repeated a year were 20 to 30 percent more likely to drop out of school than were children with similar achievement and similar backgrounds who had not been held back.[27]

So virtually all the evidence points in the same direction. Social promotion may not be a good thing, but at least so far as student achievement and the likelihood of dropping out were concerned, retention is even worse. If the goal of the opponents of social promotion in the 1980s was to improve the performance of the lowest achieving students, retention was a very poor idea. It does not help children catch up with their peers and may instead have negative effects on their achievement. In 1989 Ernest R. House, a prominent educational evaluator, summed up what the evidence had to say. "Few practices in education have such overwhelmingly negative research findings arrayed against them," House wrote. Yet retention remains popular with teachers and the public. House suspected that it had become "an entrenched ideology."[28] He may have been right. The 1990s would show that the idea of ending social promotion remained popular, and would also see the first real challenge to the evaluation evidence arrayed against the idea of retention as a way to improve student scores.

The 1990s: Evidence from Baltimore

The mid-1990s saw another surge of public concern over the practice of automatically promoting children from one grade to the next. Politicians, the media, and the public all showed acute historical blindness, apparently unaware of the 1980s movement against social promotion. Many of the arguments used earlier resurfaced. The *Economist* began a 1996 article, "It is called 'social promotion,' and it is only just being realized how much of it goes on in American schools." The assumption was that social promotion had become widespread over the past few decades, though whether it had become a problem in the 1960s or 1970s varied from one story to the next. One new argument used against social promotion was that a large number of high school graduates who went on to college were not actually ready for college work and needed to take remedial courses. In the late 1990s, for example, more than 30 percent of the students at Georgia's public universities and colleges needed to take remedial courses.[29]

Just how widespread was social promotion in the 1990s? A survey of teachers in Texas found that at least 4 percent of the state's students had been promoted the previous year without having met the official standards for advancement. If the teachers' numbers were accurate, and if the same percentages held true in other states, it would mean that 2 million children were being promoted every year without having learned what they were supposed to learn. Rudy Crew, New York City's schools chancellor, stated that if social promotion were immediately ended, at least one-third of the city's fourth and seventh graders (the grades his gradual plan to end social promotion focused on) would be held back. A National Center for Education Statistics study done in 1996 found that almost 17 percent of high

school seniors had been held back once. Another study done shortly thereafter by the National Academy of Sciences indicated that the percentage of
children held back at least once might be higher.[30] So more children were
being held back than critics of social promotion thought, but at the same
time even more students were probably being promoted despite being far
below their grade-level norms.

In the 1990s, one of the most commonly used arguments against ending
social promotion was that children who were held back more than once
were almost certain to drop out of school. As we have seen, the evidence on
this point seemed fairly strong. No one, not even those who were not especially concerned with the treatment of disadvantaged children, wanted that
to happen. As the *Economist* put it (without any noticeable sympathy for
dropouts), the children would then "join the dead-beats who roam the
streets and fill the jails." Another major rationale used to justify social promotion was that being held back—"flunking" or "failing," as children call it
among themselves, even if adults have become more careful about using
such loaded terminology—deals a serious blow to children's self-esteem.[31]
Newspaper coverage of the debate regularly cited the evaluation evidence
accurately, even in some stories that were highly critical of social promotion. In the mid-1990s, however, the evaluation picture was muddied
somewhat by findings from Baltimore.

In 1994 a significant new study of the effects of retention appeared that
was relatively favorable about its effects on students. Researchers had followed one cohort of children through the Baltimore public schools from
first grade to eighth grade. Although their study was not originally designed to examine the results of retention versus social promotion, Karl Alexander, Doris Entwisle, and Susan Dauber realized that their research had
a great deal to say about the topic. The result was their book, *On the Success
of Failure*, which looks at the effects of retention on children in Baltimore's
public schools and disagrees with the research described earlier in this
chapter. Baltimore had come out against social promotion in 1977, and retention occurred frequently in the system during the 1980s, when the study
was conducted. Approximately 800 children who were entering first grade
were randomly selected for the Beginning School Study, and *On the Success
of Failure* traces their movement through school, along with their test
scores, grades, and so on. About 40 percent of the children had been held
back at least once by the time they entered high school. More than half of
the students were African American, and most came from low-income

homes. Alexander and his colleagues found that retention was not a "cure-all," but that it appeared "to be a reasonably effective practice." Students who were held back did much better the second time around in the same grade, and for several years they continued to perform better in school than they had before being retained. Their performance remained well below that of children who were being promoted every year, but the authors argued that this was because children who were held back started school far behind. In other words, it was their lack of skills when they entered school that explained why they lagged behind, not that they had been retained in a grade once.[32]

Alexander, Entwisle, and Dauber treat prior studies on the effects of retention with some disdain. As just one example, they argue that earlier studies that used "matched" comparison groups were flawed because "it is not sensible to think that promoted children who test at the same ability level as retained children are in other ways the same." Thus Alexander and his colleagues assume schools are both rational and fair in all their promotion decisions, which is at best unlikely. Similarly, they seem to assume special education placements are always appropriate, rather than sometimes being at least partially the result of children having been retained or "labeled." Alexander and his colleagues also argue that there are a number of flaws in the earlier reviews of retention studies, such as their inclusion of some studies that occurred decades in the past. Perhaps their most important claim is that few earlier studies looked at urban settings with student populations chiefly consisting of children of color, where the problems of social promotion and retention are most pressing.[33] They also go to great lengths to demonstrate that in Baltimore children who were held back did *not* suffer any damage to their self-esteem from retention, and that their attitudes toward school actually improve after being retained. While this hardly proves that earlier studies showing that retention weakened self-esteem were wrong, it does show that retention does not automatically hurt self-esteem, which is a very important point.[34]

In general, are they right? The answer is, for Baltimore, they are probably more right than wrong. But does the study from Baltimore somehow overrule earlier findings, such as Holmes's meta-analysis? With some minor qualifications, the answer is no. Even a perfect study would not do that, and there are a number of problems with the Baltimore results. Attrition from the study was heavy: by the eighth year, 40 percent of the original sample of 800 children had left the school system, and thus were out of the study as well. Nor was this attrition random; white children were far more likely to leave the Baltimore school system altogether than were African-American children. Alexander and his colleagues made statistical adjustments for this as best they could, but it remains a problem. In addition, their knowledge of families' economic situation is based on eligibility for reduced-price meals, which left them with quite simplistic categories of high income and low income. Their argument that retained children did better (rather than worse) because of retention is based on comparisons in which they use extensive statistical adjustment to account for family factors, such as income, that affect children's achievement. Their statistical adjustments could be off, and could lead to overstating how badly retained children would have performed if they had not been held back. At one point, they write that their "best guess" is that children who had been held back in third grade had later done better in grades four through seven than they would have done otherwise. Guesses, of course, are far from proof, even when they are educated guesses. But perhaps the biggest problem Alexander, Entwisle, and Dauber faced is that, by and large, they did not know what kind of additional help was given to retained (or promoted) children. They did not know whether retained (or promoted) children received special services or attended summer school before being retained, after being retained, or not at all. Since they did not set out to study retention, this is not too surprising. Taken together, however, these issues create room for more than a little doubt about the accuracy of their arguments.[35]

Another interesting gap is that the authors make no claims whatsoever about the question of whether retention increases the likelihood that children will drop out of school. They admit that "there is already solid evidence" that being held back in the early grades increases the likelihood of dropping out in high school, but in later discussions of the impact of retention in Baltimore they ignore this.[36] Of course since they followed students to the eighth grade, their study did not include the high school years, where dropping out becomes much more common. Even if they are right that retention does not harm later achievement or self-esteem, if it significantly raises the likelihood of dropping out, as later data from Baltimore show it does,[37] then retention does some real and significant harm, which they ignore in their arguments that retention does some good. What the study by Alexander, Entwisle, and Dauber does do convincingly is show that the effects of retention can vary from place to place—and child to child. (This should not really be a surprise. Remember that one of

Holmes's findings was that a number of studies showed that retention in suburban, largely middle-class schools did not have the negative effects that the majority of studies showed.) They have shown that straightforward statements claiming "retention hurts" achievement or self-esteem are not automatically accurate, and that is an extremely important point.

The Baltimore study, giving a mild thumbs-up to retention as it did, obviously did nothing to slow down the movement against social promotion. But there is no reason to think that *any* evaluation would have had much impact on the debate over social promotion. Even a huge, flawless study showing retention to be far more damaging than Holmes's meta-analysis finds would not have had much impact on such a popular, and apparently commonsense, idea. (Bear in mind no such study exists.) Stories continued to appear in the media about individual schools or entire districts that held to tough standards and ended social promotion, and lauded the success they supposedly enjoyed by doing so. In 1998, for example, *Newsweek* ran a story on social promotion that began with a description of Nancy Ichinaga, principal of an elementary school in Inglewood, California. Ichinaga refused to practice social promotion, calling it "junk." Three-quarters of the children at her school were from families below the poverty line, but 88 percent read at or above grade level. The principal believed that her school's policy of holding children back if they were not ready for the next grade, and building self-esteem in students through their achievements, was a major reason for the school's success.[38] But the most commonly told story of the fight against social promotion came from Chicago.

Chicago

In March 1996 the long-troubled Chicago school system, which had been undergoing extensive reforms for several years, banned the social promotion of eighth graders. Instead of automatically advancing, eighth graders would have to take reading and math tests to graduate from junior high school and enter high school. Children who tested at more than two years below grade level on either math or reading would have to attend summer school, and they would not advance to high school unless their scores rose to within two years of their grade level. The policy was to go into effect immediately for children in eighth grade. The next year, the policy was to expand to include third- and sixth-grade students as well. To advance, third graders would have to score within one year of their grade level on both math and reading, and sixth graders would have to test within 1.5 years of their grade level in both subjects. In other words, children were allowed to fall behind without being held back, but only so far. Early estimates were that 9,000 eighth graders would have to attend summer school that year in an attempt to raise their achievement levels. When some parents learned that their children would not be graduating, they rose in furious protest. As a result, students who had failed the tests were allowed to participate in graduation ceremonies, but they did not receive diplomas. Students in that first year of summer school did not improve as much as was hoped. In response, the district made extensive efforts the following year to develop a curriculum that would strengthen students' grasp of the basic material covered in the standardized tests. Teachers were hired and trained specifically to use the new curriculum, with the encouraging result that more than half of summer school students earned promotion in the second year under the new policy. Even so, in the summer of 1998 more than 3,000 eighth graders (39 percent of those who had attended summer school) were headed back to try eighth grade over again.[39]

One of the most daunting problems Chicago faced was the issue of children who failed twice. Since research clearly shows that children who are held back twice are extremely likely to eventually drop out of school, school officials who want to ban social promotion are faced with a dilemma: if they retain children twice they greatly increase the likelihood of losing them altogether. Chicago met this problem by creating new schools, called transition centers, for older students who did not meet the requirements for graduation from eighth grade. Each transition center held a few hundred students, focused on core subjects, and provided extensive individual attention. Classes were small, with between fifteen and twenty children in some cases. The transition centers seemed to work. Almost two-thirds of the students at transition centers in 1997–98 graduated to regular high schools at the end of the year. Even so, 220 eighth graders returned to transition centers in the fall for their third attempt at eighth grade.[40]

To their credit, Chicago school officials see ending social promotion not as a solution in and of itself, but instead as one of many interlocking reforms intended to improve the city's schools. To help children get a better start in school, they have greatly increased the number of children attending preschool and have also provided summer classes for children who fall behind in the first and second grades. A variety of reforms have been implemented to help children succeed once in high school, including teacher-advisers and a new curriculum. Homework has been assigned every night; as a Chicago assistant superintendent put it, "There's no magic, we just re-introduced something called studying." Another Chicago school official stated that the program was restoring the credibility of the city's public schools, and claimed that in its first three years 21,000 students had moved back to the public school system from private schools.[41]

But criticisms persisted, and upset parents were not the only ones against Chicago's assault on social promotion. Academic researchers and educators aware of the evaluation evidence opposed Chicago's plan on several fronts. Evidence seemed to show that children's self-esteem was damaged when they were held back. Even more fundamentally, as we have seen, research showed that being retained once increased the likelihood that a child would drop out of school, and being held back twice was far worse, in some observers' eyes virtually assuring that a student would drop out and never graduate from high school. But presumed negative effects on the children being held back were only half of the issue for critics. The process of deciding *which children* to hold back was also attacked. Standardized tests were seen as a flawed, biased, or simplistic way of deciding which children should be retained; in particular, they were believed to be racially and culturally biased against children of color. Furthermore, critics argued, reliance on standardized tests often led schools and teachers to focus on extensive drills and teaching to the test rather than teaching for understanding and critical thinking.[42]

The attacks on Chicago's program had little discernible effect on it. In fact, the city made its standards for promotion to ninth grade stricter. In the first year of the program, eighth graders had had to read at a sixth-grade level to move on to high school. By the 1997–98 school year, moving up to the ninth grade required reading at a 7.2 grade level (the second month of seventh grade), and the standard continued to rise every year. Progress reports were being given to parents every five weeks, so if their children were behind they knew it. Given the various ways Chicago was trying to provide help for children who were struggling, the program had to be expensive. It was costing about $35 million a year. The district shifted money from other programs that were cut, and changed the way it used Title I money to pay for summer school, the transition centers, and other parts of the reform package. In late 1999, the Consortium on Chicago School Research released a study on the efforts to end social promotion. The results were mixed. Many students in the sixth and eighth grades were doing better, but many continued to struggle, and there was no evidence that the threat of retention and the extra resources were helping third-grade students who had been struggling. The study also showed that thousands of students who could have been held back were promoted through a waiver process, undermining the district's claims that the policy was being implemented evenly. School officials continued to modify their program, using the study's results for guidance, and proclaimed that the fight against social promotion was helping students achieve more. Some scholars, however, took the study's results as proof that the city's retention policy was a failure that did far more harm than good. Matters were further complicated when, in late 1999, the U.S. Department of Education's Office for Civil Rights began an investigation into whether Chicago's retention policies discriminated against minority students. The main question seemed to center around the school district's use of tests that some believed were biased; the OCR had examined state testing practices for bias, but probing a single school district such as Chicago was unusual.[43] Chicago's fight against social promotion is ambitious, but its likelihood of success remains unclear.

Other Efforts to End Social Promotion in the 1990s

Throughout the 1990s, school districts around the country moved individually against social promotion, many of them before it became a hot issue late in the decade. Cincinnati ended social promotion in 1993; in 1997 one-third of the city's children in kindergarten through third grade were held back, along with 15 percent of the students in grades four through six and 19 percent of eighth graders.[44] Similarly, Georgia's Gwinnett County ended social promotion in 1996. A new superintendent and the school board of Gwinnett, the state's second largest school system, banned social promotion as part of reforms designed to raise test scores. Beginning in the spring of 1999 children had to pass "gateway" exams to move on from the fourth, seventh, and tenth grades. A state writing test was used to determine whether fifth and eighth graders should be promoted. Children with low scores had to attend summer school to move onward, and would be held back if their work did not improve enough. At the start of each school year parents were given handbooks detailing what their children were expected to learn. Beginning in the 1998–99 school year, the system was preparing to address the problem of double repeaters with "success" or "opportunity" schools that would offer such children a different approach to the curriculum they had thus far failed to master.[45] New York City's schools chancellor Rudy Crew announced that he would end the policy of moving children from grade to grade regardless of their achievement or lack thereof, but he did not actually do so in his first years in office. In 1997 it was still city policy to automatically promote sixteen-year-olds to high school, for example.[46]

State governments also moved against social promotion as the twenty-first century approached. Louisiana, Florida, Arkansas, South Carolina, and others took action against the practice, sometimes connecting student promotion to statewide assessment tests. The plan proposed by Texas Governor George W. Bush as a cornerstone of his 1998 reelection bid was one of the most comprehensive. Bush pushed for a plan under which children would have to take the Texas Assessment of Academic Skills (TAAS) at the end of the third, fifth, and eighth grades. Third graders would have to pass the test in reading, fifth graders in reading and math, and eighth graders in reading, writing, and math. Children who did not pass the appropriate sections of the TAAS would receive remedial help. It would be up to local districts to decide how to provide that help, either through after-school classes, summer school, or some other avenue. Unlike some attacks on social promotion that had gone into effect shortly after being announced, such as Chicago's, Bush's plan was to be phased in slowly, beginning with the class entering kindergarten in the fall of 1999. The basic idea of ending social promotion enjoyed tremendous public support in Texas in early 1998. A poll showed that 92 percent of Texans agreed that no child should be allowed to advance beyond third grade without knowing how to read, and 78 percent saw social promotion as a serious problem. The public was less sure about using tests to make that decision; 44 percent favored them while 35 percent thought teacher evaluations should decide whether or not children moved on to fourth grade.[47]

Governor Bush proposed that just over $200 million in state funds be provided to schools in the following year to help them begin implementing the program. The money would be used to develop remedial programs to help struggling students, and to administer the TAAS. Children who failed to score at least 70 in their first test were to have a second and, if necessary, a third chance to take it. Children who failed their first attempt would automatically receive extensive remedial help, paid for by the state; however, the allocated state funds would clearly be inadequate to help everyone in danger of being held back. Bush's plan became less rigid practically every time he discussed it. By early 1999 he was in favor of local districts having the final say in deciding which children who failed the TAAS would be held back. Through an appeals process, even children who had failed the TAAS three times might be promoted, if the involved parents, teacher, and principal all agreed it was appropriate. Like President Bill Clinton, whose opposition to social promotion is discussed later in this chapter, Governor Bush stated that his interest was in finding out which children needed help and then helping them, not in holding children back for its own sake.[48]

Not surprisingly, some school districts were ahead of the state. Waco required students from third to eighth grade to pass the TAAS to advance in 1997–98, and more than 20 percent of the students in those grades failed. Parents in Waco were understandably upset. (One advantage of Bush's intended gradual phasing in of his program was that parents would know far in advance what was expected of their children, and what the consequences would be if they did not do well enough on the TAAS. Another advantage, as it turned out, at least from a political perspective, was that it was being implemented so slowly that Bush would be long gone from the governor's office before any negative consequences showed up, such as increased dropout rates.) In the summer of 1998, Waco increased its remedial summer school efforts, limiting classes to sixteen students and paying teachers $4 more per hour than they had earned the previous summer. Waco faced lawsuits against its approach, the results of which could dramatically affect the state's plans. One of the lawsuits argued that the TAAS is an inappropriate test to use for judging what individual students have learned, claiming that it had instead been designed to determine whether schools were teaching the desired curriculum. The next year, Houston's public schools began phasing in a plan to end social promotion that used three standards, the TAAS, the Stanford Achievement Test, and student grades. The Houston plan began with students in the first, second, and third grades, with children having to "pass" on at least two of the three measures.[49]

In California, Governor Pete Wilson and the state legislature agreed in 1998 on a gradual approach to ending social promotion that gave school districts considerable control in deciding which children should be retained. Districts had to establish promotion and retention policies at five different grade levels, including the passages to middle school and high school. The plan provided more than $100 million for summer school, after-school, and Saturday remedial programs for children who were falling behind. Even combined with $180 million already in the budget for summer school, this was expected to provide help to just 10 percent of students in grades two through nine. Unfortunately, there was reason to think that the percentage of children who were notably behind and would need help was huge, since 3 million children (more than half of the state's students) were performing below grade level. Wilson had originally wanted promotion decisions to be based on a standardized test, but the policy that was adopted allowed grades, teacher recommendations, and parents all to play a role.[50]

One of the most important questions about the ban on social promotion in California was how it would interact with the changes in bilingual education described in Chapter 2. If reading tests in English played a large role in promotion decisions, as seemed likely, children whose first language was Spanish and who were not yet fluent in English would be at a tremendous disadvantage. Tens of thousands of Spanish-speaking children might be held back. Officials at schools where many of the children were native Spanish speakers still in the process of learning English hoped that their students, if doing well in math and reading in Spanish, would not be punished for their limited English by being retained. By December 1999, administrators in Los Angeles were already looking for ways to relax their standards, prompted by the unacceptable possibility that half of the district's 710,000 students were in some danger of being held back.[51]

The Bandwagon Fills

In the late 1990s and the beginning of this century, the movement against social promotion has been much more widespread and powerful than its predecessor was during the 1970s and early 1980s. As we have seen, a number of large states and cities have acted against social promotion, as have many smaller school districts. Both Republicans and Democrats have taken the issue as their own. President Clinton was the nation's most visible proponent of ending social promotion in the late 1990s. At a 1996 conference on education attended by governors and businessmen, Clinton called on the governors to strive for high standards in their state's classes and to end social promotion. Clinton argued that retaining children in a grade was not cruel, and stated that "the worst thing you can do is send people all the way through school with a diploma they can't read." In late 1997 Clinton publicly endorsed Chicago's reforms, particularly its attack on social promotion, announcing "I want what is happening in Chicago to happen all over America." In his January 1999 State of the Union address, Clinton made ending social promotion one of his five priorities for improving education, and called for tripling the amount of federal money spent on summer schools and after-school programs to help children who were behind academically. He even proposed reducing federal education funds for districts that failed to make progress on ending social promotion and his other goals. This "do it or else" stance partially reversed the usual federal approach of offering money if schools did as the federal government urged, as with bilingual education and Clinton's class size initiative.[52]

Clinton's call to end social promotion and the national movement against it strengthened each other; he was neither leading nor following, but instead moving in sync with a popular and widespread movement that made sense to many parents and therefore appealed to most politicians. But as one would expect from a president whose first national campaign saw the term *policy wonk* becoming common parlance, Clinton's opposition to social promotion paid some attention to the evaluation evidence. After the State of the Union speech opposing social promotion, an assistant secretary of education stated that the president was not necessarily in favor of holding back large numbers of children. Instead, Clinton wanted school districts to make extensive efforts to make sure that all children learned and could earn their promotions.[53] Many educators joined politicians in opposing social promotion. In September 1997 Sandra Feldman, the new president of the American Federation of Teachers (and thus a politician as well as an educator), opposed social promotion in a speech to the National Press Club. She cited a recent survey showing that only a small percentage of schools provided tutoring or alternative teaching methods for children who were retained. Feldman argued that schools needed to identify and help children who were falling behind in school, rather than simply waiting for them to fail and then sending them through the same curriculum they had already had. In a similar vein, the president of the Houston Federation of Teachers came out in support of Texas governor Bush's plan to end social promotion.[54]

By 1998 the bandwagon against social promotion was far more crowded than it had ever been. Still, not everyone agreed that ending social promotion was an obvious and desirable goal. In an article in *Phi Delta Kappan*, education researcher Richard Rothstein wrote of the public movement against social promotion that "the politics of education is often consumed by cliches, but this crusade may be the silliest yet." Rothstein argued that it was difficult to establish what "grade level performance" should be at each grade, and that choosing a minimally acceptable standard for each grade would be "incomparably more difficult." But without such a standard, ending social promotion could not be done. Rothstein raised a number of other points. For example, in the early grades children develop at very different rates from one another, and as a result some children are "ahead" in one subject while "behind" in another.[55] Perhaps the most telling criticism of the movement to end social promotion is that the alternative stigmatizes and increases the disadvantages already faced by children from low-income families and children of color. When the House of Representatives voted against national exams in late 1997, virtually all of the House's Latino and African-American representatives opposed the tests. In Texas, advocacy groups for students of color opposed the state's reliance on the TAAS. Hispanic and African-American groups denounced the Texas policy as discriminatory and likely to increase the high school drop-out rates for children of color.[56]

Even aside from whether tests are biased against certain groups—and that is an extremely important issue—relying solely or chiefly on tests is problematic for a number of other reasons. Tests involve measurement error, which makes using one test result to decide a child's fate a highly questionable practice. With a test on which 100 is a perfect score, 70 is passing, and 69 is failing, does it really make sense to believe that a child who scores 71 knows a significant amount beyond what a child who scores 68 knows? Should that small difference in test scores, which is as likely to result from one child's being more nervous than another or some other issue that is unrelated to what was actually learned in school, cause the former student to be promoted and the latter retained? That is at best a highly problematic way of judging which students should go on to the next grade and which should not. In 1998 the National Research Council warned against using test scores to determine decisions about graduation, promotion, or placement in remedial programs.[57] And anyone who has taught at any level from grade school to college knows that test taking is a skill. Most people are moderately good at it, some people are very good at it, and some people do so poorly at it that they develop a powerful fear of tests that further decreases the likelihood that their test results will actually show what they know. Tests do play an important role in schooling, but when used as the sole criteria for advancement, they are being used in a highly questionable manner. Test scores simplify the process but makes it less fair. (Some proponents of testing might reply that test taking is an important skill. It is important while one is in school because we have chosen to make it important; once one is an adult, however, test taking rarely matters.) Relying heavily on tests is particularly questionable when they are used to make crucial decisions about children in the early primary grades. In 1998 critics of the use of tests in the battle against social promotion were joined by the National Academy of Sciences, which issued a report arguing against using standardized tests as the sole criteria for promotion decisions.[58]

Even in places that seem determined to end social promotion, the practical realities of what that entails often get in the way. In December 1997 the Oakland, California school board adopted what the *San Francisco Chronicle* called "some of the toughest high school graduation standards" in the state. Seventh- and eighth-grade students who failed in math or English would not be promoted; sixth graders who failed those core subjects would also be held back if their parents agreed. An anonymous middle school teacher questioned the policy, pointing out that often as many as one-third of her school's students failed one of those subjects. The teacher wondered where all the retained children would be taught, in schools that were already drastically overcrowded, and said that summer school would not be able to "get them up to speed." In the summer of 1999, 7,000 children who were told they had to attend summer school or be retained in a grade did *not* attend but were promoted anyway; the next spring the city's new school superintendent vowed that would not happen again. In January 1999, the superintendent of the Los Angeles Unified School District announced an ambitious plan to identify low-performing students, place them in summer school, and hold them back if the summer sessions did not help enough to justify their promotion. But by April that plan was being scaled back owing to insufficient funding and limited classroom space. Two new state laws concerning social promotion had gone into effect in the fall of 1998, requiring school districts to provide mandatory summer school and to set their own standards for promotion decisions. But the laws lacked an enforcement provision, so districts that did not hold children back were not held accountable, though they did face criticism.[59] In Chapter 3 I describe the problems California has faced trying to reduce class sizes in its urban schools; holding back huge numbers of children would directly conflict with that program in most school districts. Where would they be taught, and who would teach them? It should be obvious by now that any real attempt to end social promotion will interact with a variety of other educational issues.

For policymakers and evaluators, one of the central lessons to be drawn from the crusade against social promotion is that popular, seemingly commonsense arguments can overwhelm research evidence. Interestingly, newspapers discussing state or district attempts to end social promotion often accurately described the evidence against it. Even editorials opposing social promotion often mention the fact that research shows retention hurts rather than helps students, and that it makes their dropping out more likely. To their credit, journalists, educators, and even politicians often argue for extensive remedial efforts in the expectation that such efforts can make retention a successful policy. Whether it actually can do so remains an open question, as does where the money would come from. And studies in the mid- and late 1990s continued to show that many children nationwide were, in fact, being held back, not just children in places that had made a conscious shift in that direction. By the age of fifteen to seventeen, almost half of all Hispanic and African-American youths have apparently been held back at least once.[60]

On February 8, 1998, the *Cleveland Plain Dealer* ran articles by two of the major figures in the evaluation of retention, Lorrie A. Shepard and Karl Alexander. As mentioned, in the late 1980s Shepard wrote about the problems caused by holding children back, and in the early 1990s Alexander and his colleagues found that, in Baltimore, retention had had mixed and sometimes even positive results. But their arguments about social promotion were not a simple for-or-against political debate. In the *Plain Dealer* Shepard wrote, "Studies show that repeating a grade does not improve achievement," and argued that students who are struggling should be advanced to the next grade. But she said these students should not be left to their own devices. Instead, schools and parents should agree on an "individualized education plan" detailing specific help for each child, to increase his or her achievement. In response, Alexander described findings from Baltimore that "retention was not positively harmful." "More than that," he added, "it helped." But Alexander then pointed out that people who see him and his colleagues as "friends of retention" are mistaken. He stated that retention works "only in a narrow sense." For most children who are behind, Alexander argued that retention should be "the option of last choice." Instead of simply holding children back when they are far behind,

Alexander called for "a third way," one "that shores up their skills before problems mount."[61] Thus Shepard and Alexander offer different answers to the question "Does retention do good or harm?" But more important, and more telling for the policy debate, they both see the question as somewhat beside the point and want to focus instead on identifying children who are falling behind, and developing and implementing methods and programs to provide extensive help to those students. Others who have examined the question, including the American Federation of Teachers in a 1997 report, have also recognized the futility of assuming the issue is a choice between promotion and retention.[62]

The unfortunate fact is that millions of students in American schools are far behind where educators believe they should be in achievement, as judged by what most of their peers actually are achieving. School officials have a number of options regarding such children. One possible response to the problem is to continue doing what we have been doing, at least in terms of promotion policy, promoting some but by no means all such children to the next grade. But this may be a practice on its way out. The use of social promotion has come under extensive attack in recent years, for a variety of reasons. Social promotion allows children to fall more and more behind, and tells students that moving upward is a given rather than a reward. It is unfair to the students who are not learning, it leads to unearned and watered-down diplomas, and it can tend to dumb down the curriculum for all students, including those who are doing well. Given all these results, it is hardly surprising that the American public and the political leaders who follow public opinion have moved against the practice. If social promotion is in fact seriously reduced or halted altogether, there are three basic options from which schools and policymakers must choose.

The first option for children who are far behind is to retain them and have them repeat a grade. The research evidence on what happens to children who simply go through the same curriculum a second time is convincing, even if not unanimous: doing so generally does not help children catch up, and it does make them more likely to drop out of school later. While some opponents of social promotion seem to expect retention to help children advance despite this evidence, and others believe the threat of retention will somehow magically motivate students, most recognize that this option is not really more desirable than continuing social promotion.

Perhaps informed by the evaluation evidence that simple retention does more harm than good, most opponents of social promotion argue that students who are held back should be given extensive help to catch up. Such help should be provided before the final decision to hold back children is made; in effect, children should be given one last chance, often through summer school. Chicago's summer school program—designed for children who are about to be held back, in the hope that their test scores will rise enough for them to be promoted instead—is typical in this regard. It is this second option that started to spread across many school districts and states in the late 1990s. In many cases, however, the extra help comes too late and has limited effect. In many places, including Texas and California, the funding provided for extra help is only a tiny portion of what would be needed to help everyone in danger of being held back a grade.

The third option is to act long before any actual decisions about promotion or retention need to be made. Children who are falling behind would be identified early and given very specific and, when necessary, very extensive help. Taken to an extreme, however, this could mean that children would be receiving individual attention for much of the school day. Obviously, providing large numbers of children with highly qualified individual tutors would be prohibitively expensive. Education is a political affair fought out at local, state, and federal levels. As Chapter 5 shows, few aspects of public schooling are more contested than funding, and providing these kinds of remedial programs would require increased funding far beyond anything we have ever seriously considered. For this reason, this is the least likely of the three options to occur.

Perhaps the most useful way to look at the debate over social promotion is that it flows directly from the fact that so many children are not learning what we, as a society, believe they should learn. This can be seen as a failure on the part of schools, teachers, parents, students, or even society as a whole, but it is clearly a failure. And how to best address this failure relates to many of the issues in this book. What can be done to help very young children, especially children who are "at risk" or "not ready to learn"? Is Head Start effective? Could we do more for children before they begin school? Will smaller classes in the early grades give children a boost that will last in later years? Is more money a fundamental part of any real answer, or not—and if so, what are the best ways to use that money? What is the best way to help children from non–English-speaking families learn English at an early age? And who should decide what language they are taught in—parents, schools, or state governments? What do we do when some children are not learning effectively? The debate over social promotion starts simply, but it ends with more questions than answers. The fundamental questions remain: What are our goals for education, and how do we achieve them? Arguing over which children to hold back and which to promote does not address the real problems in our schools; instead, it avoids them.

5

Does More Money
Make Schools Better?

Schools as a whole demonstrate an inability to use available resources effectively. There is little reason to believe that an additional dollar put into a school will improve student achievement.
—ERIC A. HANUSHEK, 1981

[T]he fact that so many children attend schools with limited resources demands that policymakers examine empirical evidence
about the question of whether money matters. Our findings . . .
demonstrate that money, and the resources those dollars buy, do
matter to the quality of a child's education.
—ROB GREENWALD, LARRY V. HEDGES, AND
RICHARD D. LAINE, 1996

Education costs money. And it costs a great deal more money now than it
did in the past. There are multiple reasons for the growing cost of public
education. Most of the increase during the 1950s and 1960s came from rising teacher salaries and shrinking class sizes. More recent increases have
stemmed largely from other factors, such as skyrocketing spending for
children who need special education or compensatory help.[1] Historically,
the bulk of school funds have come from local taxes. In recent decades,
however, state governments' contributions to local school districts have
grown markedly and are now equal to the amount contributed by local
sources. Each provides roughly 45 percent of the money in school district budgets (that is the national average; some states differ dramatically).
Funds from the federal government make up most of the other 10 percent.
Public schools take up about one-third of state budgets, on average, but

they face growing competition from other public services such as Medicaid and prisons.

Many education issues revolve, at least in part, around whether schools can afford them. But money alone is not the answer to the problems of schools. A question that runs throughout this volume, and throughout debates over school funding, is whether or not education dollars are being spent efficiently. It is important to recognize that not all schools face the same costs. It costs more to educate a child who needs special education classes than it does to educate a child in mainstream classes. It generally costs more to educate disadvantaged children than children from middle-class backgrounds. Experienced teachers approaching retirement cost more than young teachers just starting out. Transportation to school, subsidized lunches, bilingual education, advanced-placement courses, and many other costs vary from one school to the next, depending on the needs of each school's particular student population.[2] And of course many schools want to provide more than the basics for their students. What school wouldn't like to have an up-to-date computer lab or a new gymnasium? (All schools want these things, actually, but for school districts struggling to pay teachers and repair crumbling buildings, even providing the basics is difficult.) All of these issues involve money. Debates about school funding are part of debates about education as a whole, whether they are openly recognized as such or not.

At the heart of debates about school finance lie two questions: Does the amount of money a school has in its budget affect student achievement, and How much is required for an "adequate" education? The answer to the first question may seem obvious—money matters, since without it schools cannot exist—but the evaluation evidence is not completely straightforward on how much (or if) money matters, beyond having enough money to pay for buildings, teachers, and basic resources such as textbooks. The second question, though different in nature, is even more complicated. We simply do not know how much is required for an adequate education, partly because there is no agreement on what that would involve.

The court system has been a major arena of conflict over school funding. Plaintiffs have brought lawsuits in both state and federal courts seeking to have numerous states' methods of financing public education found in violation of either the U.S. Constitution or state constitutions. In fact, most state finance systems have been challenged at least once in the past three decades, and in some states the cases have been in and out of court for decades. One argument is that school financing systems that provide far more money to school districts in wealthy communities than to those in poorer communities violate the principle of equal protection. Another argument is that such unequal financing violates individual state constitution guarantees regarding education, since children in poor communities receive far fewer educational resources (which presumably leads to an inferior education) than do children in affluent communities. By the late 1990s, only a few states had *not* had lawsuits brought against their school funding systems. In nineteen different states, school financing approaches had been found unconstitutional, though how much actually changed varied greatly from state to state.[3] In many places, most notably New Jersey, the conflict has expanded to become one of court against legislature. In these cases, courts order reforms but legislatures are unable to agree on how to meet those orders, or are simply unwilling to comply with court mandates.

During the 1970s and 1980s, the central goal of plaintiffs was usually to provide "equitable" funding to all school districts within a given state; in other words, to reduce or eliminate the often enormous gap between the per-pupil expenditures of schools in wealthy communities and schools in working-class and impoverished communities. In the 1990s, however, much of the effort was aimed at providing an "adequate" education for children in low-wealth districts. Neither goal has proven easily achieved.

A Brief History of Public School Funding

The U.S. Constitution does not discuss education. From the beginning of the republic, by the terms of the Tenth Amendment, schools were the responsibility of local communities and state governments.[4] In the early decades of the nation's existence states did little, leaving the education of children up to parents and their towns and cities. The beginnings of the public school system we now know came in the 1830s and 1840s. Early public schools received funds from a variety of sources, including parental contributions, local taxation, and money from the state, with the mixture varying from place to place. The battle to create public "common schools" in those years was fought district by district. For common schools to exist in any number they needed tax money directly targeted for their use, and the decision about raising taxes was usually a local one. As David Nasaw writes, "The campaign for the common schools—through the later 1830s and 1840s—was no more and no less than a campaign for public taxation." Supporters of public schools argued that people should be willing to pay taxes for them because schools were an investment in a stable and secure society. Opponents of compulsory school taxes viewed them as an assault on private property, since property owners would have to pay the taxes even if they did not have any children in school.[5] Thus opposition to taxes (new or increased) for public schools existed from the start, as did the general argument that all should pay because schools were for the good of society. Efforts to limit the money spent on schools also arose early in the development of public schools, and they played out in numerous ways. In the midnineteenth century, female teachers were already being hired in growing numbers, at least in part because their salaries were far lower than those of male teachers. As David Tyack and Elisabeth Hansot write, "City after city decided to replace male teachers with women," so that "by 1890 women held 92 percent of the teaching jobs in all cities with populations exceeding ten thousand."[6]

In the early twentieth century, roughly 80 percent of the funding for public schools came from local revenues. A new approach to funding schools developed in the 1920s that would play a role in reducing dependence on local money: foundation funding, so called because it provided the basic financial foundation for school districts. When a state created a foundation program, it required local communities to tax property and guaranteed that each district would receive a specific minimum per-pupil amount. If local property taxes did not supply enough to reach that amount, the state would supply the rest.[7]

Over the first three decades of the twentieth century, the cost of public schooling was widely discussed. Schooling was expected to be "efficient" and to be run in a businesslike manner; that is, it should not cost too much.[8] It was hardly a coincidence that this shift occurred as schools were dealing with growing numbers of immigrant children. According to Tyack, in the 1930s and 1940s a growing number of educators began to notice (and point out) that educational resources and opportunities were distributed very unevenly across the nation's communities. The most expensive schools spent many times as much on each of their students as the poorest schools. Schools that were largely rural generally spent the least, with segregated schools for African-American children having the fewest resources. James D. Anderson has shown that most of what those schools did have was contributed by African-Americans themselves, who were at the same time taxed to support white schools from which their children were excluded.[9]

From the late 1940s to the 1960s, spending on America's public schools rose dramatically. There were a number of reasons for this, including pressure by teachers, labor groups, and the cold war. The spending was not geared toward equalizing schools in different communities, regions, or states, however; inequality of school resources continued to be a basic fact of American education. Spending has continued to rise in recent decades, in large part because the services offered by schools have expanded. Schools today employ more nonteaching staff: teacher aides, counselors, and a variety of support staff. And as we shall see later in this chapter, efforts to provide more equitable funding to schools within individual states have sometimes led to higher spending. In addition, students are now far more likely to attend high school, and to graduate, than they were early in the century.[10]

For most of the nation's history, federal involvement in local education has been very limited. Attempts in Congress to increase federal involvement usually have gone nowhere; as Diane Ravitch writes, they have "traditionally foundered for three reasons: race, religion, and fear of federal control." Whether to provide federal funds to racially segregated schools in the South, and to private—especially Catholic—schools were sticking points that could not be easily resolved.[11] Once the logjam was broken by Lyndon Johnson's Great Society programs, federal spending on education shot up by 1,400 percent in the 1960s and 1970s. Spending by state and local governments on elementary and secondary schools also skyrocketed during these years, but federal spending rose most rapidly, going from 4.4 percent of total educational spending in 1960 to 9.8 percent by 1980. Much of the new money came in categorical programs that targeted disadvantaged children, most notably the Elementary and Secondary Education Act of 1965. Under President Ronald Reagan in the 1980s, the percentage of funding for elementary and secondary schools that came from the federal government reversed course, dropping to 6.2 percent by 1987.[12]

Money comes to school districts from many sources and in many forms, some with strings attached. Federal funding usually comes in categorical programs that are targeted for very specific uses. Some federal money is directed to provide compensatory education for children from disadvantaged backgrounds; other federal money is targeted toward children with disabilities. State funds can also come in categorical programs, directed to some of the same areas that federal programs target as well as such others as buying computers and repairing buildings. More fundamentally, states also usually provide a basic level of funding to all schools through foundation funding, on which other, more specific, programs, such as special education, can be built. Alternately, states can adjust for students with special needs through "pupil weighting" rather than categorical programs. In this approach, students with certain characteristics are assigned a "weight." A student requiring no special help might have a funding weight of 1.0, while a student who qualifies for a free lunch program might be at a weight of 1.2, and a student who is in special education would have a higher weight, say 2.1. In practice, what this means is that for every dollar a school district receives for the student with a pupil weight of 1.0, it receives $1.20 for the student in the free lunch program, and $2.10 for the student in special education. This approach equalizes funding between different school districts fairly efficiently, but it has drawbacks, the most notable being that it may encourage schools to label students in ways that may be inaccurate and not to the students' own advantage.[13]

The Coleman Report

In 1965 the U.S. Office of Education, at the request of Congress, conducted a detailed survey on educational opportunity. The resulting report was published in 1966, with James S. Coleman as lead author. Generally known as the Coleman Report, it was heavily publicized and has been widely cited ever since. *Equality of Educational Opportunity* examined student achievement, segregation, and a number of other issues. It found that "the great majority" of students in America attended schools that were highly segregated. Among minority children, African-Americans were, not surprisingly, the most heavily segregated, but white children were the most thoroughly segregated from other groups (which is another way of saying that children of color were allowed to mix with one another but not with white children).[14]

The report's central finding regarding student achievement was perhaps its most striking claim: that by far the strongest factor affecting how well a student did in school was the student's family background. Children from families of means (middle-class to wealthy) had high achievement, while children from low-income backgrounds had low achievement. The quality of schooling a child received seemed to make little difference.[15] This meant, if correct, that the amount of money spent on a school did not matter, since it might be able to affect school quality—which apparently did not matter much—but it could not change what actually mattered, which was student background. For decades after its publication, the Coleman Report shaped people's assumptions about why children succeeded in school. Not surprisingly, its argument led to considerable debate. Other scholars soon questioned the Coleman Report's findings.[16] Despite the report's many flaws, however, it remains a landmark in educational research, and many of its findings—right or wrong—still echo through debates about education policy.

For the purposes of this discussion, what matters is that the Coleman Report influenced the nature of school finance lawsuits. It threw into question the commonsense argument that student achievement was related to the level of school funding. The resulting doubt about that relationship was one reason that school finance lawsuits centered on questions of *fairness* when there were large disparities between what different school districts had to spend. School inputs, such as funding levels, were featured rather than school outcomes, such as student achievement, because the connection between the two was less certain after the Coleman Report.[17]

A Push for Equity: *Serrano, Rodriguez,* and Their Successors

The civil rights movement affected how schools are financed, just as it affected segregation in schools and the extent of federal involvement in public schools. Court challenges to the ways states funded their schools arose in the 1960s and 1970s out of a desire for equal educational opportunity for disadvantaged children. They were built on the conviction that states' heavy reliance on local property taxes to fund schools kept this equal opportunity out of reach, because it led to wide gaps in funding between school districts, which in turn meant differences in the quality of education. State legislatures had developed and continued this system of financing public elementary and secondary schools, and reformers believed, with good reason, that those same legislatures had little interest in changing the status quo. As a result, people seeking to change the ways schools were funded, to create more opportunity for children in disadvantaged districts, turned to the court system.

School finance cases brought in state courts based their claims on state constitutions, focusing either on the principle of equal protection or on constitutional articles regarding the education to be provided to a state's citizens. The nature of the education clauses in state constitutions varied widely, not surprisingly; it was often put to the courts to determine whether individual state constitutions mandated a more equitable school funding plan than was in place. Since the late 1960s, most states have faced at least one court challenge to their funding approach. The complaints have generally followed the same basic argument. A state government's reliance on property taxes leaves school districts with small tax bases unable to spend as much per child as wealthier communities. This results in the creation and maintenance of large gaps between schooling opportunities for children in wealthy districts and children in poor districts.[18]

School funding cases litigated in federal courts, however, have usually relied on the U.S. Constitution's equal protection clause. They argue that state financing, if it leads to wide disparities between the educational resources for children in wealthy school districts and those for children in working-class and poor districts, constitutes unfair treatment toward the latter. Related to this (though not identical) is the argument that such unequal financing causes children in the latter communities to be deprived of effective and appropriate schooling.[19]

What would become the most prominent lawsuit against how any state financed its public schools was filed in California in 1968. At the time, about one-third of the funding for California's public schools came from the state while more than half came from local property taxes. Furthermore, the way in which state aid was distributed did little to reduce the inequities between school districts created by the heavy reliance on local taxes. In the late 1960s, for example, the Beverly Hills school district spent more than twice as much per student as did nearby Baldwin Park. The plaintiffs in *Serrano v. Priest* believed that the state's dependence on property taxes to fund schools placed children from low-income neighborhoods at a severe educational disadvantage. The strategy of the plaintiffs' lawyers was to convince the courts that the system was unfair and should be declared unconstitutional, not to determine a new system; that was to be left to the legislature. They decided to sue in state court rather than federal court because the California Supreme Court, where they expected the case would eventually be decided, was viewed as more willing to consider such issues.[20]

When hearings for *Serrano v. Priest* began in Los Angeles County Superior Court in August 1968, the case received little attention. The plaintiffs used published statistics comparing the funding of rich school districts to that of poor school districts. It was easy to demonstrate that while poor districts taxed themselves at higher rates than did rich districts, they still wound up with far less money per pupil. The defense accepted the evidence regarding different funding levels from one school district to another but argued that there was no constitutional issue at stake, and asked that the case be dismissed without a trial. In early 1969 the superior court agreed and dismissed the case.[21]

The attorneys for John Serrano, Jr., and the other plaintiffs appealed that decision. The state court of appeals based its decision on a recent action by the U.S. Supreme Court in *McInnis v. Shapiro,* in which the Court had accepted a district court's decision against the plaintiffs in a school finance case. The court of appeals ruled against the plaintiffs, stating that the two cases were basically the same, and that the issue had already been settled. In early 1971, however, after further appeal, the California Supreme Court agreed to hear *Serrano v. Priest.* In the intervening period several important books making varied arguments for greater school equity had appeared. In addition, the plaintiffs' lawyers were forced by the appeals court's decision to change their approach. Before the superior court and the appeals court, they had taken what Richard Elmore and Milbrey McLaughlin call a "kitchen sink approach" by including a wide array of arguments. Before the California Supreme Court, however, they shifted to a more focused approach, arguing that the state's school finance system was unfair because the quality of education depended on the wealth of each school district.[22]

In August 1971 the California Supreme Court agreed with the plaintiffs by a six-to-one majority. It accepted virtually all of the arguments advanced by the *Serrano* lawyers, stating that the state's school funding system "invidiously discriminates against the poor because it makes the quality of a child's education a function of the wealth of his parents and neighbors." The decision recognized the right to an education as "a fundamental interest which cannot be conditioned on wealth." As a result, the court stated, "If the allegations of the complaint are sustained, the financial system must fall and the statutes comprising it must be found unconstitutional" under the equal protection clause. Not surprisingly, the court's ruling received far more attention than the case had when originally begun three years before. The court's finding, which became known as *Serrano I,* sent the case back to the California Superior Court (which had dismissed it in 1969) to determine the facts of the case.[23]

Before the superior court readdressed the case, the U.S. Supreme Court's ruling in another school-finance case, *San Antonio Independent School District et al. v. Rodriguez,* (discussed below), was issued, and the California legislature passed a new tax bill that made some changes in the way schools were financed. Both of these events had the potential to weaken the *Serrano* case. The trial in the superior court began at the end of 1972, and the court's decision was finally issued in September 1974. The court found that the objectionable features of the state's school financing system had not been eliminated, as large disparities would continue to exist in the funding levels of different school districts. As a result, the court ruled for the plaintiffs and declared the state's funding system unconstitutional by the state constitution's equal protection clause. The state legislature was given six years to develop a new system that would leave per-pupil funding differences between districts at no more than $100; the court did not specify what kind of system should be used to achieve this goal. The defendants appealed, but to no avail; in 1976 the California Supreme Court affirmed the superior court's ruling for the plaintiffs by a narrow four-to-three margin in what was known as *Serrano II.* So far as the supreme court's majority was concerned, student achievement and money were definitely related. The court stated that achievement tests did not measure everything that mattered about a child's "educational experience," but that even when tests were used to measure educational quality, "differences in dollars do produce differences in pupil achievement." Wealthier districts had "a substantial advantage in obtaining higher quality staff, program expansion and variety, beneficial teacher-pupil ratios and class sizes, modern equipment and materials, and high-quality buildings."[24]

The legislature's first attempt to change the school funding formula in late 1972—partly in response to *Serrano I*—was really a tax bill with some additional funding for schools, and it did not satisfy the courts. Developing a formula that would meet the court's mandate was chiefly a political problem; coalitions in support of school finance reform changed over time and never had as much strength as the *Serrano* plaintiffs and lawyers would have liked. Even so, the legislature's next attempt was a more plausible response to the state supreme court's affirmation of *Serrano II* and included a more effective equalizing approach that shifted tax revenues from wealthy school districts to disadvantaged ones. Governor Jerry Brown signed the bill into law in September 1977. Not everyone agreed that it was a good law, though; one *Serrano* lawyer called it "a gigantic fraud."[25]

Before the new law was fully in place, however, came the death knell for better school funding for poor school districts, and for quality public education in California in general: Proposition 13. The statewide referendum, passed in June 1978 by a two-thirds majority of California voters, placed strict limits on local property taxation, thereby making the 1977 school funding law, S.B. 65, impossible to implement. With the new limits on local property taxation, the state share of public school spending shot up to 70 percent the next year. Over the next few years funding levels did even out somewhat between wealthy and disadvantaged school districts in California, but it was because funding in general was dropping, not because poor school districts were receiving greatly increased funding. In other words, what equalization occurred was through "leveling down," not leveling up.[26]

In 1983 the California Superior Court found that the state government was in compliance with the *Serrano* rulings. Just over 93 percent of the state's public elementary and secondary schools were receiving virtually the same amount of per-pupil funding, as required by the court's 1974 ruling, and the court viewed the 6.8 percent of schools falling outside the range to be an acceptably small proportion. Although the court found against the plaintiffs and for the state regarding the question of whether schools were equitably funded, it also noted that the state's schools did not receive enough money to provide an excellent education. (And indeed they did not. Between the 1960s and the 1980s, California went from having one of the highest per-pupil expenditure levels in the nation to having one of the lowest; student test scores followed suit.) In 1986 the state court of appeals upheld the 1983 ruling.[27]

The most significant school finance case to enter federal courts and then reach the U.S. Supreme Court was *San Antonio Independent School District et al. v. Rodriguez.* The plaintiffs in the case were children in Texas school districts with low property values. They claimed that the sizable school funding gap between affluent and poor communities caused by dependence on property taxes violated the U.S. Constitution's equal protection clause. They compared two school districts, Alamo Heights and Edgewood, both in the San Antonio area. The state provided approximately $220 per pupil to each school district. In Alamo Heights, a residential area of considerable means, property values were high, leading to a local contribution of another $333 per pupil, for a total of $558 for each student. Edgewood, an inner-city community, taxed itself at a higher rate for its schools than did Alamo Heights, but because property values in Edgewood were quite low, its contribution amounted to only $26 per pupil. Combined with state money, Edgewood had a total of $248 per pupil, which was less than half what Alamo Heights had to spend on each of its students. The plaintiffs found this system of financing public education discriminatory, and believed it unfairly provided an inferior education for children from less affluent communities.[28]

The federal court in Texas that heard the case agreed with the *San Antonio v. Rodriguez* plaintiffs, finding that education was a "fundamental interest" and that Texas's system violated the Fourteenth Amendment's equal protection clause. When the case reached the United States Supreme Court, however, it found a less hospitable audience under new Chief Justice Warren Burger. Elmore and McLaughlin write that "there was a growing sentiment among school finance lawyers that *San Antonio v. Rodriguez* was the wrong case at the wrong time." And so it was; the Supreme Court found for the defendants and reversed the district court's ruling by a narrow five-to-four margin.[29]

The Court's 1973 ruling in *San Antonio v. Rodriguez* is one of the most important in the history of school finance legislation. The Court upheld Texas's method of funding its schools. One of the central reasons for this ruling was that the Court found that the facts in evidence did not show that most poor people lived in poor districts, and that therefore there was no basis to view the system as discriminatory. Texas's system of financing its schools was upheld; rather than discriminatory, it was seen by the Court as a legitimate system that protected local control of public education. Nothing in the Constitution stated that school systems must be comparable to one another, either within states or between states. The Court went so far as to state that there was no fundamental right to education in the Constitution. This was a dramatic step backward from its ruling two decades earlier in *Brown v. Board of Education of Topeka*, where the Court had found education to be a highly important government function.[30]

The Supreme Court's ruling that highly unequal funding of different school districts within a state was constitutional made it difficult—though not impossible—for later efforts to challenge state methods of financing public education in federal courts. In a later ruling in another case, *Papason v. Allain,* the Court stated that its ruling in *Rodriguez* should not automatically protect any and all variations in state methods for financing schools. They might be unconstitutional under the equal protection clause if it could be shown that they were not rationally connected to an important state interest. By and large, however, the Supreme Court's various rulings continued to leave control of education funding in the hands of state legislatures. As a result, since *Rodriguez* most legal challenges to state school financing plans have been made in state courts.[31]

In the 1970s and 1980s, at least six states faced challenges to their school funding systems based on equal protection clauses in their state constitutions. Most states survived the challenge; only Connecticut was found to be in violation of its state constitution. Challenges to how states financed their public schools based on federal equal protection law fared just as poorly in the 1970s and 1980s. Only Wyoming's system was deemed unconstitutional. The Wyoming Supreme Court found education to be a fundamental right, and that the state had failed to prove that its method of financing schools served a compelling interest; as a result, the court declared the state's school funding system unconstitutional. Courts that supported existing funding systems that led to wide disparities from one district to another did so for a variety of reasons. Some doubted that funding levels were closely related to student achievement, while others considered local control to be more important than equitable funding, or were hesitant to intrude on educational issues because they were the prerogative of the legislature.[32]

Across the 1980s things began to shift slightly in favor of plaintiffs who sought more equitable school funding arrangements. By the late 1980s, nine states had had their school financing systems deemed unconstitutional by the courts for one reason or another. In many of these states, legislative solutions had not proven satisfactory and court cases continued to argue that the school funding methods in place were unconstitutional. In a few states, legislatures changed their approach to funding public schools because of the threat of lawsuits. In most states, however, courts found school finance systems to be constitutional. They did not do so because school funding was equitable, but instead because neither equal protection nor state education clauses required that funding be equitable across all school districts.[33]

While these lawsuits often accomplished far less than their initiators and supporters had hoped, some did have an impact. In 1970 in California, local taxes supplied far more money to overall spending on public elementary and secondary schools than did state funds. By 1986, that relationship had reversed dramatically, with state revenues supplying almost three times as much money as local revenues. In fact if the state had not stepped in after Proposition 13's assault on property taxes, California's schools, already struggling, would have been complete disasters. More important (at least to the *Serrano* plaintiffs), during that same period the percentage of education spending from the state of California that went to equalizing spending across school districts rose considerably. The same thing occurred in other states, such as New Jersey and Connecticut, in which courts ruled against state practices for financing schools.[34]

In the 1970s and 1980s there seemed to be little rigorous evidence showing that increasing school resources did in fact lead to higher student achievement, so the legal battles for more equitable funding might seem misguided. But plaintiffs seeking more funding for schools in lower-income communities knew that those same schools had older textbooks, inferior or nonexistent labs, inferior classroom spaces, and many other deficiencies when compared with more affluent schools. It seemed obvious to these plaintiffs, and to many others, that improving each of these areas would help students. Where courts have ruled in favor of lawsuits seeking more equal funding, they have agreed with this commonsense view rather than with what the evidence seemed to say about increased school funding. As William Camp, David Thompson, and John Crain wrote in 1990, "The courts have ruled that in the absence of convincing evidence to the contrary, a positive link between resource allocation and student achievement must be assumed."[35] Even so, it is important to understand what evaluation has had to say. What did the evidence actually show in the 1980s? How has that changed in the 1990s?

Evidence: From "Does Money Matter?" to "How Does Money Matter?"

Hundreds of studies have been done on the relationship between school funding levels and student achievement. One approach, known as production-function or input-output studies, examines the relationship between various inputs to education, including funding, and measurable outcomes. Other inputs besides funding that such studies often take into account include parental education and income, teacher experience, class size, and the demographics of the school as a whole. Some examine individual schools or groups of schools, while others look at school districts or even larger units. The results of these studies vary dramatically, as does their quality. Because of the varied nature of the studies done on school funding and their findings, the best way to try to understand what the evidence has to say is to review all of the studies together (or at least all of the higher-quality studies). The most influential figure in debates about school finance in the 1980s was Eric Hanushek, a professor of economics and political science at the University of Rochester, who did just that. In 1981 Hanushek published a journal article titled "Throwing Money at Schools," which argued (if the title isn't enough of a clue) against the movement to increase school budgets. Hanushek began by pointing out that spending on education had risen sharply over several decades, during which time student achievement seemed to stagnate or even decline. Such an argument, however, is based on a simplistic understanding of historical change and is virtually meaningless, because numerous other issues that affect student achievement were also changing during that time. But Hanushek soon turned to the substance of his research, which was built on more solid ground.[36]

Hanushek looked at the results of twenty-nine studies that examined, in one form or another, the relationship between school expenditures and student outcomes. Within the twenty-nine studies there were a total of 130 analyses of the effect of money on achievement. The studies varied greatly. Some looked at multiple districts, while others focused on one school district; some used standardized tests to judge outcomes, while other used grades, dropout rates, or other factors. Some of the studies were of secondary school, others of elementary school; some looked at individual students, while others looked at the aggregate scores of students within a school or a school district. To understand what all these studies taken together meant, Hanushek used a method known as vote counting. For each of the seven "inputs" to schooling he was interested in—per-pupil expenditure, teacher experience, teacher-pupil ratio, and four others—he counted the number of studies that showed a statistically significant positive relationship with student achievement.[37]

An example may make Hanushek's approach easier to understand. Out of the 130 separate analyses Hanushek examined, 55 included per-pupil expenses. Of those 55, only 5 showed a statistically significant relationship in which higher expenditures and high student performance went together. At the same time, 3 of those 55 analyses showed that higher per-pupil expenditures were related to *lower* student performance. In the remaining 47 studies, the relationship between student performance and per-pupil expenditures was not statistically significant. Hanushek reported that in 23 of the cases higher expenditures related (very weakly) to higher student performance, while in 13 cases they related (again weakly) to lower student performance. In 11 of the analyses, the relationship between the two was not described by the authors of the original studies, except to say that it was not statistically significant.[38]

Hanushek's conclusion, quite understandably, was that the evidence did not show that increasing spending on schools led to higher student achievement. Of the seven "input" factors he examined for a relationship to student performance, the only one for which a number of the studies showed a significant connection to high performance was teacher experience. Out of the 104 analyses looking at teacher experience, 36 found it to be statistically significant: 30 of those found it related to higher student performance, and 6 found it related to lower student performance. Surprisingly, Hanushek nonetheless dismissed the importance of teacher experience, writing that if it "actually had a significant beneficial effect, it is unlikely that so few studies would pick up that fact." He concluded that "higher school expenditures per pupil bear no visible relationship to higher student performance," though he admitted that money might perhaps have a positive impact in some circumstances. Hanushek also stated that this showed that school finance lawsuits, seeking more money as the way to improve schools, were off target. This argument might have seemed nonsensical to many teachers and to reformers seeking to improve public schools, especially schools in disadvantaged inner-city and rural areas. But Hanushek was not going by what *seemed* obvious; he was basing his conclusion on studies others had done examining the effects of funding on education. In the Reagan era this argument appealed tremendously to conservatives nationwide, especially coming from a professor asserting that he had proof. Hanushek became a well-known expert in some conservative circles, and he testified as an expert in school finance cases.[39]

Hanushek published several more articles on school finance, including an influential work in 1989 in which he summarized the findings of thirty-eight studies on the relationship between school inputs and student performance that contained a total of 187 separate analyses. Once again he used the vote-counting approach in reviewing and summarizing the studies. After examining this larger pool of evidence, Hanushek's conclusions were basically the same as they had been in 1981: "Variations in school expenditures are not systematically related to variations in student performance." Teacher experience once again showed the strongest relationship to higher student achievement. Of the 150 analyses of this relationship, 40 found a statistically significant relationship demonstrating that more teacher experience related to higher student performance (while 10 found higher teacher experience significantly related to lower student achievement). As he had in 1981, however, Hanushek downplayed this evidence. Hanushek was emphatic that money did not make a difference: *"There is no strong or systematic relationship between school expenditures and student performance."* As a result, he claimed, court cases seeking higher, and more equitable, levels of funding for schools in disadvantaged communities, such as those described earlier in this chapter, were "misguided." (He did argue—based on other research and against the findings of the Coleman Report—that teachers and schools could make a difference: *"Teachers and schools differ dramatically in their effectiveness."*[40]

Hanushek's work was extremely influential, but not everyone was convinced by his arguments. Morton Hunt tells the story of how Richard Laine, a graduate student at the University of Chicago concerned with school reform, did not believe Hanushek's results, and subsequently took a class on research methods taught by Larry Hedges, an expert on research synthesis, so that he would understand Hanushek's methods. Laine quickly found that Hanushek's approach, vote counting, was not a very well respected research method. Laine convinced several other graduate students to collaborate with him on a meta-analysis of the studies Hanushek had used; he believed the far more sophisticated statistical methods of meta-analysis would give them a more rigorous and accurate result than Hanushek's approach.[41]

The seminar paper Laine and his colleagues wrote, based on a meta-analysis of the same data Hanushek had synthesized to argue that money did not matter, had markedly different conclusions. Instead of no effects, they found that every additional $100 spent per pupil (in 1989 dollars) would increase student achievement by one-fifth of a standard deviation, a significant gain. With help from Hedges, Laine and Rob Greenwald expanded their examination of the data. The result was published in 1994 in *Educational Researcher,* the same journal that had published Hanushek's influential review five years earlier.[42]

Hedges, Laine, and Greenwald's meta-analysis examined the same seven inputs to schooling—per-pupil expenditure, teacher experience, teacher salary, teacher-student ratio, teacher education, facilities, and administrative inputs—as had Hanushek in his 1989 article. But their results were very different. First they took on Hanushek's interpretation of his vote-counting results. Hedges and his colleagues pointed out that if per-pupil expenditure and student achievement were truly unrelated, then only 5 percent of the studies Hanushek examined would have had statistically significant outcomes, half of them positive relationships and half of them negative. But for teacher experience (which Hanushek had dismissed), 35 percent of the studies had statistically significant results, which was seven times what would be expected if there were no connection. To Hedges, Laine, and Greenwald, even vote counting, if done properly, showed that money *did* matter.[43]

But that argument was a prelude to the main event, their own meta-analysis of the same data Hanushek had used in his review. Whereas Hanushek had concluded that *none* of the seven inputs he examined was positively related to student outcomes, Hedges, Laine, and Greenwald found that *most* of the inputs were related to student performance. The evidence was strongest for the impact of per-pupil expenditures and teacher experience. In sum, Hedges and his colleagues found that the data, which Hanushek had decided showed money did not affect student achievement, led to "exactly the opposite conclusion," that "expenditures are positively related to school outcomes."[44]

Hanushek disagreed, in an article published in the next issue of *Educational Researcher*. His tone throughout showed a certain disdain for the meta-analytic approach taken by Hedges, Laine, amd Greenwald; he referred to "their statistical manipulations and their zeal." Hanushek criticized meta-analysis in general, and the way they had employed it in particular. He reiterated his belief that since expenditures had gone up dramatically over several decades but test scores had not, money could not matter—an argument that was naive at best and moreover showed a misunderstanding of historical change, educational complexity, or perhaps both. Astoundingly, Hanushek then replied that they had asked "the wrong question" and that "policy interpretations do not depend really on the statistical issues." He reiterated his belief that money made little or no difference in most cases, and that the idea that money could (or might have to) be part of the solution was "misleading and potentially dangerous."[45] Hedges, Laine, and Greenwald replied in the same journal issue, defending meta-analytic technique in general, their specific use of it, and the policy conclusions they had drawn from it.[46] On technical (and logical) grounds they had the better of the debate, though what any individual reader takes from the debate may depend largely on which argument that reader wants to be true.

That was not the last of it. In 1996 Greenwald, Hedges, and Laine published another meta-analysis on the effects of school finance, and Hanushek was again given the opportunity of replying, this time in the same journal issue. Greenwald and his colleagues brought together sixty research studies for their meta-analysis. They included twenty-nine of the thirty-eight studies Hanushek had used in 1989 (and they had used in 1994), along with thirty-one more studies found after an exhaustive search. The results differed in minor ways from those of two years earlier, but their overall conclusion was similar: a variety of resources were related to student performance, and the connection was strong enough "to suggest that moderate increases in spending may be associated with significant increases in performance." Greenwald, Hedges, and Laine were careful to point out that they did "not argue that money is everything. How we spend the money and the incentives we create for both children and teachers are equally important." Confident that they had answered the question "Does money matter?" they argued for the need to answer another, "How does money matter?"[47]

Hanushek agreed that the latter question was more important and admitted, more than he had in the past, that when resources were used efficiently by schools, they did in fact make a difference. He continued to question the meta-analytic approach on a variety of technical grounds, however. And more interesting, he seemed to put words in their mouths, claiming (among other things) that Greenwald and his colleagues assumed schools were working well. The heart of Hanushek's criticism was that their selection process biased their results to find stronger effects on student achievement than actually exist; in fact they seem to have taken pains to avoid selection bias. Hanushek even claimed that meta-analysis was not an appropriate approach to examining studies from different settings, but so long as a meta-analysis is done properly, that is actually one of the main strengths of the method, and one of the reasons it was developed. All in all, in his response he sometimes comes across more as someone determined to defend his position than someone taking part in an unbiased debate over either research methods or school resources.[48]

Who is right? Hedges, Laine, and Greenwald. While meta-analysis is not a perfect technique, and can be performed poorly, their use of it seems sound, and far more rigorous than Hanushek's vote counting. Hanushek's approach to studying the data is seriously flawed. As Richard Light and David Pillemer put it, vote counting "ignores sample size, effect size, and research design. Serious errors can result."[49] Hanushek's unwillingness to acknowledge that even vote counting showed teacher experience to be related to improved student performance casts a harsh light on any claims to impartiality on his part.[50] Of course, he is right to say that increasing school funding will not *automatically* improve student achievement. Hedges, Laine, and Greenwald do not claim that, only that it often does make a difference. But to make effective education policy we need to know far more than their work shows; as they all agree, we need to know how to use money wisely, and unfortunately school finance evaluations offer limited guidance on that question.

New Jersey

No court case, and no state, bridges the struggle over school financing in the years from the 1970s to the late 1990s as dramatically as New Jersey. In 1970 a lawsuit was brought against New Jersey's method of financing its public schools. The suit, *Robinson v. Cahill,* argued that children attending school in districts with low property values were at a strong disadvantage compared with children in more affluent areas, much as the *Serrano* plaintiffs argued in California. The New Jersey state constitution states that children should receive a "thorough and efficient system of free public schools." According to the plaintiffs, the extremely unequal funding of some schools meant that the system as a whole fell short of that constitutional mandate.[51]

New Jersey courts agreed with the plaintiffs, capped off by the state supreme court's ruling of 1973. The plaintiffs' argument contained a claim that equal protection was being violated, but the New Jersey Supreme Court did not agree. Regarding the education article in the state constitution, however, the high court ruled in the plaintiffs' favor. The court maintained in *Robinson v. Cahill* that the state's funding method violated the constitutional clause guaranteeing a "thorough and efficient system" of schools for the state's children. The wide disparities between the funding levels of different school systems in New Jersey meant that this was not being provided. In the long run, this reliance on a constitutional guarantee regarding education would have different implications than the reliance on equal protection in California's *Serrano* decisions. In the short run, however, in the decision that became known as *Robinson I,* the court gave the legislature until the end of 1974 to develop a remedy for the unequal funding, and it had to be in place by July 1975. When the legislature delayed, the court extended its deadlines.[52]

By 1975, however, the New Jersey Supreme Court decided that it had waited long enough and developed orders for redistributing state funds. The legislature finally acted before the court's order went into effect, passing the Public School Education Act in the same year. The act provided a long list of educational goals, but it was not fully funded. The court approved the act while recognizing that it needed to be funded, and withheld full approval until it was actually in place so that its results could be examined. In the summer of 1976, the court shut the state's public school system down briefly because the legislature had not yet funded the act appropriately. The legislature, which had been opposing the governor's call for a state income tax to provide the needed funds, gave in after a week and created the income tax. State funding for elementary and secondary education rose by 40 percent between 1975–76 and 1976–77. By 1981 the New Jersey school budget was more than twice what it had been five years before. Where California achieved *relative* equalization—enough to satisfy the court system—by lowering funding (due largely to Proposition 13), New Jersey tried to achieve it by increasing funding.[53]

In New Jersey, however, wide disparities continued to exist among the funding levels of different school districts, and as a result a new court challenge to the financing system arose in 1981. The Education Law Center filed *Abbott v. Burke* on behalf of twenty students living and attending public schools in Camden and three other disadvantaged communities. The plaintiffs claimed that local property taxes still supplied the bulk of funding for public schools, and that as a result there were still large differences in funding levels between different school districts. To the plaintiffs, this showed that the school financing system was still in violation of the state constitution, because it did not provide them with a "thorough and efficient" education. (They also believed it violated the equal protection clauses of the state and federal constitutions.) In 1984, after a lower court had dismissed the case, an appeals court reversed the lower court's dismissal and sent the case back to the chancery division; in 1985, the state supreme court reversed the appellate court decision and sent the case to the state's commissioner of education. The commissioner subsequently rejected the idea that there is a strong relationship between per-pupil expenditure and the quality of education; subsequent educational reforms enacted in the late 1980s did not try to equalize funding across the state.[54]

By 1990 the case was again before the New Jersey Supreme Court, which unanimously ruled for the plaintiffs. "We find that under the present system the evidence compels but one conclusion: the poorer the district and the greater its need, the less the money available, and the worse the education. That system is neither thorough nor efficient," and therefore the Public School Education Act of 1975 was declared unconstitutional "as applied to poorer urban school districts." The court's *Abbott II* decision focused on students in twenty-eight of the state's poor school districts, and left much of the state's system intact. The court was very specific, stating that students in those school districts could benefit from a quality education, deserved to receive one, and that the state should spend as much for the basic education of those children as it did in the wealthiest districts. Unlike the commissioner of education, the court believed that money mattered. It stated that "the decisions regularly made by school districts, the Commissioner, and the Board are based on the premise that what money buys affects the quality of education"; as a result, the court agreed with "the conventional wisdom" that money was an important factor in educational quality. Money alone, however, would not suffice: "substantial, far-reaching change" was also required in the targeted districts. The shift in focus from the ruling in *Robinson I* in 1973 was dramatic. Then, students all deserved a basic, minimum level of education. The 1990 *Abbott II* ruling went far beyond that, implying that the state might have to spend *more* per pupil in disadvantaged school districts to provide something approaching legitimate equal educational opportunity.[55]

The New Jersey legislature responded to the court's ruling with the Quality Education Act of 1990, which it amended in 1991. The original act would have distributed more money from state coffers to disadvantaged school districts than to wealthier ones. After this met strong resistance around the state, however, Governor James Florio and Democrats in the legislature agreed to a revision that took one-third of the additional money that had been targeted to education and shifted it to relieve property taxes. In response, the Education Law Center asked the state supreme court to intervene and set a deadline for the legislature to develop a new plan to equalize funding. By the summer of 1992 the case was in court again, this time in superior court. In its defense, the state argued that the earlier ruling, that funding should be "guaranteed," should not be taken as literally as the plaintiffs believed. It admitted that the Quality Education Act did not create parity among all the state's school districts but believed that it had done enough to start things moving in the right direction. The superior court disagreed and found the Quality Education Act unconstitutional. In 1994 the state supreme court agreed in its *Abbott III* ruling, but in recognition of the increase in funding to poor districts since 1990, the court announced it would intervene only if the state did not reach "substantial equivalence" by 1997.[56]

But the persistence of the Education Law Center, and the resistance of New Jersey politicians to requests to fully equalize funding (and antagonize many of the state's voters in the process), meant that both sides were soon back in court. In 1996 the state supreme court denied a motion by the plaintiffs, partly because the legislature was debating how to change the school finance system. After passage of the Comprehensive Educational Improvement and Financing Act of 1996, the plaintiffs renewed their motion. This time the New Jersey Supreme Court agreed to hear the case. In May 1997 the court again found for the plaintiffs, ruling the state's new effort unconstitutional. The court pointed out that the state had had seven years since the *Abbott II* ruling to equalize funding, and more than two decades since *Robinson I,* and had still failed to do so. Tired of waiting, the court called for allocating several hundred million dollars in additional funds to disadvantaged school districts by September. The state's next efforts focused on both whole-school reform and more equitable funding, and finally met the court's approval, although the court did order the state to provide more extensive kindergarten and preschool programs. Most observers thought that *Abbott v. Burke* had finally come to an end. But when the state moved slowly to make kindergarten and preschool classes more readily available in twenty-eight "special needs districts," the Education Law Center went back to court.[57]

A Push for Adequacy: Courts and Legislatures in the 1990s

In the midst of the New Jersey saga, the 1980s ended with the legal tide in school finance cases turning in favor of plaintiffs. In 1989 and 1990 five different state high courts ruled on whether their state's school funding methods were constitutional, and only one court (Wisconsin) upheld the existing method. Along with New Jersey, courts in Texas, Kentucky, and

Montana ruled against the ways in which schools were financed. Perhaps partly because of these triumphs by plaintiffs, the 1990s saw "a new wave of litigation" that expanded the kinds of issues raised in discussing state school funding methods.[58]

In Kentucky, a court ruling led to an overhaul of the state's public school system that went far beyond funding issues. In *Rose v. Council for Better Education, Inc.*, the plaintiffs claimed that Kentucky's method of financing its schools violated the state constitution, which stated that the legislature was to provide "an efficient system of common schools." The lower court agreed, even writing that many of Kentucky's children were "suffering from an extreme case of educational malnutrition." The case was appealed to the Kentucky Supreme Court, which agreed with the lower court's ruling and then went well beyond it by declaring the *entire Kentucky public school system* to be unconstitutional.[59]

The Kentucky legislature's response was a far cry from the New Jersey legislature's reluctance. The Kentucky Education Reform Act of 1990 not only changed how the state's elementary and secondary schools were financed, it also changed how they were governed, and sought to improve student achievement through a variety of coordinated measures. By 1993 school funding had risen by 19 percent (adjusted for inflation). At least as important, equity between districts had improved, with the advantage the highest per-pupil expenditure areas had over the lowest dropping from 2.5 times to 1.6 times. (One of the ways the legislature raised funding was by increasing the state sales tax.) By the late 1990s there had been impressive changes in the structure of Kentucky's educational system, although practice in classrooms was changing less rapidly.[60]

The impact of the Kentucky Supreme Court's ruling was felt in other states throughout the 1990s. The greatest effects have been seen in Alabama and Massachusetts, where courts "have directly followed the Kentucky precedent" by declaring their state's public schools to fall short of state constitutional guarantees. Both states even used the Kentucky Supreme Court's ruling about what an adequate education entailed.[61] Significant changes in school financing were not limited to courts and legislatures in the 1990s. In 1994 Michigan voters approved a fundamental change in how the state's public schools were financed. They voted to replace property taxes with an increase in the state sales tax and cigarette tax. The new system also included minimum per-pupil spending amounts and placed upper limits on what school districts could spend.[62]

New Jersey is not the only state where efforts to make school funding more equitable have moved back and forth from courts to legislatures over several decades. Sizable disparities among the funds available to different school districts still existed in California in the 1990s. On several occasions a number of school districts joined forces to take the state to court. In one instance, more than one hundred school districts joined together, but they dropped their lawsuit because they were unable to raise the necessary money. (Meanwhile, the state appropriated $1.8 million to fight the prospective lawsuit.) In 1979 the West Virginia Supreme Court described the overarching goals that an acceptable public school system would seek to meet. Four years later a lower court approved the educational "master plan" of the state's legislature and education department. By 1997, however, the state's supreme court was again involved, ruling that the plan had not been completely followed and ordering that it had to be followed the next year.[63]

In Ohio in 1991, plaintiffs filed a lawsuit charging that their schools were not providing an adequate education. The court ruled in their favor, depending on the Kentucky ruling describing an adequate education. (In the 1970s the Ohio Supreme Court had denied a challenge to the state's school funding approach that had been based on an equity argument.) The case was appealed to the state's highest court, which ruled for the plaintiffs in 1997, criticizing the state's dependence on property taxes and giving the legislature a year to adopt a better school funding approach.[64] The Ohio legislature's response did not start by looking at how to make funding more equitable, however. Instead, it replied more to the lower court's argument about an adequate education than to the supreme court's ruling regarding equitable funding. The legislature used what is known by some as the "successful schools" approach. This method seeks to identify schools with student test scores that are well above average, adjusted for the composition of the student body. The state's foundation level of funding is then based on the per-pupil average within those successful schools.[65]

One of the greatest ongoing differences between schools in wealthy districts and those in disadvantaged districts is the state of their buildings. America's school buildings are, in many instances, in a state of desperate need. By the mid-1990s there was a need for well above $100 *billion* in repairs, and that figure has undoubtedly grown since then. On average, local taxes pay for about four-fifths of the construction of new school buildings. Given the limited wealth of some communities, this clearly increases inequity between school districts. Many states do pass school construction bonds, which account for the remaining 20 percent of construction funding. While helpful, however, that 20 percent is not nearly enough to make up for the tremendous disparity between what wealthy districts and disadvantaged districts can afford to spend on school buildings. In 1994 an Arizona court addressed this issue, ruling the state's school financing system unconstitutional because it did not provide more equitably for educational facilities. In a subsequent decision the Arizona Supreme Court, by a three-to-two margin, refused to limit its ruling to building and maintenance issues because it saw them as symptomatic of broader problems in the state's public schools. Over the next three years, the court rejected two different school financing plans the state legislature developed in response.[66]

By the late 1990s, nearly twenty state courts had found the school funding mechanisms within their states to be unconstitutional, and lawsuits were ongoing in a number of other states, including New York.[67] While lawsuits have usually not managed to lead to truly equitable public school systems, even in the states where courts found state finance systems unconstitutional, they have had an impact. State attempts to reduce inequality between school districts have succeeded somewhat, estimated in the range of 19 percent to 37 percent. They are also believed to have led to approximately a 12 percent increase in per-pupil spending in low-income school districts, and a smaller increase in moderate-income school districts. And of course they have led to some reduction in local control of public schools.[68]

The ironic thing about all the efforts within states such as New Jersey to create more equitable funding among their school districts is that there may be even greater inequality *between* states than there is *within* states. One estimate holds that well over half of the variation in spending per student across the nation comes from the differences between states, not the differences between wealthy and poor districts within individual states. The gap between states diminishes somewhat if the different costs from one state to another are taken into account (land, construction costs, and teacher salaries all run far higher in New York than in rural states, for example), but it remains a major reason for the differences between school districts' budgets.[69]

The shift of focus in court cases in the 1990s, from equity to adequacy, is a promising one for the future of disadvantaged students. Equity cases tend to focus on educational inputs, while adequacy cases tend to focus more on educational outcomes (how students are actually performing).[70] Given the uncertainty about the effects of greater inputs, effort focused more on what schools achieve with their students is likely to lead to greater impacts on student achievement. Kentucky may show the difference between equity and adequacy most clearly. If the main concern is equity, all students should have somewhat similar educational opportunities, but those do not have to be very impressive. As in California in the 1980s, the gap between rich districts and poor districts can be closed by leveling funding, even if that means shifting both funding and the quality of education downward. (Other equity cases have led to more spending in low property-wealth districts, however; the problem in California was related to Proposition 13, not just reliance on the equity argument.)

In cases where adequacy is required by courts, however, there may be a greater likelihood that school funding will be leveled upward. When adequacy is defined as meaning all children should be provided with a school that gives them a legitimate chance at educational success, it can lead to more financing and school reform in ways that equity cases have not. But the two issues overlap; Paul Minorini and Stephen Sugarman are correct to argue that the difference between the two approaches is not necessarily very large.[71]

History clearly shows that a court ruling ordering a legislature to change how schools function does not mean that huge changes will result. Court rulings about education are often resisted by legislatures, by school officials, or by significant portions of the public. Resistance to *Brown v. Board of Education* (and to subsequent local court orders that established busing) is the most well known example, but there was also considerable resistance in some places to school funding rulings that called for more equitable treatment. New Jersey is probably the most obvious example of how legislatures and the voting public can effectively resist court decisions, but similar roadblocks have been thrown up elsewhere. And the effects of Proposition 13 in California are a striking example of how other factors can make court rulings almost irrelevant.

What about in schools themselves? What difference does money make? The evaluation evidence is not completely clear-cut. In the 1980s, Eric Hanushek's work was considered close to definitive, and Hanushek himself became a major figure in school finance cases. In the 1990s, however, Hedges, Greenwald, and Laine performed several meta-analyses that show per-pupil expenditures do make a real difference in student achievement, and their work is more rigorous and compelling than Hanushek's. Both sides of the debate, however, would probably agree that money does not solve a school's problems by itself; it has to be used intelligently. For many schools in disadvantaged communities, or with student populations where large percentages of the children live in poverty, more money is necessary but clearly not sufficient. At any rate, the evidence about whether money matters has played a generally limited role in school finance decisions. Legal arguments have played a far greater role, as has evidence about the disparity between the funding levels of different school districts. Furthermore, many judges have relied more on what seemed to them the obvious connection between money and quality of education than on expert testimony one way or the other.

In a way, the debate over whether money matters is misleading; it is about whether an extra few hundred dollars per child will have a meaningful impact on a school that already has buildings, teachers, and resources. But suppose one were to make a more radical comparison, between a school that has only a few hundreds dollars per student and one with tens of thousands of dollars per student. In the first case, school might consist of hundreds of students in one leaky auditorium, lectured at by an inexperienced teacher, without textbooks, a library, or computers to broaden their educational experience. In the second case, classes might hold only a handful of students each, taught by people with years of teaching experience, with advanced lab equipment and a computer for every student. Taken to such extremes, it becomes obvious that money does not just matter, it matters a great deal. In the real world, however, increases in funding will generally be by hundreds of dollars per student, not thousands, and many different programs compete for that extra money.

Every issue in this book is, in a very real way, partly about money. Chapter 1 shows that Head Start, an extremely popular program with mixed evaluation results, has never reached anywhere near the "full funding" status promised by the twentieth century's last two presidents. Chapter 2 shows the difficulty of finding successful methods for teaching language-minority children; at the least, such methods probably will require highly trained teachers and small classrooms, both of which are expensive. Chapter 3 shows that smaller classes, which are the most expensive of the issues detailed in this book, also have the strongest support in the evaluation literature. Chapter 4 shows that the debate over whether to promote children automatically or retain them in a grade if they are not advancing quickly enough is something of a false issue; the real need seems to be more extensive help as children start to fall behind, which is another very expensive offering. And there are any number of educational reforms not discussed in this book, many (but not all) of which cost money. We need to know which have the most impact on what kind of student, and we need to know how various reform possibilities interact. To have the kind of quality schooling many of us *claim* we want for all children, we will need to spend more money than we do now. But we cannot spend infinite amounts, so we need to know what will pay off most regularly and most effectively.

Even if the evidence were to become crystal clear about how to build superb schools in every school district, it would be an extraordinarily difficult thing to do, in part because the financing of schools would remain, fundamentally, a political issue. To increase school budgets, taxes have to be increased somewhere; should they be local property taxes, or state sales or income taxes, or should the federal government greatly increase its contribution? How can the public—most of which does not have children of school age—be convinced that more money should go to schools rather than their own more direct needs? Perhaps the first step is wider recognition by politicians and citizens that, while money will not automatically make a difference, it is a necessary component of any true educational reform, especially when it comes to our most troubled schools.

Conclusion

The conclusions you draw from this book may come as much from what you believed before you began reading it as from the evidence and arguments presented here. A reader who considers education to be society's top priority may come away with several ideas about what needs to be done. Such a reader might conclude that schools need more money, especially schools whose populations largely come from disadvantaged families or do not speak English. That small classes should be provided in the early grades. That preschool programs need to be high-quality programs. That children who are falling behind in school need to be identified and provided with extensive and intensive help, whether they are promoted to the next grade or not.

A reader who favors local control and believes we are already spending enough money on education but are spending it foolishly, or who believes that the central problem faced by schools is the students themselves and their families, might take away a very different set of lessons. Such a reader could easily conclude that Head Start does not have much apparent effect on children's cognitive future, so why open more centers? Small classes may help a little, but going small enough to matter a lot is extremely expensive, and in any event there are not enough good teachers around to staff all those additional classes. There does not seem to be any especially good way to teach children who do not speak English, so why not take the most straightforward route and simply immerse them in English? And perhaps more money would help schools help children more effectively, but what should that money be spent on to get the most bang for the buck? Lacking better and more specific knowledge, why pour more money into schools?

By acknowledging that readers' earlier assumptions may shape how they interpret this book, I do not mean to throw up my hands and say, "Take what you will." I believe that a number of lessons flow from these chapters, for liberal and conservative alike. Some are about what works in classrooms, some are about how educational policy is made and how it could be made more intelligently, and some are about how we go about knowing what "works." While these lessons do not lead to a blueprint, they should be taken into account when concerned parties think about or discuss education, and when they act to change it.

In the 1990s, Head Start policy seemed to be heading in the right direction by trying to develop stricter standards and higher quality programs. That makes far more sense than expanding the program to include more children without worrying much about quality; simply being in a preschool program is probably not worth much for a child's future unless the program is a good one. That said, once higher standards are in place (and can be met consistently), politicians should finally do what they have been promising since the late 1980s: provide Head Start for every eligible child. This book has shown how little we really know about how to help disadvantaged children in school, and the difficulty of finding enough money to provide high-quality schooling and individual attention to every child throughout their years in school. Given this, giving every child a boost at the beginning, even if it is a small one, seems likely to be money well spent. Head Start programs can play an important role, but only if they are all brought up to the level of the best preschool programs now in existence.

No issue shows the political nature of education and education reform more blatantly than bilingual education. The practice was developed in a highly politicized community in the 1960s and the Bilingual Education Act of 1968 was passed in part because of a serious education problem (the high dropout rate of Hispanic children), but also because the approach was being pushed by a rapidly growing voting bloc. Neither of these facts, of course, necessarily means that teaching language-minority children in their own language was or is a bad idea. But every major development in policies shaping how LM children are taught, from the Lau remedies of the 1970s to California's move away from bilingual education in the late 1990s, has been driven by politics. Supporters and opponents of these policies both claim, erroneously, to have evidence on their side.

Even if there had been strong evidence supporting one approach or another to language-minority students, it probably would have had little or no impact on the debate. The simple fact is that in some instances, broader societal conflicts shape schooling. It seems to me that two lessons can be drawn from the actual evaluation evidence on bilingual education. The first is that we have done a poor job of teaching LM children, whether through their native languages, English, or a combination. The second, which partially explains the first, is that teaching LM children effectively, particularly if they come from poor or working-class homes, is very difficult. The quality of the program they are in matters a great deal, but that is not what we have paid attention to. Compared to program quality and teacher quality, the specific nature of the programs students are in may not matter very much at all from an educational perspective, but that is where most of the energy has gone.

In contrast, the evidence that smaller classes have a positive, long-lasting impact on student achievement is very strong. If reducing class size were easy, disagreements over just how powerful it is would not matter; we would simply do it. But it is far from easy. In fact, there are few educational reforms that cost anything approaching what reducing class size does. Hiring additional teachers is expensive enough, and building or buying additional classroom space is also expensive. To make matters worse, quality teachers and sound school buildings are both areas in which we have fallen far behind where we should be, if providing a good education to all our children is really a central goal of American society (as voters' polls continually show it to be). We do not have enough qualified teachers right now; uncertified teachers are working in classrooms throughout the nation. And repairing or replacing inadequate and aging school buildings nationwide would cost more than $100 billion.

Smaller classes are thus both a necessity and a luxury: a necessity for children who are already falling behind at six or seven years of age, and whom we have too few ways to help, and a luxury because implementing them in a widespread manner is so expensive. This combination of factors leads to the most straightforward conclusion of this book. We should provide smaller classes to disadvantaged children in the first few grades, whatever the cost of providing decent classroom space, and we should provide incentives to make sure that good teachers are staffing those smaller classrooms. Otherwise, much of the money we are already spending on public education may go to waste.

The tumult over social promotion is an excellent example of the broader problems behind efforts to improve education: it is related to a real problem (that large numbers of children are not learning very much in school), yet the proposed solution completely misses the point. To their credit, some of the politicians who loudly oppose the practice also advocate giving extra help to children before they need to be retained. But prohibiting social promotion, especially by requiring specific test scores, is relatively easy. Of course it may not survive the next wave of school reform. Providing extensive, specialized instruction that will help children learn what we want them to learn requires ongoing effort and extensive resources.

There is no simple solution, because the problem reveals where our schools are at their weakest: in teaching children who are struggling. Freshman in high school should be able to read moderately well, write coherent sentences, and multiply and divide; can anyone doubt that? A high school diploma should, as opponents of social promotion insist, mean that the recipient has a certain level of skill. But simply insisting that children need to "pass" one test to be promoted a grade, or to graduate, does nothing except place the blame for failing to learn squarely where, in most cases, it least belongs: on the child who is failing. And providing a little help here and there, or extensive help for eight weeks in one summer, will not solve the underlying problem. Addressing this problem effectively requires a host of interlocked reforms, including some described in this book. We do not yet know what all those reforms need to look like, nor have we made as much headway as I would like in finding out.

Like reducing class size, providing enough extra help to boost children who are struggling to the point where they can *earn* promotions and a high school diploma is extremely expensive. Unfortunately, like the conflict over bilingual education, the debate over school funding has a long and overheated history. Unlike the teaching of language-minority children, where there is no strong evidence favoring one way or the other, the evidence that money does matter is very persuasive. Additional money, if spent directly in classrooms (through better teachers and smaller classes, for example), does make a difference. But the search for more money brings schools into conflict with one another, and brings education into conflict with numerous other institutions and social services, as well as with the desire of taxpayers to lighten their burden and the need of politicians to please those same taxpayers.

Courts have played a central role in school finance, but there are very strict limits on what court orders alone can achieve. As Richard Elmore and Milbrey McLaughlin wrote in 1982 about *Serrano v. Priest,* "Courts are limited agents of reform."[1] Nowhere has this been more evident than in New Jersey, where numerous rulings for the plaintiffs in two different lawsuits led to only limited change over several decades. (The most famous education lawsuit of all, *Brown v. Board of Education,* also faced stiff resistance in many places, and schools remain highly segregated even now in some parts of the nation.) Thus, providing additional money to schools through the courts has proven difficult, though more so in some places than in others. To make matters worse, it is also true that we still do not really know what are the best ways to spend money to achieve the strongest results. But the fact that more money is needed and can make a difference, especially in schools where a majority of students come from disadvantaged backgrounds, seems clear.

The cases described in this book have different lessons for different interested parties. For parents, the evidence from Head Start and the Perry Preschool program shows, it seems to me, two fundamental things: a high-quality preschool education can help children in the long run, and most Head Start centers are not of a very high quality. Getting one's child enrolled at a Head Start center (or in another preschool program) is a beginning, not an end. At the least, parents need to be conscious of teacher experience and quality, class size, and a program's health care components.

Similarly, parents of language-minority children might be better advised to call for highly trained teachers than for one approach or another. And parents who know about Project STAR might be automatically inclined to push for small classes, especially if their children are in the early grades. But they should remember that dropping from a class of thirty to a class size of twenty-seven might not really help, and if other things are sacrificed in the process, the change might even be harmful. To make a real difference, classes probably need to be under twenty students (though twenty-seven would be better—possibly far better—than thirty-eight or forty, especially in the early grades). And parents should recognize that a small student-teacher ratio achieved by adding a teacher's aide is *not* the same as a small class. Finally, teacher quality matters: children may not be better off in a class of twenty with a mediocre teacher than in a larger class with a better teacher, and they may even be worse off. We simply do not know.

The lesson for school officials and teachers from various efforts to teach language-minority children is that they need to do a better job of implementing whatever programs they put in place. Unfortunately, factors that have a huge influence on program quality are often beyond school officials' immediate control. Most notably, the lack of qualified teachers hinders virtually every one of the bilingual approaches currently in use. Perhaps the most compelling lesson in these pages for teachers and school officials is that they should be wary of advocates for a specific program who tell them that "the evidence shows" the advocate is right. Supporters and opponents of both Head Start and bilingual education, for example, all claim that the evidence is on their side, and all are wrong. The evidence on both of those topics is generally of low quality and is very murky indeed.

It is (or at least should be) the role of federal and state education officials to disseminate the evidence on a variety of educational issues. This requires those same officials to be nonpartisan, or at least to seek out nonpartisan reviews of the evidence on each topic, and then to make the results widely available. Historian Maris Vinovskis has looked at the history of federal education research and its current practice, and has suggested changes in the Office of Educational Research and Improvement that would make it more effective.[2] Structural changes, a larger high-quality staff, and better funding could certainly make a difference. The bigger issue, however, may be one of attitude, both on the part of the public as to what it accepts from its elected officials, and on the part of those officials.

It would be wishful thinking to expect politicians to make evidence a leading determinant in the policies they choose to advocate. Being re-elected drives most politicians, not the public good; or to be somewhat less cynical, politicians define the public good largely in the terms espoused by those who voted for them, by the stand of their political party, and by those who fund their campaigns. In either case, evidence about what works is usually well down the list of factors influencing policy. But as several of these chapters show, most notably Chapter 3 on class size, in the right circumstances evaluation can have a powerful influence on policy decisions. If money is available and there is a strongly felt need to improve schools, the right evaluation at the right time can help determine how that money is spent, and that is no small thing.

Opponents of President Clinton's federal plan to hire more teachers for smaller classrooms argued that states should be able to determine for themselves how to spend the money they receive from the federal government. Whether state control is always a good thing is not at all clear. Even a quick glance at the specific plan adopted by California to reduce class size shows that local control can be far less intelligent than federal oversight, at least on class-size issues. California reduced class sizes in a politically savvy way that gained widespread middle-class support, but in a way that may not help disadvantaged children much. So far as using smaller classes as a reform to help student learning, other states and the federal government have developed far more thoughtful plans that target the students who gain the most, disadvantaged children. So perhaps it is not the *level* of government making educational decisions that matters as much as how well thought out the decisions are. In the case of the evidence on class size, the federal government and a number of other states have tailored programs that seem likely to gain the maximum benefit for the money being spent. California and states that have not adopted class-size legislation have not. (For that matter, there is certainly something to be said for local control, but given the size of most states, how "local" are many state departments of education?)

Clinton's successor, President George W. Bush, has no interest in smaller classes, and as many people at the state and local level feared in the late 1990s, the federal program seems unlikely to continue. President Bush came into office pushing for two major education programs: high-stakes testing and vouchers. Congress agreed readily with the idea of mandating tests, but quickly dispatched the idea of vouchers. These differing congressional views, embracing testing while dismissing vouchers, are certainly not based on the evidence. There is little solid evidence that high-stakes testing will have positive results; as Chapter 4 showed in discussing social promotion, if tests are used to keep large numbers of children from being promoted from one grade to the next, the main effect will probably be high dropout rates. There is also very little evidence showing what the effects of vouchers would be. Several large studies on the effects of school vouchers were initiated in the 1990s, but they are not designed to actually say *why* vouchers might make a difference for some children. Even if their results come back and *seem* compelling, they will not say anything about why children benefited from private schools, or what public schools might do to improve; they will be useless as guides to public policy.

Congress, like Bush and most of the public, thinks testing will somehow make schools, teachers, and students all try harder, even though there is no evidence on which to base that belief. Unlike Bush, the majority in Congress see vouchers as a threat to the public school system, and believe the popular support for vouchers is small enough to discount. In both cases, the decision was political, not based on any real knowledge of education or how to improve schools or student performance.

One lesson for politicians is that if they really want to find out what works in education, they should seek nonpartisan reviews of the evaluation evidence. In most instances, the evidence is not clear-cut. Even when it seems relatively straightforward, it often lacks the specifics needed to describe exactly how programs should be implemented. But in almost every case the evidence has something to say, even if that is simply that advocates of one approach or another are speaking from their emotional or political positions, not from evidence.

The federal government and, in particular, state governments can and should sponsor large, carefully conducted experiments similar to Tennessee's Project STAR. Imagine a large, controlled, randomized experiment that features three or four different approaches to teaching language-minority children. Such an experiment could be conducted in any state with a big immigrant population. School officials would have to be willing to randomize children into different settings, sometimes against their parents' wishes. But bear in mind that, right now, many LM children are being taught in settings other than what their parents desire. If program quality were stressed in *each* option, with qualified teachers and small classes, teacher and parental agreement to an experiment might be achievable. One program could place children in two-way bilingual programs, another in transitional bilingual, another in structured immersion. If serious efforts were made to assure that all the involved teachers were qualified, and if the programs and evaluation were carefully designed, following children through high school to see how they do in later years would tell us far, far more than we currently really know. Of course, the results of such an experiment would be of little use to LM children now in, or about to enter, school. But we have been working blind, with only heated opinions to guide us, for three decades in efforts to teach LM children effectively. (Before that, one might say we were working blindfolded.) Trying to develop more and better knowledge, even if we would not have it for another six or eight or ten years, could make a big difference for children in the future. Not ideal, perhaps, but it would be more than we have now, or are likely to ever have with our current approach, which is bickering based on political and cultural opinion.

For a variety of reasons, including their generally limited size and relative lack of funding, school districts themselves are a less promising locale for ambitious experiments designed to produce evidence of interest to the entire nation. For example, an experiment conducted in Los Angeles would tell us little about the effects of a reform on rural children. An experiment conducted in schools throughout California (or any sizable state), however, might offer important lessons for the rest of the country.

There are also lessons here for evaluators. The powers that be who are concerned with the quality of education evaluation and interested in learning from future evaluations still cannot agree on what "good" evaluations look like. The decades-old debate between proponents of qualitative and quantitative research goes on, perhaps more heartily in education evaluation than in any other arena of evaluation. In 1999 the American Academy of Arts and Sciences sponsored a conference on how to improve education evaluation. The main thrust of the conference was that there needed to be more large-scale randomized experiments performed in education evaluation. At roughly the same time, officials in the U.S. Department of Education also stated the need for more excellent education evaluations to guide policy decisions. But the government officials put forth a very different vision of what such evaluations would look like than that presented at the American Academy of Arts and Sciences conference. Rather than large experiments, the DOE wanted more high-quality *qualitative* evaluations.

Whatever approach is taken, the task will remain difficult. Both Head Start and bilingual education show the problems involved in evaluating complex educational programs. At this point, it would be difficult—more likely impossible—to perform a large randomized experiment on either issue with a control group not participating in any special program. Parents would be unlikely to risk allowing their children to be randomized out of preschool altogether, for example. But we could still learn more about each program than we have in the past. For example, a state government could offer two preschool settings, one with high educational content, another with a more play-oriented, parent-involved approach. If it was made clear that both programs would receive high funding and support, many parents might be willing to have their children randomly placed in one of the two settings. A third kind of program could also be added. Children could then be followed into their school years, much as in the Perry Preschool program. While the lack of a control group would keep such an evaluation from showing what the effects of preschool were compared with no preschool, the evaluation would distinguish between two or three different approaches. If each approach were instituted with care, it would certainly be reasonable to assume that the one showing the *worst* results in later schooling would be doing at least as well as a control group receiving no preschool would have done. It would also be reasonable to assume that children in the higher performing groups had gained from their preschool experience.

Another important point about educational evaluation is that, in many cases, it should follow children for a number of years after the program being studied. This is difficult and expensive, but it pays off. The Perry Preschool had a very small student population but it received tremendous attention, in large part because it followed children into adulthood. Project STAR's findings are far more powerful than they would have been otherwise because a follow-up study has tracked children all the way into high school. Studies of bilingual education that track children only while they are in their respective programs, or for a year or so afterward, miss much of what really matters: whether a program leads to children doing well in school in later years. No matter how well designed an evaluation may be otherwise, if it stops tracking children when the educational program under study ends, or shortly thereafter, it will have little useful to say to education policymakers.

The lesson, in a nutshell, for evaluators: think boldly, and think long-term. And, somehow, find champions in state government. Project STAR offers lessons that go beyond what it tells us about class size.

It should be clear by now that politics is often at the heart of education, and of arguments about how to change or "reform" education. The heavily political nature of education can be very harmful at times. It certainly clouds the picture when one is trying to determine what works in some of the areas discussed in this book, particularly bilingual education. Partisan attacks from both sides of the debate misrepresent both stances and the evidence.

But getting politics out of education, as has been tried at several points in American history, is not necessarily desirable. Politics is driven by passion as often as by cynicism, by a desire to do what is right as often as by a desire to gain power. The influence of politics on education has often led to what I would consider desirable goals, such as the *Brown* case's attempt to integrate schools, and efforts to provide meaningful education to children who came to school with limited or nonexistent English skills. That some of the efforts may eventually have developed methods that many see as objectionable, such as busing, does not invalidate their initial importance.

One of the central questions about how to reform (and presumably improve) schools is, Who should make be making decisions: parents, voters, educators, politicians, or other groups? And at what level should decisions be made: individual schools, school districts, states, or the federal government? There is considerable reason to believe that top-down reforms do not work very well.[3] Yet local control can mean discrimination or regimentation. This problem—that reform from above and local control both have serious pitfalls—makes paying careful attention to evaluation evidence all the more important.

If we really want to improve our schools, one of the things we need to do is pay better attention to what evidence exists. But another thing we need to do is recognize that we will never have *absolute* knowledge. We will never know that a particular curriculum is the best we can offer children, nor will we know exactly how to train teachers most effectively. There will be no one-size-fits-all answer to how to teach language-minority children well, or how to help children who are falling behind in first grade. Education, and people, are too complicated and varied for that to be possible. We need to act on incomplete knowledge; we also need to recognize that that is better than acting on what "feels right" or is politically popular.

Education reform runs in cycles. Perhaps the most surprising thing about the past two decades is how powerful the focus on education has remained. Yet we have jumped from one reform to another, with mixed results at best. Battles over curriculums will continue, as will debates over the desirability and likely effect of supposed panaceas such as vouchers. No one would think of running for president or governor now without laying claim to being an education leader. But there are many things that are certain in politics, especially that talk is cheap. It is time to try a different tack. School officials, teachers, and parent groups should push for more knowledgeable education reform—and for the long-term planning we will need to guide us on any number of issues. We have run blind for too long as it is.

NOTES

SUGGESTED READINGS

INDEX

Notes

Introduction

1. National Commission on Excellence in Education, *A Nation at Risk: The Imperative for Educational Reform: A Report to the Nation and the Secretary of Education.* (Washington, D.C.: National Commission on Excellence in Education, April 1983).
2. Michael B. Katz, *Reconstructing American Education* (Cambridge, Mass.: Harvard University Press, 1987), pp. 130–154.
3. David B. Tyack, *The One Best System: A History of American Urban Education* (Cambridge, Mass.: Harvard University Press, 1974), p. 270; Katz, *Reconstructing American Education*, pp. 111–118.
4. George F. Madaus, Daniel L. Stufflebeam, and Michael S. Scriven, "Program Evaluation: A Historical Overview," in George F. Madaus, Michael S. Scriven, and Daniel L. Stufflebeam, eds., *Evaluation Models: Viewpoints on Educational and Human Services Evaluation* (Boston: Kluwer-Nijhoff, 1983), pp. 8–9; Milbrey W. McLaughlin and D. C. Phillips, eds., *Evaluation and Education: At Quarter Century,* Ninetieth Yearbook of the National Society for the Study of Education, pt. 2 (Chicago: University of Chicago Press, 1991), p. x; W. James Popham, *Educational Evaluation,* 3rd ed. (Boston: Allyn and Bacon, 1993), p. 2; Ellen Condliffe Lagemann, *An Elusive Science: The Troubling History of Education Research* (Chicago: University of Chicago Press, 2000), pp. 141–144.
5. McLaughlin and Phillips, eds., *Evaluation and Education,* pp. 1–2.
6. Ralph W. Tyler, *Educational Evaluation: Classic Works of Ralph W. Tyler,* compiled and edited by George F. Madaus and Daniel L. Stufflebeam (Boston: Kluwer Academic Publishers, 1989), p. 1; Madaus, Stufflebeam, and Scriven, "Program Evaluation," pp. 10–11.
7. Carl F. Kaestle and Michael S. Smith, "The Federal Role in Elementary and Sec-

217

ondary Education, 1940–1980," *Harvard Educational Review* 52 (4), Nov. 1982, pp. 392–396; Tyler, *Educational Evaluation,* p. 1; Madaus, Stufflebeam, and Scriven, "Program Evaluation," pp. 11–12.

8. Robert F. Boruch, "The President's Mandate: Discovering What Works and What Works Better," in McLaughlin and Phillips, eds., *Evaluation and Education,* pp. 150–155.

9. McLaughlin and Phillips, *Evaluation and Education,* pp. x–xi.

10. Lee J. Cronbach, "Course Improvement through Evaluation," *Teachers College Record* 64 (8), May 1963, pp. 672–683.

11. Marshall Kaplan and Peggy L. Cuciti, eds., *The Great Society and Its Legacy: Twenty Years of U.S. Social Policy* (Durham: Duke University Press, 1986), pp. 1–4; William R. Shadish, Jr., Thomas D. Cook, and Laura C. Leviton, *Foundations of Program Evaluation: Theories of Practice* (Newbury Park, Calif.: Sage Publications, 1991), pp. 22–25; Madaus, Stufflebeam, and Scriven, "Program Evaluation," pp. 12–13; Michael B. Katz, *In the Shadow of the Poorhouse: A Social History of Welfare in America* (New York: Basic Books, 1986), pp. 264–265.

12. Madaus, Stufflebeam, and Scriven, "Program Evaluation," pp. 12–13; Shadish, Cook, and Leviton, *Foundations of Program Evaluation,* pp. 22–25; Milbrey Wallin McLaughlin, *Evaluation and Reform: The Elementary and Secondary Education Act of 1965, Title I* (Cambridge, Mass.: Ballinger Publishing Company, 1975).

13. Ernest R. House, "Trends in Evaluation," *Education Researcher,* April 1990, p. 24.

14. Madaus, Stufflebeam, and Scriven, "Program Evaluation," pp. 13–14.

15. Madaus, Stufflebeam, and Scriven, "Program Evaluation," pp. 14–15; House, "Trends in Evaluation," p. 25; Richard J. Light and David B. Pillemer, *Summing Up: The Science of Reviewing Research* (Cambridge, Mass.: Harvard University Press, 1984), p. 154.

16. Madaus, Stufflebeam, and Scriven, "Program Evaluation," pp. 13–14.

17. Michael Scriven, "The Methodology of Evaluation," in Ralph W. Tyler, Robert M. Gagne, and Michael Scriven, eds., *Perspectives of Curriculum Evaluation* (Chicago: Rand McNally, 1967), pp. 39–83.

18. Marvin C. Alkin, "Evaluation Theory Development: II," in McLaughlin and Phillips, eds., *Evaluation and Education,* pp. 97–98.

19. Carol H. Weiss, "The Politicization of Evaluation Research," *Journal of Social Issues* 26, 1970, pp. 57–68; Carol H. Weiss, "Where Politics and Evaluation Research Meet," in Dennis J. Palumbo, ed., *The Politics of Program Evaluation,* Sage Yearbooks in Politics and Public Policy 15 (Beverly Hills: Sage Publications, 1987), pp. 47–70 (based on a paper Weiss presented in 1973).

20. Carol H. Weiss, "The Circuitry of Enlightenment: Diffusion of Social Science Research to Policymakers," *Knowledge: Creation, Diffusion, Utilization* 8 (2), Dec. 1986, pp. 274–281.

21. Shadish, Cook, and Leviton, *Foundations of Program Evaluation*, pp. 28–29; Madaus, Stufflebeam, and Scriven, "Program Evaluation," pp. 15–16.

22. Carol H. Weiss, *Evaluation*, 2nd ed. (Upper Saddle River, N.J.: Prentice Hall, 1998), pp. 9–33; Shadish, Cook, and Leviton, *Foundations of Program Evaluation*, p. 171.

23. Henry M. Levin, "Cost Effectiveness at Quarter-Century," in McLaughlin and Phillips, eds., *Evaluation and Education*, pp. 189–197.

24. Gene V. Glass, "Primary, Secondary, and Meta-Analysis of Research," *Educational Researcher* 10, 1976, pp. 3–8; Light and Pillemer, *Summing Up*, p. 3; Thomas D. Cook, "Lessons Learned in Evaluation over the Past Twenty-Five Years," in Eleanor Chelimsky and William R. Shadish, eds., *Evaluation for the Twenty-First Century: A Handbook* (Thousand Oaks, Calif.: Sage Publications, 1997), pp. 36–39.

25. Robert E. Slavin, "Meta-Analysis in Education: How Has It Been Used?" *Educational Researcher*, Oct. 1984, pp. 6–26.

26. Madaus, Stufflebeam, and Scriven, "Program Evaluation," pp. 16–18; Michael Scriven, "Beyond Formative and Summative Evaluation," in McLaughlin and Phillips, eds., *Evaluation and Education*, p. 58; Shadish, Cook, and Leviton, *Foundations of Program Evaluation;* House, "Trends in Evaluation," pp. 24–28.

27. House, "Trends in Evaluation," p. 26.

28. Cook, "Lessons Learned in Evaluation," p. 32.

1. What Difference Does Head Start Make?

1. Maris A. Vinovskis, *Education, Society, and Economic Opportunity: A Historical Perspective on Persistent Issues* (New Haven: Yale University Press, 1995), pp. 17–44; Maris A. Vinovskis, "School Readiness and Early Childhood Education," in Diane Ravitch and Maris A. Vinovskis, eds., *Learning from the Past: What History Teaches Us about School Reform* (Baltimore: Johns Hopkins University, 1995), pp. 243–245.

2. Catherine J. Ross, "Early Skirmishes with Poverty: The Historical Roots of Head Start," in Edward Zigler and Jeanette Valentine, eds., *Project Head Start: A Legacy of the War on Poverty* (New York: The Free Press), 1979, pp. 28–31.

3. J. McVicker Hunt, *Intelligence and Experience* (New York: The Ronald Press Company, 1961); Edward Zigler and Karen Anderson, "An Idea Whose Time Had Come: The Intellectual and Political Climate," in Zigler and Valentine, eds., *Project Head Start*, pp. 6–7.

4. Hunt, *Intelligence and Experience*, p. 363.

5. Edward Zigler and Susan Muenchow, *Head Start: The Inside Story of America's Most Successful Educational Experiment* (New York: Basic Books, 1992), pp. 12–13; Edward F. Zigler and Sally Styfco, "Head Start and Early Childhood Intervention: The Changing Course of Social Science and Social Policy," in Edward

F. Zigler, Sharon Lynn Kagan, and Nancy W. Hall, eds., *Children, Families, and Government: Preparing for the Twenty-First Century* (New York: Cambridge University Press, 1996), p. 138.

6. Michael B. Katz, *The Undeserving Poor: From the War on Poverty to the War on Welfare* (New York: Pantheon Books, 1989), pp. 79–81.

7. Lisbeth B. Schorr, *Within Our Reach: Breaking the Cycle of Disadvantage* (New York: Anchor Press, 1988), pp. 184–185; Zigler and Muenchow, *Head Start*, p. 2.

8. Schorr, *Within Our Reach*, pp. 184–187; Zigler and Muenchow, *Head Start*, pp. 4–5; Zigler and Anderson, "An Idea Whose Time Had Come," pp. 10–11.

9. Zigler and Muenchow, *Head Start*, pp. 2–4; Schorr, *Within Our Reach*, pp. 185–187.

10. Zigler and Muenchow, *Head Start*, pp. 7–8; Zigler and Anderson, "An Idea Whose Time Had Come," pp. 13–15; Schorr, *Within Our Reach*, p. 187; Zigler and Styfco, "Head Start and Early Childhood Intervention," pp. 133–134.

11. Zigler and Muenchow, *Head Start*, pp. 14–20; Zigler and Styfco, "Head Start and Early Childhood Intervention," p. 136.

12. Zigler and Muenchow, *Head Start*, pp. 21–26.

13. Zigler and Styfco, "Head Start and Early Childhood Intervention," p. 134; Schorr, *Within Our Reach*, p. 190.

14. Schorr, *Within Our Reach*, pp. 188–189.

15. Zigler and Muenchow, *Head Start*, pp. 29–31.

16. Schorr, *Within Our Reach*, pp. 188–190.

17. Zigler and Muenchow, *Head Start*, pp. 40–45.

18. June Solnit Sale, "Implementation of a Head Start Preschool Education Program: Los Angeles, 1965–1967," in Zigler and Valentine, eds., *Project Head Start*, pp. 178–186.

19. Zigler and Muenchow, *Head Start*, pp. 48–53.

20. Zigler and Styfco, "Head Start and Early Childhood Intervention," pp. 135–138; Zigler and Muenchow, *Head Start*, pp. 26–27.

21. Zigler and Muenchow, *Head Start*, pp. 56–59.

22. Ibid., pp. 60–64.

23. *The Impact of Head Start: An Evaluation of the Effects of Head Start Experience on Children's Cognitive and Affective Development* (Westinghouse Learning Corporation/Ohio University, April 1969), p. 0–1; Edward Zigler, "Project Head Start: Success or Failure?" in Zigler and Valentine, eds., *Project Head Start*, p. 496.

24. Zigler and Muenchow, *Head Start*, pp. 68–69.

25. *Impact of Head Start*, pp. 1–8.

26. Zigler and Styfco, "Head Start and Early Childhood Intervention," p. 134.

27. Zigler and Muenchow, *Head Start*, pp. 69–71.

28. Marshall S. Smith and Joan S. Bissell, "Report Analysis: The Impact of Head Start," *Harvard Educational Review* 40 (1), Winter 1970.

29. Zigler and Styfco, "Head Start and Early Childhood Intervention," pp. 148–149.

30. Schorr, *Within Our Reach,* p. 190.

31. Zigler and Styfco, "Head Start and Early Childhood Intervention," pp. 139–140.

32. Steven Waldman, "The Stingy Politics of Head Start," *Newsweek,* Sept. 1990 (Fall/Winter Special Edition), p. 78.

33. "Whatever Happened to . . . ; Operation Head Start: Still Going Strong," *U.S News and World Report,* Aug. 22, 1977, p. 67; Thomas Toch, "Large Increases in Preschool Enrollment Linked to Head Start," *Education Week,* Aug. 25, 1982; Waldman, "Stingy Politics of Head Start."

34. Zigler and Styfco, "Head Start and Early Childhood Intervention," p. 139; Consortium for Longitudinal Studies, *As the Twig Is Bent: Lasting Effects of Preschool Programs* (Hillsdale, N.J.: Lawrence Erlbaum Associates, 1983).

35. "A High Grade for Head Start," *Newsweek,* Oct. 8, 1979, p. 102; Spencer Rich, "Lasting Gains Provided by Preschool Programs," *Washington Post,* Nov. 30, 1979, p. A23.

36. *Head Start in the 1980s: Reviews and Recommendations* (Washington, D.C.: U.S. Department of Health and Human Services, 1980).

37. Ibid.

38. Ibid.

39. "It Really Is a Head Start," *Newsweek,* Dec. 22, 1980, p. 54; "Preschool Training Gets a Better Report Card," *Business Week,* Dec. 29, 1980, p. 28.

40. L. J. Schweinhart and D. P. Weikart, *Young Children Grow Up: The Effects of the Perry Preschool Program on Youths through Age 15* (Ypsilanti, Mich.: High/Scope Press, 1980), pp. 1–10.

41. Ibid., pp. 17–20.

42. Ibid., pp. 20–23.

43. Ibid., pp. 31–44.

44. Ibid., pp. 37–54.

45. Ibid., pp. 69–72.

46. Ibid.

47. Waldman, "Stingy Politics of Head Start"; Zigler and Styfco, "Head Start and Early Childhood Intervention," p. 141; Spencer Rich, "House Money Bill Drops Extension of Head Start," *New York Times,* July 2, 1981, p. A10; Edward F. Zigler, "Head Start's 'Perils of Pauline,'" *New York Times,* Jan. 29, 1982, p. A27; "Report Shows Federal Net Missing Poor Kids," *Chicago Tribune,* Oct. 3, 1986, p. 3.

48. Consortium for Longitudinal Studies, *As the Twig Is Bent.*

49. John R. Berrueta-Clement et al. *Changed Lives: The Effects of the Perry Pre-school Program on Youths through Age 19* (Ypsilanti, Mich.: High/Scope Press, 1984), pp. 21–41.

50. Ibid., pp. 43–58.

51. Ibid., pp. 61–75.

52. Ibid., pp. 83–92.

53. Ibid., p. 109.

54. Ibid., pp. xiv–xv.

55. Anne Bridgman, "Early-Childhood Education: States Already on the Move," *Education Week,* Oct. 16, 1985; Deborah L. Gold, "Head Start: Where Does It Fit in Preschool Movement?" *Education Week,* April 6, 1988.

56. Gordon Witkin, "Great Society: How Great Has It Been?" *U.S. News and World Report,* Sept. 24, 1984, p. 31.

57. Sar Levitan and Clifford Johnson, "Did the Great Society and Subsequent Initiatives Work?," in Marshall Kaplan and Peggy L. Cuciti, eds., *The Great Society and Its Legcay: Twenty Years of U.S. Social Policy* (Durham: Duke University Press, 1986), pp. 77–78

58. "Breaking the Poverty Cycle," *Los Angeles Times,* Feb. 13, 1988, Metro, p. 8.

59. "Everybody Likes Head Start," *Newsweek,* Feb. 20, 1989, p. 49; Gold, "Head Start: Where Does It Fit?"; Deborah L. Cohen, "Head Start Benefits Children, Parents, Study Finds," *Education Week,* April 25, 1990.

60. Edward Zigler, Sally J. Styfco, and Elizabeth Gilman, "The National Head Start Program for Disadvantaged Preschoolers," in Edward Zigler and Sally J. Styfco, eds., *Head Start and Beyond: A National Plan for Extended Childhood Intervention* (New Haven: Yale University Press, 1993), p. 11.

61. Gene I. Maeroff, "Education: Despite Head Start 'Achievement Gap' Persists for Poor," *New York Times,* June 11, 1985, p. C1.

62. Sherry Sontag, "For the Parents, Too, Head Start Can Provide Life Opportunities," *New York Times,* July 4, 1985, p. C1.

63. Warren Richey, "Head Start Has Less Money for Children because of Staff Pay Issue," *Christian Science Monitor,* Aug. 8, 1985, p. 5; Robert Marquand, "A Head Start on First Grade for Disadvantaged Kids," *Christian Science Monitor,* Mar. 28, 1986, p. B3; "Vital Jobs, Meager Pay," *Christian Science Monitor,* June 5, 1990, p. 20.

64. Howard LaFranchi, "Where the Candidates Stand on Education," *Christian Science Monitor,* Oct. 26, 1988, p. 3; Don Phillips, "House Votes to Increase Funding for Head Start," *Washington Post,* Mar. 22, 1989, p. A4.

65. "Everybody Likes Head Start."

66. Lawrence J. Schweinhart and David P. Weikart, "A Fresh Start for Head Start?" *New York Times,* May 13, 1990, Section 4, p. 19.

67. Neal R. Peirce, "Bush's New Head Start Budget Is Just a Start," *National Journal,*

Feb. 10, 1990, p. 345; Waldman, "Stingy Politics of Head Start"; Lynn Olson and Julie A. Miller, "The 'Education President' at Midterm: Mismatch between Rhetoric, Results?" *Education Week,* Jan. 9, 1991; "Budget Deal's Failures and Hopes . . . Including a Promise to Head Start," *Chicago Tribune,* Nov. 9, 1990, p. 22; "Bush Signs Bill to Expand Head Start Program Fivefold," *New York Times,* Nov. 4, 1990, p. 32.

68. Susan Chira, "Head Start Today: 25 Years of Lessons Learned—A Special Report," *New York Times,* Feb. 14, 1990, p. A1.

69. "House Backs Measure to Expand Head Start to Cover All Eligible," *Education Week,* May 23, 1990; Peter West, "Panel Calls for Overall Strategy to Assess Head Start," *Education Week,* Nov. 21, 1990; Zigler and Styfco, "Head Start and Early Childhood Intervention," pp. 141–146.

70. Douglas Jehl, "Bush Proposes $600-Million Hike in Head Start Program," *Los Angeles Times,* Jan. 22, 1992, p. A1; "Give All Poor Children a Head Start," *St. Louis Post-Dispatch,* Jan. 30, 1992, p. C2; "More Funds for Head Start; Investing in Young Children Pays Off," *San Diego Union-Tribune,* Jan. 24, 1992, p. B8; "Kid Corps; Head Start Deserves Bush's Big Boost," *Columbus Dispatch,* Jan. 24, 1992, p. 6A.

71. David Maraniss, "Clinton Accuses Bush of Forsaking Education," *Washington Post,* May 15, 1992, p. A22.

72. Collin Nash, "Starting Out Strong," *Los Angeles Times,* April 13, 1992, p. B1; "For Head Start, Two Steps Back," *New York Times,* June 30, 1992, p. A22.

73. Sandra Evans, "Va. Proposes to Expand Preschool Education," *Washington Post,* Dec. 14, 1988, p. D3; William Raspberry, "Head Start: A Program That Works," *Washington Post,* Jan. 19, 1990, p. A21.

74. Diego Ribadeneira, "Most of State's Poor Miss Out on Preschool," *Boston Globe,* Aug. 20, 1992, p. 31; Deborah L. Cohen, "Preschool Access Linked to Where a Family Lives," *Education Week,* Sept. 15, 1993.

75. Zigler and Styfco, "Head Start and Early Childhood Intervention," p. 145; Jason DeParle, "Social Investment Programs: Comparing the Past with the Promised Payoff," *New York Times,* Mar. 2, 1993, p. A18; Michael Kramer, "The Political Interest: Getting Smart About Head Start," *Time,* Mar. 8, 1993, p. 43.

76. Kramer, "Political Interest: Getting Smart About Head Start."

77. Jason DeParle, "Sharp Criticism for Head Start, Even by Friends," *New York Times,* Mar. 19, 1993, p. A1; Julie A. Miller, "Plan to Boost Head Start Will Address Quality as Well as Scope, Shalala Says," *Education Week,* Mar. 10, 1993; Alan Miller, "Fine Tuning Head Start," *San Diego Union-Tribune,* April 9, 1993, p. B6.

78. Rochelle L. Stanfield, "Lobbying Nonstop for Head Start," *National Journal,* April 30, 1993, p. 831.

79. John Hood, "Caveat Emptor: The Head Start Scam," *USA Today Magazine,* May, 1993, p. 75.

80. "Head Start Has Become a Free-Fire Zone," *Newsweek,* April 12, 1993, p. 57.

81. Lawrence J. Schweinhart, Helen V. Barnes, and David P. Weikart, *Significant Benefits: The High/Scope Perry Preschool Study through Age 27* (Ypsilanti, Mich.: The High/Scope Press, 1993).

82. Ibid., pp. 235–238.

83. Steve Barnett, "Does Head Start Fade Out?" *Education Week,* May 19, 1993.

84. Debra Viadero, "'Fade-Out' in Head Start Gains Linked to Later Schooling," *Education Week,* April 20, 1994.

85. "Shalala Calls for Refocusing, Re-energizing the Head Start Program," *Children Today,* Dec. 22, 1993, p. 4; Barbara Vobejda, "Head Start Expansion Is Urged," *Washington Post,* Jan. 13, 1994, p. A4.

86. "Senate Backs Major Expansion of Head Start, Starting at Birth," *New York Times,* April 22, 1994, p. A28; David E. Rosenbaum, "Facing Limit on Spending, House Reduces Clinton's Requests," *New York Times,* July 12, 1994, p. A13; Deborah L. Cohen, "Clinton Expected to Sign Widely Hailed Head Start Bill," *Education Week,* May 18, 1994; Linda Jacobsen, "Head Start Programs Back on Track in Denver under New Management," *Education Week,* Sept. 17, 1997; "Clinton Signs Head Start Expansion," *Washington Post,* May 19, 1994, p. A1; "Clinton Signs Expansion Bill for Head Start," *Los Angeles Times,* May 19, 1994, p. A17.

87. Phillip Lutz, "Head Start Expanding Despite Problems," *New York Times,* Aug. 7, 1994, Section 13LI, p. 1; Kay Mills, "Head Start Advocates Tout Program's Success," *Dallas Morning News,* Oct. 27, 1995, p. A46; "Low Salaries Hurting Head Start Programs," *Phoenix Gazette,* Jan. 20, 1995, p. A6.

88. Government Accounting Office, "Head Start: Research Provides Little Information in Impact of Current Program" (Report Number HEHS-97–59, April 15, 1997).

89. James Bennet, "Political Memo: In Evolution of Clinton, A Few Echoes Survive," *New York Times,* Feb. 6, 1997, p. B8.

90. Karen MacPherson, "Congress Examining Head Start: Expanded Funding Linked to Proof of Program's Effect," *Pittsburgh Post-Gazette,* Mar. 27, 1998, p. A10; "Better, Not Bigger, Head Start Sought," *Arizona Republic,* Oct. 28, 1998, p. A7.

91. Marjorie Coeyman, "Head Start Loses Some Elbow Room," *Christian Science Monitor,* Aug. 18, 1998, p. B4.

92. Joan Lowy, "Program for Poor Children Imperiled," *Orange County Register,* Aug. 28, 1998, p. A29.

93. Linda Jacobson, "Advocates Question Bush Plan to Revamp Head Start," *Education Week,* Dec. 1, 1999.

94. Barnett, "Does Head Start Fade Out?"

95. Erik W. Robelen, "Budget Agreement Gives Ed. Department Largest-Ever Increase," *Education Week*, Dec. 18, 2000.

2. Is Bilingual Education a Good Idea?

1. Jonathan Yardley, "The Hard Lessons of Bilingual Education," *Washington Post*, Oct. 24, 1994, p. B2.

2. Susan Walton, "Research and the Quest for 'Effective' Bilingual Methods," *Education Week*, Feb. 8, 1984; Christine H. Rossell and Keith Baker, *Bilingual Education in Massachusetts: The Emperor Has No Clothes* (Boston: Pioneer Institute, 1996), pp. 6–8.

3. A parent quoted in the *Los Angeles Times* in 1996 is representative of how many bilingual supporters, including parents, teachers, school officials, and even academics, view its detractors. She stated that Spanish was "a treasure" and that "those who are opposed to Spanish are racists who want to keep us down." Richard Lee Colvin, "Battle Heats Up over Bilingual Education," *Los Angeles Times*, April 8, 1996, p. A1.

4. "Bilingual Education Has Taken Shape along Two Federal Tracks," *Education Week*, April 1, 1987.

5. The official phrase for children whose English is limited or nonexistent, and who speak another language, is "limited English proficiency," abbreviated as LEP. I have chosen to use language-minority (LM) instead, because it shows more respect for children's native languages. I will use LEP when referring to government statistics or categories that employ that abbreviation.

6. James Crawford, *Bilingual Education: History, Politics, Theory and Practice*, 3rd ed. (Los Angeles: Bilingual Educational Services, 1995), pp. 30–32, 177–193.

7. Carl F. Kaestle, *Pillars of the Republic: Common Schools and American Society, 1780–1860* (New York: Hill and Wang, 1983), pp. 164–166; Jonathan Zimmerman, "'A Babel of Togues,'" *U.S. News and World Report*, Nov. 24, 1997, p. 39; Richard Rothstein, "Bilingual Education: The Controversy," *Phi Delta Kappan*, May 1998, p. 672.

8. Kaestle, *Pillars of the Republic*, pp. 165–166; Rothstein, "Bilingual Education: The Controversy."

9. Zimmerman, "'A Babel of Tongues'"; Judith Rosenberg Raftery, *Land of Fair Promise: Politics and Reform in Los Angeles Schools, 1885–1941* (Stanford, Calif.: Stanford University Press, 1992), p. 65; Crawford, *Bilingual Education*, p. 26; Rothstein, "Bilingual Education: The Controversy."

10. Crawford, *Bilingual Education*, pp. 32–34; Zimmerman, "'A Babel of Tongues'"; Rothstein, "Bilingual Education: The Controversy"; Paul Taylor,

"Parents' Disenchantment with Bilingual Education Found Rising," *Washington Post*, April 9, 1984, p. A2.

11. Crawford, *Bilingual Education*, pp. 35–37; "School's Pioneer Bilingualism Gives Way to Changing Times," *Education Week*, Jan. 11, 1984.

12. Melinda Burns, "'New Federalism' vs. Bilingual Education," *Christian Science Monitor*, May 10, 1982, p. 23; Melanie Markley, "One Mind, Two Voices: Advocates Split on Bilingual Teaching Tactics," *Houston Chronicle*, June 4, 1995, p. A33; Ernest Holsendolph, "The Reagan Effect; Bilingual Funds: A Problem in Any Language," *New York Times*, Nov. 14, 1982, Special Section, p. 47.

13. Rossell and Baker, *Bilingual Education in Massachusetts*, pp. 16–17.

14. Crawford, *Bilingual Education*, pp. 40–41; M. Beatriz Arias and Ursula Casanova, *Bilingual Education: Politics, Practice, and Research*, Ninety-second Yearbook of the National Society for the Study of Education, pt. 2 (Chicago: University of Chicago Press, 1993), pp. x–xi; Richard Rodriguez, "Bilingualism, Con: Outdated and Unrealistic," *New York Times*, Nov. 10, 1985, Section 12, p. 63.

15. *Lau v. Nichols* is in Keith A. Baker and Adriana A. de Kanter, eds., *Bilingual Education: A Reappraisal of Federal Policy* (Lexington, Mass.: Lexington Books, 1983), pp. 205–211; Beatrice F. Birman and Alan L. Ginsburg, "Introduction: Addressing the Needs of Language-Minority Children," in Baker and de Kanter, eds., *Bilingual Education*, p. xi; Crawford, *Bilingual Education*, pp. 42–46; Cynthia Gorney, "The Suit That Started It All; The Lau Case: When Learning in a Native Tongue Became a Right," *Washington Post*, July 7, 1985, p. A12.

16. Birman and Ginsburg, "Introduction," pp. ix–xiii; "Lau remedies" are in Baker and de Kanter, eds., *Bilingual Education*, pp. 213–221; Crawford, *Bilingual Education*, pp. 46–47; Muriel Cohen, "Bilingual Education; More than 20 Years after Being Made Law, It's Still Controversial—In Any Language," *Boston Globe*, Dec. 4, 1994, p. B1; "Administration Scraps Bilingual Education Rules," *Washington Post*, Feb. 3, 1981, p. A1; July 7, 1985; Rochelle L. Stanfield, "Are Federal Bilingual Rules a Foot in the Schoolhouse Door?" *National Journal*, Oct. 18, 1980, p. 1736.

17. Marshall Ingwerson, "Bilingual Education; Its Goal: To Teach English Quickly and Efficiently, Leading to a Generation Fluent in Two Languages," *Christian Science Monitor*, Aug. 23, 1983, p. 13; Gorney, "The Suit That Started It All."

18. Ingwerson, "Bilingual Education; Its Goal"; Rossell and Baker, *Bilingual Education in Massachusetts*, p. 5; Crawford, *Bilingual Education*, pp. 162–163.

19. Crawford, *Bilingual Education*, pp. 42–47; Rossell and Baker, *Bilingual Education in Massachusetts*, pp. 18–19; Michael A. Rebell and Arthur R. Block, *Educational Policy Making and the Courts: An Empirical Study of Judicial Activism* (Chicago: University of Chicago Press, 1982), pp. 175–196; Rosalie Pedalino

Porter, "The Politics of Bilingual Education," *Society*, Sept. 19, 1997, p. 31; James Ylisela Jr., "Bilingual Bellwether at Bay," *Christian Science Monitor*, Jan. 13, 1983, p. 23; "When It Takes Two Languages to Teach the Three R's . . . ," *U.S. News and World Report*, July 7, 1975, p. 67; Edward B. Fiske, "The Controversy over Bilingual Education in America's Schools," *New York Times*, Nov. 10, 1985, Section 12, p. 1; Charlotte Libov, "Bilingual Programs Are Under Attack," *New York Times*, Feb. 22, 1987, Section 11CN, p. 1; Joseph Berger, "Whose Language? Bilingualism in the Schools—A Special Report; School Programs Assailed as Bilingual Bureaucracy," *New York Times*, Jan. 4, 1993, p. A1; Dennis A. Williams, "Chicanos in Ferment," *Newsweek*, Oct. 5, 1981, p. 76; Keith B. Richburg, "Bilingual Education: Carrot and Stick; Bennett Would Shift Program to Give Localities Flexibility," *Washington Post*, Sept. 27, 1985, p. A23.

20. "When It Takes Two Languages to Teach the Three R's . . ."

21. Ibid.; Hope Aldrich, "Districts Vying for Limited Supply of Bilingual Instructors," *Education Week*, March 23, 1983.

22. Malcolm N. Danoff et al., *Evaluation of the Impact of ESEA Title VII Spanish/English Bilingual Education Programs* (Palo Alto, Calif.: American Institutes for Research, 1978); Crawford, *Bilingual Education*, pp. 104–106; J. David Ramirez et al., *Final Report: Longitudinal Study of Structured Immersion Strategy, Early-Exit and Late-Exit Transitional Bilingual Education Programs for Language-Minority Children*, 2 vols. (San Mateo, Calif.: Aguirre International, Feb. 1991), vol. 1, p. 22.

23. Danoff et al., *Evaluation of the Impact of ESEA Title VII Spanish/English Bilingual Education Programs*; Crawford, *Bilingual Education*, p. 49.

24. Birman and Ginsburg, "Introduction," p. xiii; "Administration Scraps Bilingual Education Rules"; Charles R. Babcock, "Bell Easing Up on Native-Language Teaching Rules," *Washington Post*, April 24, 1982, p. A11; Marjorie Hunter, "U.S. Education Chief Bars Bilingual Plan for Public Schools," *New York Times*, Feb. 3, 1981, p. A1; "Bell Strikes Down Bilingual Regulations," *National Journal*, Feb. 7, 1981, p. 241; Williams, "Chicanos in Ferment."

25. Pat Bauer, "U.S. Tells Fairfax Bilingual Classes Are Not Required," *Washington Post*, Dec. 31, 1980, p. A1; Fred M. Hechinger, "About Education; U.S. Ruling Fuels Controversy over Bilingual Teaching," *New York Times*, Jan. 20, 1981, p. C4; Janet Elder, "New Programs Are Widening Scope of Bilingual Education," *New York Times*, Jan. 2, 1986, p. C1. In 1975 there had only been 50 foreign-born students in public schools in Fairfax County, the nation's tenth largest school system. By 1985–86 the number had skyrocketed to 14,000 foreign-born children, accounting for fifty-seven different languages.

26. Rosalie Pedalino Porter, *Forked Tongue: The Politics of Bilingual Education* (New York: Basic Books, 1990), pp. 146–149; "Educating the Melting Pot," *U.S. News and World Report*, March 31, 1986, p. 20.

27. Hechinger, "About Education; U.S. Ruling Fuels Controversy over Bilingual Teaching"; Stanfield, "Are Federal Bilingual Rules a Foot in the Schoolhouse Door?"

28. Crawford, *Bilingual Education*, pp. 110–116; Keith A. Baker and Adriana A. de Kanter, "Federal Policy and the Effectiveness of Bilingual Education," in Baker and de Kanter, eds., *Bilingual Education*, p. 41.

29. There is evidence for the effectiveness of structured immersion in Canada, but whether it is even remotely pertinent to the debate in the United States is unclear. It seems successful in helping Canadian children who already speak the majority language to learn another language, which is very different from what it would be asked to do in the United States: teach the majority language, English, to children speaking other languages. Crawford, *Bilingual Education*, pp. 110–116, 139–143; Baker and de Kanter, "Federal Policy and the Effectiveness of Bilingual Education," pp. 49–53.

30. Birman and Ginsburg, "Introduction," p. xii.; "Educating the Melting Pot"; Marshall Ingwerson, "Bennett's Proposals Spotlight Bilingual Education's Mixed Record," *Christian Science Monitor*, Oct. 3, 1985, p. 8.

31. Robert E. Barnes with Ann M. Milne, "The Size of the Eligible Language-Minority Population," in Baker and de Kanter, eds., *Bilingual Education*, pp. 3–32; "A Battle in Any Language," *Newsweek*, Dec. 15, 1980, p. 93; "Teach Immigrants in Their Own Language?" *U.S. News and World Report*, Oct. 3, 1983, p. 51; Judith Heffner, "The Battle over Bilingual Education," *Scholastic Update*, Sept. 21, 1984, p. 30; "For Learning or Ethnic Pride?" *Time*, July 8, 1985, p. 80; Crawford, *Bilingual Education*, pp. 88–89.

32. Ylisela, "Bilingual Bellwether at Bay."

33. "California Program Grapples with Problems, Scores Successes," *Education Week*, April 1, 1987; "Bilingual Education an Emotional Issue," *San Diego Union-Tribune*, June 10, 1984, p. A1; Pamela Moreland, "Bilingual Program Takes a New Tack," *Los Angeles Times*, June 30, 1985; Bill Billiter, "County's Bilingual Debate Goes On; Educators View State Law as Too Restrictive, Call for Some Changes," *Los Angeles Times*, Sept. 27, 1985, Metro, p. 1.

34. Moreland, "Bilingual Program Takes a New Tack"; "Bilingual Plan Backed in Los Angeles," *New York Times*, May 10, 1988, p. A20.

35. Crawford, *Bilingual Education*, pp. 215–217; Robert Marquand, "Model Bilingual Education," *Christian Science Monitor*, Sept. 25, 1987, p. 21. For much more on the Oyster School, see Rebecca D. Freeman, *Bilingual Education and Social Change* (Philadelphia: Multilingual Matters, 1998).

36. Mary Willix Farmer, "Students in Bilingual Grade School Get Basics Twice," *Christian Science Monitor*, April 4, 1983, p. 16; Siobhan Gorman, "A Bilingual Recess," *National Journal*, Jan. 30, 1999, p. 258; "Two-Way Bilingual Study: Learning a Foreign Language," *New York Times*, Nov. 24, 1986, p. B12; Lisa Leff,

"Where Bilingual Education Is a Two-Way Street," *Washington Post*, March 13, 1994, p. B1; "Multitude of Approaches Typify 'Two-Way' Immersion Method," *Education Week*, Jan. 20, 1988.

37. Willig excluded three studies from Canada that Baker and de Kanter had included, one study from the Philippines, and one study from the United States that looked mainly at preschool and after-school programs. Ann C. Willig, "A Meta-Analysis of Selected Studies on the Effectiveness of Bilingual Education," *Review of Educational Research* 55 (3), Fall 1985, pp. 270–272.

38. Willig, "Meta-Analysis of Selected Studies," pp. 269–277.

39. Lynn Olson, "Shocking Waste of Youths Cited in Study of Hispanic Schooling," *Education Week*, Dec. 12, 1984; James Hertling and Susan Hooper, "District Officials Criticize Bennett's Call For Flexible Bilingual-Education Policy," *Education Week*, Oct. 9, 1985; James J. Lyons, "Commentary: Bilingual-Policy Initiative 'Doesn't Make Sense,'" *Education Week*, Oct. 23, 1985; "'A Failed Path,' Bennett Blasts Bilingualism," *Time*, Oct. 23, 1985, p. 55; "Educating the Melting Pot"; Keith B. Richburg, "Plan to Change Bilingual Aid Rekindles Debate," *Washington Post*, Jan. 25, 1986, p. A3; Lee May, "Latinos Assail Bilingual Education Plans," *Los Angeles Times*, Jan. 25, 1986, p. 3.

40. Lynn Olson, "Many Bilingual Pupils Unaided, Study Finds," *Education Week*, Jan. 8, 1986.

41. Neal R. Peirce, "California's Big Debate: English Spoken Here?" *National Journal*, Oct. 11, 1986, p. 2461; Libov, "Bilingual Programs Are under Attack"; "Bilingual Education: Clash of the Ideologues," *Economist*, Jan. 24, 1987, p. 26; "With Schools Becoming Towers of Babel, California Stumbles Along without a State Bilingual Education Program," *California Journal*, June 1, 1993, Feature section; Richard C. Paddock, "Deukmejian Vetoes Bill on Bilingual Education," *Los Angeles Times*, Oct. 1, 1986, p. 1; Richard C. Paddock, "Deukmejian Vetoes Bill to Revive Bilingual Program," *Los Angeles Times*, July 25, 1987, p. 1.

42. U.S. General Accounting Office, *Bilingual Education: A New Look at the Research Evidence*, Briefing Report to the Chairman, Committee on Education and Labor, House of Representatives, March 1987; "Bilingual-Education Boost," *Los Angeles Times*, June 24, 1986, Metro, p. 4.

43. Irvin Molotsky, "New and Old School Chiefs Differ on Issues and Styles," *New York Times*, Sept. 22, 1988, p. A22; Lori Silver, "Education Dept., in Shift, Favors Bilingual Education," *Los Angeles Times*, Aug. 26, 1989, p. 1.

44. "Bilingual Education: Clash of the Idelogues"; Dick Kirschten, "Speaking English," *National Journal*, June 17, 1989, p. 1556.

45. "Bilingual Plan Backed in Los Angeles"; Elaine Woo, "Eastman School Touted for Bilingual Innovations," *Los Angeles Times*, Aug. 31, 1989, Nuestro Tiempo ed., p. 8.

46. Rene Sanchez, "D.C. School Chief's First Test: Bilingual Education," *Washing-*

ton Post, Nov. 12, 1988, p. B9; Rene Sanchez, "D.C. Bilingual Education Compromise Struck," *Washington Post,* Dec. 10, 1988, p. B8.

47. Ramirez et al., *Final Report,* vol. 1; Crawford, *Bilingual Education,* pp. 148–149.

48. Ramirez et al., *Final Report,* vol. 1.

49. Ibid., pp. 35–56.

50. Ramirez et al. *Final Report,* vol. 2, p. 645.

51. Ramirez et al., *Final Report,* vol. 2, pp. 646–667; Nanette Asimov, "Education Study Finds Flaws in 'English-Only,'" *San Francisco Chronicle,* Feb. 12, 1991, p. A2.

52. Peter Schmidt, "Panel Faults Methods of E.D.'s Bilingual-Education Studies," *Education Week,* Aug. 5, 1992.

53. Ramirez et al., *Final Report,* vol. 1, pp. 90–91; ibid., vol. 2, p. 33.

54. Ibid., vol. 1, pp. 182, 421–422.

55. Ibid., pp. 370–376.

56. "Sommers Pushes Bilingual-Education Bill: Critics See It as Attempt to Avoid Lawsuit," *Seattle Times,* Feb. 12, 1993, p. C1; Ruben Sosa Villegas, "Group Files Complaint against DPS," *Denver Rocky Mountain News,* June 13, 1994, p. 3N.

57. Jon Nalick, "Westminster Tackles State on Bilingualism," *Los Angeles Times,* March 14, 1995, p. B1; Tina Nguyen, "Study Shows Gains from Classes Based in English," *Los Angeles Times,* Oct. 2, 1997, p. B1.

58. Lynn Schnailberg, "Board Relaxes Bilingual-Ed. Policy in Calif.," *Education Week,* Aug. 2, 1995; Amy Pyle, "State Panel OKs Flexible Bilingual Education Policy," *Los Angeles Times,* July 14, 1995, p. A1; Nick Anderson, "Bilingual Debate Intensifies," *Los Angeles Times,* April 13, 1997, p. A1; Teresa Moore, "State Expands Schools' Choices on Bilingual Education," *San Francisco Chronicle,* July 15, 1995, p. A15.

59. Amy Pyle, "Bilingual Schooling Is Failing, Parents Say," *Los Angeles Times,* Jan. 16, 1996, p. B1; Amy Pyle, "80 Students Stay Out of School in Latino Boycott," *Los Angeles Times,* Feb. 14, 1996, p. B1; "Lessons of a School Boycott," *Los Angeles Times,* Feb. 26, 1996, p. B4; Lynn Schnailberg, "Parents Worry Bilingual Ed. Hurts Students," *Education Week,* Feb. 28, 1996.

60. As one of many examples, the Jan. 13, 1996, issue of the *Los Angeles Times* began an article on early information released about the study by calling it "the most comprehensive national study of bilingual education ever conducted." See Amy Pyle, "Bilingual Classes Boost Performance, Study Finds," *Los Angeles Times,* Jan. 13, 1996, p. A1. The op-ed piece, by Texas representative Gene Green and Delia Pompa, director of DOE's Office of Bilingual Education and Minority Language Affairs, appeared in the *Houston Chronicle,* April 3, 1997, p. 33.

61. Wayne P. Thomas and Virginia Collier, "School Effectiveness for Language Minority Students," disseminated by National Clearinghouse for Bilingual Education, George Washington University, Dec. 1997.

62. Ibid.

63. Ibid., pp. 9–53.

64. Ibid., pp. 15–16.

65. Ibid., pp. 27–30.

66. Ibid., p. 51.

67. At times it is obvious that Thomas and Collier are so determined to influence policymakers that they make claims that are, at best, problematic. Their continued assertions that they only looked at "well-implemented" programs, when they did not have enough evidence to know this in many cases, is one example. Another is their claim that independent school districts, who remain unnamed, have verified their findings: they write that "thus far, at least three large school systems" have done so (see Thomas and Collier, "School Effectiveness for Language Minority Students," p. 29). Why "at least"? Was it three? Four? How can they not know how many school systems have done so? Or is it that the school systems they refer to have actually found results that are more equivocal? Or that these school systems' methods were so shaky that Thomas and Collier are a little uncomfortable with their results? Vagueness like this does not help their case; at other times they are assertive in ways their research methods simply do not merit.

68. Jay P. Greene, "A Meta-Analysis of the Effectiveness of Bilingual Education," sponsored by the Tomas Rivera Policy Institute, University of Texas at Austin, March 1998.

69. Ibid.

70. Amy Pyle, "Education; Campaign Targets Bilingual Education," *Los Angeles Times,* July 9, 1997, p. B2; Mark Z. Barabak, "The Times Poll; Little Support for Bilingual Classes Found," *Los Angeles Times,* Oct. 15, 1997, p. A1; Betsy Streisand, "Is It Hasta La Vista for Bilingual Ed?" *U.S. News and World Report,* Nov. 24, 1997, p. 36.

71. Streisand, "Is It Hasta La Vista for Bilingual Ed?"; Laurel Shaper Walters, "The Bilingual Education Debate," *Harvard Education Letter* 14 (3), May/June 1998, p. 1; Gregory Rodriguez, "English Lesson in California: In the Face of a Ballot Challenge, Support for Bilingual Education Is Wavering," *The Nation,* April 20, 1998, p. 15; Amy Pyle, "Pressure Grows to Reform Bilingual Education in State," *Los Angeles Times,* May 22, 1995, p. A1.

72. Lynn Schnailberg, "Calif. Board Revises Policy for LEP Students," *Education Week,* April 15, 1998; Peter Baker, "Education Dept. Faults Anti-Bilingual Measure," *Washington Post,* April 28, 1998, p. A3; "Calif. Rejection a Big Blow to Bilingualism," June 4, 1998, p. A16; "Prop. 227 Foes Vow to Block It Despite Wide Vote Margin," *Los Angeles Times,* June 4, 1998, p. A1.

73. Thomas D. Elias, "California Teachers to Defy Bilingual Ban," *Washington Times,* July 13, 1998, p. A1; Thomas D. Elias, "California Schools Find Ways to Evade Anti-Bilingual Vote," *Washington Times,* Sept. 13, 1998, p. A2; Mary Ann

Zehr, "Prop 227 Makes Instruction Less Consistent, Study Says," *Education Week,* May 3, 2000.

74. Elias, "California Schools Find Ways to Evade Anti-Bilingual Vote"; "Judge Refuses to Stand in Way of Prop. 227, *Los Angeles Times,* July 16, 1998, p. A1.

75. Nanette Asimov, "Judge Delivers Large Bilingual Education Win," *San Francisco Chronicle,* Aug. 28, 1998, p. A21; "Bilingual Teaching Backers Win Key Court Decision," *Los Angeles Times,* Aug. 28, 1998, p. A1; Chuck Squatriglia, "Court Strengthens Ban on Bilingual Education," *San Francisco Chronicle,* Sept. 28, 1999, p. A18.

76. Kate Folmar, "Parents Overwhelmingly Request Bilingual Classes," *Los Angeles Times,* Sept. 26, 1998, p. B1; Kate Folmar, "Word Getting Out on Bilingual Class Waivers," *Los Angeles Times,* Oct. 8, 1998, p. B1; "Bilingual Classes Still Thriving in Wake of Prop. 227," *Los Angeles Times,* Oct. 22, 1998, p. A1; Lynn Schnailberg, "Parents Ask for Waivers to Put Students Back in Bilingual Ed.," *Education Week,* Nov. 11, 1998; Lynn Schnailberg, "Calif.'s Year on the Bilingual Battleground," *Education Week,* June 2, 1999; Lynn Schnailberg, "Interpretations of Prop. 227 Vary Widely, Experts Say," *Education Week,* June 2, 1999; Zehr, "Prop. 227 Makes Instruction Less Consistent."

77. Lynn Schnailberg, "Caution Urged in Interpreting Calif. Scores," *Education Week,* Aug. 4, 1999; Liz Seymour, "One-Language Rule Produces Winners," *Los Angeles Times,* Feb. 16, 1999, p. B1; Siobhan Gorman, "California's Language Wars, Part II," *National Journal,* July 31, 1999; Maureen Magee, "San Diego Student Test Scores Climb," *San Diego Union-Tribune,* June 29, 1999, p. A1; Chris Moran, "Students' Scores Improve in County, State," *San Diego Union-Tribune,* July 23, 1999, p. A1.

78. Kathy Renolds, "Quality, Not Speed, Is Key in Bilingual Programs," *Arizona Republic,* Aug. 26, 1998, p. EV6; Hector Tobar, "English-Only Push Revisits Arizona's Cultural Divide," *Los Angeles Times,* March 7, 1999, p. A1; Abby Goodnough, "New York Region Steps Up Efforts for Bilingual Classes," *New York Times,* June 15, 1998, p. B1; Melinda Tuhus, "Law Supports Bilingual Education," *New York Times,* July 11, 1999, Section 14CN, p. 3.

79. Cynthia Gorney, "For Teachers, 10 Years of Trial and Error," *Washington Post,* July 8, 1985, p. A1; Barbara Koh, "Making New Maps for the Labyrinth of Learning," *Los Angeles Times,* Jan. 31, 1991, p. B1; Jane Perlez, "Hundreds of Bilingual School Jobs Go Begging," *New York Times,* Aug. 21, 1986, p. B1; Susan Headden, "Only English Spoken Here," *U.S. News and World Report,* Sept. 25, 1995, p. 44; Peter Schmidt, "Calif. Is Short 14,000 Bilingual Teachers, Panel Finds," *Education Week,* June 19, 1991.

80. Elaine Woo, "Revival of State Law Sought," *Los Angeles Times,* Feb. 10, 1988, p. 1; Carol Steinberg, "For L.I., Surge of Foreign Pupils," *New York Times,* Oct. 20, 1985, Section 11LI, p. 1; Kathleen Kennedy Manzo, "Rural N.C. to Get Aid for LEP-Student Influx," *Education Week,* Jan. 27, 1999.

81. Melissa M. Turner, "Washington Stirs the Multilingual Melting Pot; Limited Federal Aid," *National Journal,* Dec. 19, 1987, p. 3240; Crawford, *Bilingual Education,* pp. 88–89.

82. Rossell and Baker, *Bilingual Education in Massachusetts,* pp. 113–131; Peter Schmidt, "New Bilingual-Ed. Rules to Expand N.Y. Program," *Education Week,* Dec. 6, 1989.

83. Porter, *Forked Tongue,* pp. 66–67; Susan Headden, "Tongue-Tied in the Schools," *U.S. News and World Report,* Sept. 25, 1995, p. 44; Berger, "Whose Language? Bilingualism in the Schools"; Linda Chavez, "Bilingual Education Gobbles Up Kids, Taxes," *USA Today,* June 15, 1994, p. A15.

84. Rossell and Baker, *Bilingual Education in Massachusetts,* pp. 115–116; Amy Pyle, "English Fluency Moves Up the Priority Ladder," *Los Angeles Times,* July 31, 1995, p. B1; Amy Pyle, "Bilingual Students Post Gains in English," *Los Angeles Times,* Oct. 17, 1995, p. B1; "Public Education: California's Perilous Slide," *Los Angeles Times,* May 18, 1998, p. R2.

85. Mary Ann Zehr, "For Bilingual Ed. Programs, Three Is Magic Number," *Education Week,* Nov. 17, 1999.

86. Paul Van Slambrouck, "Texas Debates Blueprint for 'Model' Bilingual Classes," *Christian Science Monitor,* May 28, 1981, p. 6.

87. Rossell and Baker, *Bilingual Education in Massachusetts,* p. 71; Porter, *Forked Tongue,* pp. 5–6; Berger, "Whose Language? Bilingualism in the Schools."

88. Rossell and Baker, *Bilingual Education in Massachusetts,* pp. 20–22; Kate Zernike, "State Board Eases Rules on Bilingual Education," *Boston Globe,* May 13, 1997, p. A1.

89. *Digest of Education Statistics, 1998.*

90. Catherine E. Snow, M. Susan Burns, and Peg Griffin, eds., *Preventing Reading Difficulties in Young Children,* National Research Council (Washington, D.C.: National Academy Press, 1998), pp. 28–29, 100–133.

91. Porter, *Forked Tongue.*

92. Joetta L. Sack, "Riley Endorses 'Dual Immersion' Programs," *Education Week,* March 22, 2000.

93. Crawford, *Bilingual Education,* pp. 195–196.

94. Birman and Ginsburg, "Introduction," p. xvii.

3. Does Class Size Matter?

1. Barbara Nye, Larry V. Hedges, and Spyros Konstantopoulos, "The Effects of Small Classes on Academic Achievement: The Results of the Tennessee Class Size Experiment," unpublished paper, p. 3; Howard Kurtz, "The Candidates' Lesson Plan: Education Becomes a Hot Theme in Campaign Ads," *Washington Post,* July 4, 1998, p. A1.

2. Jeremy D. Finn and Charles M. Achilles, "Tennessee's Class Size Study: Find-

ings, Implications, Misconceptions," *Educational Evaluation and Policy Analysis* 21 (2), Summer 1999, pp. 104–105.

3. Leanne Malloy and David Gilman, "The Cumulative Effects on Basic Skills Achievement of Indiana's Prime Time—A State-Sponsored Program of Reduced Class Size," *Contemporary Education* 60 (3), Spring 1989, p. 169.

4. Reed Ueda, *Avenues to Adulthood: The Origins of the High School and Social Mobility in an American Suburb* (Cambridge: Cambridge University Press, 1987), pp. 20–22; Gene V. Glass et al., *School Class Size: Research and Policy* (Beverly Hills: Sage Publications, 1982), pp. 17–18; Bryce E. Nelson, *Good Schools: The Seattle Public School System, 1901–1930* (Seattle: University of Washington Press, 1988), p. 17.

5. David Tyack, Robert Lowe, and Elisabeth Hansot, *Public Schools in Hard Times: The Great Depression and Recent Years* (Cambridge: Harvard University Press, 1984), pp. 38, 146–147.

6. Glass et al., *School Class Size*, p. 23; Tommy M. Tomlinson, *Class Size and Public Policy: Politics and Panaceas* (Washington, D.C.: U.S. Department of Education, Programs for the Improvement of Practice, March 1988), pp. 14–18.

7. "Why the Surge in Teachers' Strikes," *U.S. News and World Report*, Sept. 18, 1978, p. 79; "Chicago, Philadelphia Teachers Reach Pacts; Seattle Still Out," *Education Week*, Sept. 11, 1985.

8. Glass et al., *School Class Size*, p. 25.

9. Ibid., pp. 33–44.

10. Ibid., pp. 44–50.

11. Mary Lee Smith and Gene V. Glass, *Relationship of Class-Size to Classroom Processes, Teacher Satisfaction and Pupil Affect: A Meta-Analysis* (San Francisco: Laboratory of Educational Research, 1979); Glass et al., *School Class Size*, pp. 51–65.

12. Glass et al., *School Class Size*, pp. 67–74.

13. Malloy and Gilman, "Cumulative Effects on Basic Skills Achievement of Indiana's Prime Time," p. 169; Educational Research Services, *Class Size Research: A Critique of Recent Meta-Analyses* (Arlington, Va.: Educational Research Services, 1980).

14. Fred M. Hechinger, "Are Smaller Classes Really Much Better," *New York Times*, June 24, 1980, p. C4.

15. Tyack, Lowe, and Hansot, *Public Schools in Hard Times*, pp. 203–208; Lucia Solorzano, "Schools Open—With a Lean Year Ahead," *U.S. News and World Report*, Sept. 6, 1982, p. 43.

16. Maggie Locke, "Fairfax Officials Seek Flexibility in Law Limiting Class Size," *Washington Post*, Feb. 3, 1977, p. Va. 3.

17. Hechinger, "Are Smaller Classes Really Much Better"; Gene I. Maeroff, "Unmanageable Class Size Still City School Problem," *New York Times*, March 15, 1981, p. 42; Joyce Purnick, "Few Schools Reduce First-Grade Classes to Size

City Wants," *New York Times* Oct. 29, 1984, p. A1; Joyce Purnick, "City Schools Miss Goal for Class Size," *New York Times* Nov. 22, 1984, p. B3; Gene I. Maeroff, "City High Schools Meeting Class-Size Target," *New York Times* March 3, 1985, p. 36.

18. Nathaniel Sheppard, Jr., "Nation's Schools in Fiscal Squeeze as Students Return to Classrooms," *New York Times,* Sept. 5, 1982, p. 36.

19. Tomlinson, *Class Size and Public Policy,* pp. 3–9.

20. Ibid., pp. 1–21.

21. Barbara Vobejda, "NEA Poll Indicates Teacher Shortage," *Washington Post,* July 5, 1987, p. A13.

22. David Schaefer, "Pittsburgh Public Schools Enjoy Big Budgets, Sharp Programs," *Seattle Times,* May 22, 1990, p. B1.

23. Malloy and Gilman, "Cumulative Effects on Basic Skills Achievement of Indiana's Prime Time," pp. 170–171; "Most Schools Adopt Primetime," UPI, Aug. 13, 1984, Regional News, Indiana; Andrea Neal, "ISTA, Governor Pleased with Education Progress," UPI, March 2, 1984, Regional News, Indiana; "Commission Loosens Requirements for Prime Time," UPI, May 3, 1984, Regional News, Indiana.

24. "Most Schools Adopt Primetime"; Jeremy D. Finn, *Class Size and Students at Risk: What Is Known? What Is Next?* (U.S. Department of Education, Office of Educational Research and Improvement, 1998), p. 6; Malloy and Gilman, "Cumulative Effects on Basic Skills Achievment of Indiana's Prime Time," pp. 171–172.

25. Howard Dukes, "Study Raises Questions about Prime Time," *South Bend Tribune,* April 17, 1994, p. C5.

26. Andrea Neal, "The Merits of Smaller Class Size," *Indianapolis Star,* Nov. 16, 1995, p. A12.

27. "Early Grades: Actions to Reduce Class Size," *Education Week,* Oct. 16, 1985.

28. Tomlinson, *Class Size and Public Policy,* pp. 23–29; Robert Rothman, "Class Size No Panacea, Says Study," *Education Week,* April 6, 1988.

29. Tomlinson, *Class Size and Public Policy.*

30. Joseph Berger, "Is There an Optimum Class Size for Teaching?" *New York Times,* April 6, 1988, p. B9; "Is Small Beautiful?" *Washington Post,* April 9, 1988, p. A24.

31. Gary W. Ritter and Robert F. Boruch, "The Political and Institutional Origins of a Randomized Controlled Trial on Elementary School Class Size: Tennessee's Project STAR," *Educational Evaluation and Policy Analysis* 21 (2), Summer 1999, pp. 112–114; Jeremy D. Finn and Charles M. Achilles, "Answers and Questions about Class Size: A Statewide Experiment," *American Educational Research Journal* 27 (3), Fall 1990, pp. 558–559; Nye, Hedges, and Konstantopoulos, "Effects of Small Classes on Academic Achievement," pp. 5–7; Frederick Mosteller, "The Tennessee Study of Class Size in the Early School

Grades," *The Future of Children* 5 (2), Summer/Fall 1995, pp. 115–119; Barbara Nye, Larry V. Hedges, and Spyros Konstantopoulos, "The Long-Term Effects of Small Classes: A Five-Year Follow-Up of the Tennessee Class Size Experiment," *Educational Evaluation and Policy Analysis* 21 (2), Summer 1999, pp. 127–142.

32. Mosteller, "Tennessee Study of Class Size in the Early Grades," pp. 114–115; Finn and Achilles, "Answers and Questions about Class Size," pp. 559–561; Nye, Hedges, and Konstantopoulos, "Effects of Small Classes on Student Achievement," pp. 6–8; Finn, *Class Size and Students at Risk*, pp. 6–10.

33. Nye, Hedges, and Konstantopoulos, "Effects of Small Classes on Students Achievement," pp. 11–36.

34. Finn and Achilles, "Answers and Questions about Class Size," pp. 561–568; Finn, *Class Size and Students at Risk*, pp. 7–10; Mosteller, "Tennessee Study of Class Size in the Early School Grades," pp. 116–120; Gerald W. Bracey, "Research Oozes into Practice: The Case of Class Size, *Phi Delta Kappan*, Sept. 1995, p. 89.

35. Nye, Hedges, and Konstantopoulos, "Long-Term Effects of Small Classes," pp. 127–142; Finn, *Class Size and Students at Risk*, pp. 10–11; Mosteller, "Tennessee Study of Class Size in the Early School Grades," p. 125; Richard Locker, "Benefits of Smaller Class Sizes Tracked," *Commercial Appeal* (Memphis), Jan. 29, 1994, p. B1; Finn, *Class Size and Students at Risk*; "The Beauty of Small Classes," *San Francisco Chronicle*," May 4, 1999, p. A22.

36. Sue Allison, "Pricetag High for Class Size Reduction," UPI, Dec. 3, 1989, Regional News, Tennessee; Nancy Weil, "Smaller Classes Found to Make Big Difference in Tennessee," *St. Petersburg Times*, March 7, 1993, p. A9.

37. Finn, *Class Size and Students at Risk*, p. 12.

38. Reed Branson, "Tennessee Schools Face Early Cuts in Class Sizes," *Memphis Commercial Appeal*, June 4, 1992, p. B1.

39. Vicki Brown, "Audit Finds Spending Up, Smaller Classes in State," *Chattanooga Free Press*, June 2, 1997, p. A7; Mary Buckner Powers, "Tennessee Districts Scramble to Meet Reduced Class Size Law," *Engineering News-Record*, Oct. 12, 1998, p. 12.

40. Barbara Esteves-Moore, "Williamson's Reduced Class Sizes Attract International Attention," *Tennessean*, Feb. 10, 1998, p. 5W; Paul Donsky, "School Still Out on Advantages of Smaller Classes," *Tennessean*, Nov. 2, 1998, p. A1.

41. Nancy Weil, "Critics: Smaller Classes No Guarantee of Success," *St. Petersburg Times*, March 7, 1993; Donsky, "School Still Out on Advantages."

42. Eric A. Hanushek, "Money and Education: Making America's Schools Work," *Current*, March 1995, p. 9; Eric A. Hanushek, "Some Findings from an Independent Investigation of the Tennessee STAR Experiment, and from Other Investigations of Class Size Effects," *Educational Evaluation and Policy Analysis* 21 (2), Summer 1999, pp. 143–163.

43. David G. Savage, "Legislators Like Teachers' Proposal but Balk at the Cost," *Los*

Angeles Times, Nov. 8, 1985, Metro, p. 1; Jennifer Kerr, "State's Education Grades Not All A's, But Improved," *Los Angeles Times,* Dec. 15, 1985; George Neill, "Loss of Funds Cited in Deterioration of California Schools," *Education Week,* Feb. 24, 1982.

44. Tara Weingarten, "Vista Seeks Year-Round Classes to Cut Crowding," *San Diego Union-Tribune,* May 15, 1986, p. B3; J. Harry Jones, "Grossmont Teachers Say Classes Too Big," *San Diego Union-Tribune,* Nov. 13, 1986, p. B5; Kathlyn Russell, "Class-Size Bill Worries Educator," *San Diego Union-Tribune,* Sept. 12, 1987, p. B6; "Early Grades: Actions to Reduce Class Size"; William Snider, "Official Asks Year-Round Schedule for Los Angeles Schools," *Education Week,* Oct. 16, 1985; John L. Mitchell, "Year-Round Schools Have Little Support," *Los Angeles Times,* April 26, 1990, p. J1; Tina Griego, "Schools Bulge Despite Yearlong Schedule," *Los Angeles Times,* April 29, 1990, p. J1; Andrew Horan, "District Combines Grade Levels to Even Class Size," *Orange County Register,* Nov. 5, 1987, Community, p. 3.

45. Michael Smolens, "Teachers Buy TV Ads to Appeal for School Funds," *San Diego Union-Tribune,* Oct. 12, 1987, p. A1; Dan Walters, "Debate over Public Education Is Just Beginning," *San Diego Union-Tribune,* Nov. 15, 1988, p. B9; Richard Lacayo, "Schools Out—Of Cash," *Time,* April 5, 1993, p. 34.

46. "Students, Students Everywhere and Nary a Place to Sit," *Los Angeles Times,* Sept. 5, 1989, Metro, p. 1.

47. Walters, "Debate over Public Education Is Just Beginning"; Douglas Shuit, "Deukmejian Cites Cutting Class Size as Prop. 98 Goal," *Los Angeles Times,* Dec. 4, 1988, p. 3; Douglas Shuit, "Hart, Teacher Groups at Odds over Prop. 98 Funds," *Los Angeles Times,* Dec. 16, 1988, p. 3; William Trombley, "Deukmejian Offers an Extra $97 Million for Schools," *Los Angeles Times,* Aug. 24, 1990, p. 3.

48. Linda Stewart, "OC Pupils Suffer as Class Size Balloons," *Orange County Register,* Feb. 4, 1990, p. A1; William Trombley, "No Simple Answer to Class Size Problem," *Los Angeles Times,* Aug. 26, 1990, p. A3; Adrianne Goodman, "Schools Want Cost-of-Living Boost of 4.76%," *Los Angeles Times,* Aug. 30, 1990, p. B1; Sandy Banks, "Busing Fails to Ease Load on Schools," *Los Angeles Times,* Oct. 23, 1990; Sharon Spivak, "Cost of Cutting Classroom Size Too High: Wilson," *San Diego Union-Tribune,* Sept. 11, 1990, p. A4.

49. Sandy Banks, "Cuts Leave Year-Round Schools in State of Chaos," *Los Angeles Times,* July 20, 1991, p. A1; Denise Hamilton, "Impact of Cuts on Schools Is Uneven," *Los Angeles Times* Aug. 29, 1991, p. J1; Sandy Banks, "School Board OKs Deepest Cuts in a Decade," *Los Angeles Times* Sept. 11, 1991, p. B1; Edmund Newton, "Speaking Volumes: Rowland Teachers Make a Protest Statement about Class Sizes By Keeping Quiet for a Day," *Los Angeles Times,* May 22, 1992, p. B1; William Trombley, "Cuts Imperil School Gains, Honig Warns," *Los Angeles Times* June 11, 1992, p. A3; Diane Seo, "Booked Solid," *Los Angeles Times* Sept. 27, 1992, p. 18; Catherine Gewertz, "Class Sizes Grow,

But at Slower Pace," *Los Angeles Times,* April 30, 1993, p. B1; Kurt Pitzer, "Calabasas; District OKs Cuts, Increased Class Sizes," *Los Angeles Times,* June 24, 1993, p. B3; Nanette Asimov, "New Cuts Merely Continue State Schools' Downward Spiral," *San Francisco Chronicle,* Sept. 3, 1992, p. A21.

50. Teri Sforza, "Weber Wants Smaller Classes in Southeast," *San Diego Union-Tribune,* Nov. 20, 1991, p. B1; Sharon L. Jones, "Trustees Pass Plan to Reduce Class Size," *San Diego Union-Tribune* Feb. 2, 1994, p. B1.

51. Richard Lee Colvin, "Wilson to Propose Cutting Class Size in 1st, 2nd Grades," *Los Angeles Times,* May 19, 1996, p. A1; "Doing More with Less," *California Journal,* June 1, 1997; Marcos Breton, "Plan to Cut Class Sizes Will Stretch System, Educators Say," *Sacramento Bee,* May 20, 1996, p. A1; Brad Hayward, "Class Size Clash May Stall Budget," *Sacramento Bee,* June 30, 1996, p. A1; Brad Hayward, "Wilson Presses Fight on Class Size," *Sacramento Bee,* July 2, 1996, p. A3; Deborah Anderluh, "Shrinking of Class Sizes No Easy Task," *Sacramento Bee,* July 14, 1996, p. A1.

52. "Doing More with Less"; "Does Class Size Matter?," *U.S. News and World Report,* Oct. 13, 1997, p. 22; Greg Lucas, "Potential Flaws in Wilson's Education Plan," *San Francisco Chronicle,* May 20, 1996, p. A1; Jan Ferris, "Smaller Class Sizes Yield Good Results," *Sacramento Bee,* Dec. 6, 1996, p. A1; "No Magic Number for Class Sizes?" *San Diego Union-Tribune,* Sept. 16, 1996, p. A3.

53. Elaine Woo and Dan Morain, "Budget Battle Flares over Bid to Cut Class Size," *Los Angeles Times,* July 2, 1996, p. A3; Daryl Kelley, "Educators Praise State Plan to Reduce Class Sizes," *Los Angeles Times,* July 4, 1996, p. B1; Elaine Woo, "Accord Reached to Cut Class Size in Schools," *Los Angeles Times,* July 4, 1996, p. A1; Hayward, "Wilson Presses Fight on Class Size"; Anderluh, "Shrinking of Class Sizes No Easy Task."

54. "Does Class Size Matter?"; Daryl Kelley, "Educators Praise State Plan to Reduce Class Sizes"; Woo, "Accord Reached to Cut Class Size in Schools"; Richard Lee Colvin, "Districts Race to Build Classroom Space," *Los Angeles Times,* Aug. 5, 1996, p. A3; Amy Pyle, "Principals Try to Clear Hurdles to Cut Class Size," *Los Angeles Times,* Aug. 24, 1996, p. B1; Tina Nguyen, "Future of O.C. Smaller-Class Push in Doubt," *Los Angeles Times,* Oct. 14, 1996, p. A1; Kate Folmar, "Districts to Divide $4.42 Million for Classroom Space," *Los Angeles Times,* Oct. 24, 1996, p. B1; Richard Lee Colvin, "State Says It Can't Cover Class Reduction Costs," *Los Angeles Times,* Oct. 24, 1996, p. A3; Robert C. Johnston, "Calif. Scurries to Find Space for Students," *Education Week,* Oct. 9, 1996; Anderluh, "Shrinking of Class Sizes No Easy Task"; Ryan McCarthy, "School Districts Relish Challenge of Slashing Class Sizes," *Sacramento Bee,* Aug. 8, 1996.

55. Max Vanzi, "Assembly OKs Plan to Make It Easier to Become a Teacher," *Los Angeles Times,* July 12, 1996, p. A3; Amy Pyle, "Rules Eased as Schools Hunt

New Teachers," *Los Angeles Times*, July 27, 1996, p. A1; "Teacher Shortage Causes Districts to Play Hardball," *Los Angeles Times*, Aug. 22, 1996, p. B1; Elaine Herscher, "Quest to Cut Class Size," *San Francisco Chronicle*, Aug. 15, 1996, p. A17; "Does Class Size Matter?"; Lillian Salazar Leopold, "Rush On to Hire More Teachers," *San Diego Union-Tribune*, Aug. 2, 1996, p. A1.

56. Richard Lee Colvin and Amy Pyle, "Many Districts Manage to Meet Class-Size Goals," *Los Angeles Times*, Sept. 3, 1996, p. A1; Colvin, "State Says It Can't Cover Class Reduction Costs."

57. Richard Lee Colvin, "95% of Eligible School Districts to Cut Class Sizes," *Los Angeles Times*, Dec. 3, 1996, p. A3; "Learning Their Lesson," *San Francisco Chronicle*, Feb. 14, 1997, p. A21; Nanette Asimov, "Mixed Marks for Reducing Class Size," *San Francisco Chronicle*, July 9, 1997, p. A11.

58. Amy Pyle, "Schools Get OK to Trim Class Sizes in Kindergarten and Third Grade," *Los Angeles Times*, Aug. 5, 1997, p. B3; Duke Helfand, "Class Cuts May Not Aid Kindergartners," *Los Angeles Times*, Sept. 9, 1997, p. B1; Amy Pyle, "Class-Size Reduction Program Nears Goal," *Los Angeles Times*, Jan. 13, 1998, p. B1; Jan Ferris, "School Districts Struggle to Cut More Class Sizes," *Sacramento Bee*, Aug. 18, 1997, p. A1; Jon Engellenner, "Rookie Teachers Put to Test as Schools Reform," *Sacramento Bee*, June 21, 1998, p. A1; "Smaller Classes Can Mean Unseasoned Teachers," *San Diego Union-Tribune*, April 21, 1998, p. B2.

59. Jon Engellenner, "CSU to Ease Admission to Teacher Training," *Sacramento Bee*, July 16, 1998, p. A4; Nick Anderson, "An Exploration of Ideas, Issues and Trends in Education," *Los Angeles Times*, Nov. 25, 1998, p. B2.

60. Janine DeFao, "Class Size Drops for Many K–3 Students," *Sacramento Bee*, June 23, 1998, p. B1.

61. Tina Nguyen, "O.C. Schools Struggling to Keep Up with Upkeep," *Los Angeles Times*, Aug. 31, 1997, p. A1; Helfand, "Class Cuts May Not Aid Kindergartners"; Peter Schrag, "California: A State Slouching toward Mediocrity," *Sacramento Bee*, Sept. 17, 1997, p. B9; "Classes Packed for Coming Year," *San Francisco Chronicle*, Sept. 8, 1998, p. A1.

62. "Does Class Size Matter?"; Donna Foote, "California's Space Race," *Newsweek*, Aug. 31, 1998, p. 57.

63. Janine DeFao, "Schools Face Cloud of Uncertainty," *Sacramento Bee*, Aug. 25, 1998, p. B1; Dan Smith, "Wilson Blasts Teachers Union, Pushes Prop. 8," *Sacramento Bee*, Sept. 12, 1998, p. A3; Tina Nguyen, "State Budget Extends Class-Size Reductions," *Los Angeles Times*, Oct. 12, 1998, p. B1; Greg Lucas, "Easier Passage of Local School Bonds Asked," *San Francisco Chronicle*, May 6, 1999, p. C18.

64. Tina Nguyen, "$1-Billion Question: Do Smaller Classes Work?," *Los Angeles Times*, March 10, 1997, p. A1; Nick Anderson, "Class-Size Cuts Carry a Price,

Educators Say" *Los Angeles Times*, April 8, 1997, p. B1; Lisa Fernandez, "Smaller Classes Reaped Benefits, Simi Poll Shows," *Los Angeles Times*, Sept. 7, 1997, p. B5; Susan Deemer, "Growth in Skills Attributed to Class Size," *Los Angeles Times*, Oct. 22, 1997, p. B3; Janine DeFao, "Smaller Classes Post Gains on Test," *Sacramento Bee*, Nov. 25, 1997, p. A1; Lori Olszewski, "Oakland Schools Show Big Gains in Early Grades," *San Francisco Chronicle*, Aug. 17, 1998, p. A13.

65. DeFao, "Class Size Drops for Many K–3 Students."

66. Janine DeFao, "Smaller Classes, Higher Scores?" *Sacramento Bee*, Dec. 29, 1998, p. B1; Lynn Olson, "Slight Gains Found from Calif. Class-Size Program," *Education Week*, June 23, 1999.

67. Cheryl Gamble, "Fla. Class-Size Mandate Sends Districts Scurrying," *Education Week*, Oct. 11, 1995.

68. UPI, May 24, 1989, Regional News, Arizona-Nevada; UPI, June 29, 1989, Regional News, Arizona-Nevada; Steve Friess, "Governor Details Education Proposal," *Las Vegas Review-Journal*, Jan. 15, 1997, p. A1.

69. Natalie Patton, "Class-Size Reduction Still a Miller Priority," *Las Vegas Review-Journal*, Jan. 24, 1997, p. A8; "Smaller Classes, Revisited," *Las Vegas Review-Journal*, Feb. 5, 1997, p. B10; "Flunking the Test," *Las Vegas Review-Journal*, May 1, 1997, p. B8; Sean Whaley, "Democrats Ask Guinn to Protect Public Education," *Las Vegas Review-Journal*, Jan. 14, 1999, p. B4; Jan Ferris, "Smaller Classes Really Better?" *Sacramento Bee*, March 24, 1997, p. A1.

70. Alex Molnar et al., "Evaluating the SAGE Program: A Pilot Program in Targeted Pupil-Teacher Reduction in Wisconsin," *Educational Evaluation and Policy Analysis* 21 (2), Summer 1999, pp. 165–177; *Education Week*, Oct. 18, 2000; J. R. S. Owczarski, "District Seeks State Aid," *Milwaukee Journal Sentinel*, Nov. 23, 1995, Neighbors, p. 3; Daynel L. Hooker, "MPS Launches Program to Reduce Class Sizes," *Milwaukee Journal Sentinel*, Sept. 2, 1996, p. 4; Curtis Lawrence, "Fighting to Stay Small," *Milwaukee Journal Sentinel*, May 7, 1997, p. 1; Joe Williams, "Study Touts Class-Size Program," *Milwaukee Journal Sentinel* Dec. 9, 1997, p. 1; Joe Williams, "MPS to Get $1 Million from Program to Reduce Class Size," *Milwaukee Journal Sentinel* Oct. 2, 1998, p. 1; "Reducing Class Size Increases Achievement," *School Planning and Management*, March, 1998, p. 20; Rochelle L. Stanfield, "The Value of Small Classes," *National Journal*, March 7, 1998, p. 508.

71. Betsy White, "State Expels 15 Who Check Limits on Size of Classes," *Atlanta Journal and Constitution*, Sept. 6, 1991, p. C3; Robert Anthony Watts, "DeKalb School Board Cuts Class Size," *Atlanta Journal and Constitution* Nov. 12, 1991, p. C1.

72. Diane R. Stepp, "Schrenko Plan to Reduce Class Size Too Costly, Schools Say," *Atlanta Journal and Constitution*, Aug. 25, 1995, p. C3.

73. John F. Harris, "Terry Offers Plan for Poor Schools," *Washington Post*, Sept. 8,

1993, p. B4; Peter Baker, "Va. Votes School Disparity Bill," *Washington Post,* Feb. 25, 1994, p. C5; Joel Turner, "Allen Set to Increase Funding for Schools," *Roanoke Times & World News,* Dec. 27, 1995, p. C1.

74. Kent Jenkins, Jr., "Class Size: A Cutting Edge Issue?" *U.S. News and World Report,* Nov. 17, 1997, p. 5; Ledyard King, "Nominees Stand Grades Apart on Education," *Roanoke Times & World News,* Oct. 26, 1997, p. A1; Ledyard King, "Crowded, Decaying Schools Get Little Attention from Candidates," *Virginian-Pilot,* Oct. 28, 1997, p. A1; Ledyard King, "Adding Teachers Is the Answer, Gilmore Says," *Virginian-Pilot,* July 22, 1998, p. B2.

75. Nick Chiles, "Thousands of Teachers Sick of Crowded Classes," *Newsday,* Oct. 16, 1991, p. 20; Edna Negron, "Coping with Cuts," *Newsday,* Aug. 12, 1994, p. A8; Joseph Berger, "Shift of Funds from Schools Is Protested," *New York Times,* April 29, 1992, p. B1; Maria Newman, "Detailing Price of Cuts, Cortines Proposes Larger Class Sizes," *New York Times* July 14, 1995, p. B1; Michael Cooper, "Schools' Bind: More Pupils, Less Money," *New York Times,* Sept. 10, 1995, Section 13, p. 13; Kristen King, "Schools Mull Bigger Classes," *New York Daily News,* July 19, 1995, Suburban, p. 1.

76. "Schools Split at Seams, Gyms & Bathrooms Used as Classrooms," *New York Daily News,* Sept. 6, 1996, p. 7; Vivian S. Toy, "New York's Schools Are Planning a Test of All-Year Classes," *New York Times,* Sept. 18, 1996, p. A1; Jacques Steinberg, "Survey Suggests Class Sizes Exceed the Official Averages," *New York Times,* April 14, 1997, p. B1; Romesh Ratnesar, "Class Size Warfare," *Time,* Oct. 6, 1997, p. 85; "Does Class Size Matter?"

77. Somini Sengupta, "Albany School Aid Largesse Faces Harsh Realities in City," *New York Times,* Aug. 1, 1997, p. A1; Joanne Wasserman, "Jumbo Classes Found by Study, Many Have 30 Kids, or More" *New York Daily News,* Aug. 27, 1998, p. 5; Nancie L. Katz, "Poor Schools First for Smaller Classes," *Daily News,* Oct. 6, 1998, p. 21.

78. Lizabeth Hall, "Boar Approves Hiring 2 Elementary Teachers," *Hartford Courant,* June 14, 1994, p. D4; Cindy Rodriguez, "Town to Add Full-Time Teacher to Cut Second-Grade Class Sizes," *Hartford Courant* Sept. 8, 1994, p. B3; Fran Silverman, "Plainville Students Given Option to Move to Smaller Class Size," *Hartford Courant* Sept. 25, 1995, p. B1.

79. Finn, *Class Size and Students at Risk,* pp. 1–31.

80. David J. Hoff, "Clinton Seeks Teacher Hires, Smaller Classes," *Education Week,* Feb. 4, 1998; David J. Hoff, "Clinton's 100,000-Teacher Plan Faces Hurdles," *Education Week,* Feb. 4, 1998; Thomas Toch, "Stealing Republican Thunder," *U.S. News and World Report,* Feb. 9, 1998, p. 61; "This Is Job for States," *USA Today,* Jan. 28, 1998, p. 12A.

81. Barb Albert, "Indiana Mixed on Teacher Initiative," *Indianapolis Star,* April 5, 1998, p. B1; Barb Albert, "Fed Money to Hire Teachers Carries Risks," *Indianapolis Star,* Nov. 2, 1998, p. A1; Anemona Hartocollis, "Educators Say

Clinton's Plan on Class Size Faces Problems," *New York Times,* Jan. 29, 1998, p. A1; "This Is Job for States"; *Los Angeles Times,* April 6, 1999.

82. Stanfield, "Value of Smaller Classes"; Rochelle L. Stanfield, "Education Wars," *National Journal,* March 7, 1998, p. 506; David Young, "Bricks and Mortar Do Matter," *South Bend Tribune,* June 5, 1998, p. 9; Janet Hook, "$500-Billion Budget Accord Is Reached," *Los Angeles Times,* Oct. 16, 1998, p. A1.

83. Chester E. Finn, Jr., and Michael J. Petrilli, "The Elixir of Class Size," *Weekly Standard,* March 9, 1998, p. 16.

84. Gil Klein, "Funds Would Add 525 State Teachers," *Richmond Times,* Oct. 17, 1998, p. B6; Finn, Jr., and Petrilli, "Elixir of Class Size"; "Cutting Class Sizes," *Indianapolis Star,* Nov. 16, 1998, p. A10.

85. "Shrinking Classes," *Sacramento Bee,* Feb. 11, 1998, p. B6.

86. Glen Martin, "Study Finds Toxic Air in Portable Classrooms," *San Francisco Chronicle,* May 27, 1999, p. A19; Martha L. Willman, "Study Cites Schoolroom Toxin Risks," *Los Angeles Times,* May 28, 1999, p. B1.

4. Is Social Promotion a Problem?

1. "A Drive to Make High-School Diplomas Mean Something," *U.S. News and World Report,* June 21, 1976, p. 47; "Holding Students Back," *New York Times,* April 22, 1998, p. A26; Nick Anderson, "Anti-'Social Promotion' Bills Signed," *Los Angeles Times,* Sept. 24, 1998, p. A3; "End Routine Social Promotion," *Houston Chronicle,* April 15, 1999, p. A34.

2. "A Drive to Make High-School Diplomas Mean Something"; "Ending Social Promotion," *Sacramento Bee,* Nov. 6, 1997, p. B6; "Hey, Crew, Get a Move On," *New York Daily News,* March 11, 1998, p. 32.

3. "Free Pass Fails Kids," *USA Today,* Feb. 18, 1998, p. A14; "Retaining Kids No Answer," ibid.

4. Carl F. Kaestle, *Pillars of the Republic: Common Schools and American Society, 1780–1860* (New York: Hill and Wang, 1983), pp. 132–133; David B. Tyack, *The One Best System: A History of American Urban Education* (Cambridge, Mass.: Harvard University Press, 1974), pp. 44–46; Michael B. Katz, *Reconstructing American Education* (Cambridge, Mass.: Harvard University Press, 1987), pp. 44–45.

5. Reed Ueda, *Avenues to Adulthood: The Origins of the High School and Social Mobility in an American Suburb* (New York: Cambridge University Press, 1987, p. 79).

6. Joel Perlmann, *Ethnic Differences: Schooling and Social Structure among the Irish, Italians, Jews and Blacks in an American City, 1880–1935* (New York: Cambridge University Press, 1988), pp. 16–17; Tyack, *One Best System,* pp. 199–204; Paul Davis Chapman, *Schools as Sorters: Lewis M. Terman, Ap-*

plied Psychology, and the Intelligence Testing Movement, 1890–1930 (New York: New York University Press, 1988), pp. 44–45; Richard Rothstein, "Where Is Lake Wobegon, Anyway? Social Rather than Merit Promotions of Students to Higher Grades," *Phi Delta Kappan,* Nov. 1998, p. 195.

7. Perlmann, *Ethnic Differences,* pp. 95, 176–181.
8. Chapman, *Schools as Sorters,* pp. 24–27.
9. Rothstein, "Where Is Lake Wobegon, Anyway?"
10. "A Drive to Make High-School Diplomas Mean Something."
11. Ibid.
12. Tom Mirga, "In Jacksonville's Integrated Schools, The Quest for Excellence Paid Off," *Education Week,* Sept. 21, 1981.
13. Bart Barnes, "Making a High School Diploma Mean Something," *Washington Post,* May 15, 1977, p. A1.
14. Ibid.
15. Lawrence Feinberg, "Rubber Diplomas?; Va. Superintendent Loses Fight against Social Promotions," *Washington Post,* Feb. 16, 1982, p. C1.
16. Lynn Olson, "Is Retention without Remediation Punishment?" *Education Week,* June 12, 1985; "Making School Promotions Count," *Washington Post,* March 29, 1980, p. A12; Judith Valente, "D.C. School Competency Plan Voted," *Washington Post,* April 29, 1980, p. C1; Kenneth Bredemeier, "D.C. Outlines New Rules on Student Promotions," *Washington Post,* June 1, 1980, p. B1.
17. "Happy Ending to Social Promotions," *Washington Post,* June 8, 1981, p. A14; Feinberg, "Rubber Diplomas?"; "Making the Grade," *Washington Post,* May 30, 1985, p. A20.
18. Sally Reed, "Doubts on Ending 'Social Promotion,'" *New York Times,* Nov. 16, 1980, Section 12, p. 27; Gene I. Maeroff, "$63 Million Aimed at Programs for Students Who Are Left Back," *New York Times,* Dec. 16, 1980, p. C1; Thomas Toch, "'Promotion Gates' Are Raising Both Standards and Concerns," *Education Week,* Sept. 15, 1982; Ernest R. House, "Policy Implications of Retention Research," in Lorrie A. Shepard and Mary Lee Smith, eds., *Flunking Grades: Research and Policies on Retention* (New York: Falmer Press, 1989), pp. 202–203.
19. "Exit from a Dead End?" *New York Times,* March 20, 1983, Section 4, p. 6; Joyce Purnick, "Alvarado to Ease Promotion Policy," *New York Times,* May 11, 1983, p. A1; Hope Aldrich, "New N.Y.C. Chancellor Reverses Promotion Policy," *Education Week,* May 18, 1983; Thomas Toch, "Making the Grade Harder," *U.S. News and World Report,* Oct. 5, 1998, p. 59; House, "Policy Implications of Retention Research," p. 203.
20. House, "Policy Implications of Retention Research," pp. 202–204; Ernest R. House, "Flunking Students Is No Cure-All," *New York Times,* Jan. 30, 1999, p. A13.
21. "A Drive to Make High School Diplomas Mean Something."

22. Ibid.
23. Lorrie A. Shepard and Mary Lee Smith, "Synthesis of Research on Grade Retention," *Educational Leadership,* May 1990, pp. 84–87; Cindy Currence, "Making the Grade: A Kindergarten Summer School in Minneapolis," *Education Week,* Aug. 22, 1984.
24. C. Thomas Holmes and Kenneth M. Matthews, "The Effects of Nonpromotion on Elementary and Junior High School Pupils: A Meta-Analysis," *Review of Educational Research* 54 (2), Summer 1984, pp. 225–228.
25. Ibid., pp. 225–232.
26. C. Thomas Holmes, "Grade Level Retention Effects: A Meta-Analysis of Research Studies," in Shepard and Smith, eds., *Flunking Grades,* pp. 16–28.
27. James B. Grissom and Lorrie A. Shepard, "Repeating and Dropping Out of School," in Shepard and Smith, eds., *Flunking Grades,* pp. 34–61; Shepard and Smith, "Synthesis of Research on Grade Retention," p. 85.
28. House, "Policy Implications of Retention Research," p. 204.
29. "Effortless Rise," *Economist,* Feb. 10, 1996, p. 33; Patricia King, "Politics of Promotion," *Newsweek,* June 15, 1998, p. 27; "End Social Promotion," *Atlanta Journal and Constitution,* Feb. 9, 1998, p. A8.
30. "Effortless Rise"; "Politics of Promotion"; Karen Kelly, "Retention vs. Social Promotion: Schools Search for Alternatives," *Harvard Education Letter,* Jan./Feb. 1999, p. 1.
31. "Effortless Rise"; "Politics of Promotion."
32. Karl L. Alexander, Doris R. Entwisle, and Susan L. Dauber, *On the Success of Failure: A Reassessment of the Effects of Retention in the Primary Grades* (New York: Cambridge University Press, 1994).
33. Ibid., pp. 17–19, 97.
34. Ibid., pp. 156–187.
35. Ibid., pp. 31–45, 78–110, 131.
36. Ibid., p. 20.
37. Debra Viadero, "Ending Social Promotion," *Education Week,* March 15, 2000.
38. "Politics of Promotion."
39. Toch, "Making the Grade Harder"; Caroline Hendrie, "Summer School Booms in Chicago," *Education Week,* Aug. 7, 1996; Rosalind Rossi, "Thousands Face Summer School," *Chicago Sun-Times,* March 28, 1996, p. 9; Rosalind Rossi, "Some Kids Are Still Not Making the Grade," *Chicago Sun-Times,* Aug. 13, 1998, p. 10; Ronald Brownstein, "Clinton Calls for End to 'Social Promotion' in Schools," *Los Angeles Times,* Oct. 29, 1997, p. A7; Kent Fischer, "Chicago Schools Take a Stand for 'Old-Fashioned' Standards," *St. Petersburg Times,* May 17, 1998, p. A12.
40. Toch, "Making the Grade Harder"; Rob Hotakainen, "In Other States; You Don't Work, You Don't Pass," *Star Tribune,* Jan. 19, 1998, p. A7; Rossi, "Some Kids are Still Not Making the Grade."

41. Toch, "Making the Grade Harder"; Fischer, "Chicago Schools Take a Stand for 'Old-Fashioned' Standards"; Melanie Markley, "New HISD Rules Designed to End Social Promotions," *Houston Chronicle,* July 26, 1998, p. A1.

42. Hotakainen, "In Other States; You Don't Work, You Don't Pass."

43. "Learn a Lesson From Other Cities," *New York Daily News,* April 20, 1998, p. 28; Fischer, "Chicago Schools Take a Stand for 'Old-Fashioned' Standards"; Debra Viadero, "OCR Probing Social Promotion in Chicago," *Education Week,* Dec. 8, 1999; Debra Viadero, "Study Looks at Retention Policy in Chicago," *Education Week,* Jan. 12, 2000.

44. John Ritter, "When Kids Don't Make the Grade," *USA Today,* Aug. 18, 1997, p. A3.

45. Diane R. Stepp, "School System Goes Back to Basics," *Atlanta Journal and Constitution,* Dec. 31, 1995, p. 1; "End Social Promotion," *Atlanta Journal and Constitution,* Feb. 9, 1998, p. A8; Doug Cumming, "Promotion Policies Low in Esteem," *Atlanta Journal and Constitution,* Feb. 25, 1999, p. A1; Patti Puckett, "Getting Students Up to Speed," *Atlanta Journal and Constitution,* Feb. 25, 1999, p. J1; Patti Puckett, "Focus on Making the Grade," *Atlanta Journal and Constitution,* March 2, 1999, p. B1.

46. "Schools Pass Kids—and the Buck," *Daily News,* June 29, 1997, p. 54; "Hey, Crew, Get a Move On."

47. Robert C. Johnston, "Texas Governor Has Social Promotions in His Sights," *Education Week,* Feb. 11, 1998; Caroline Hendrie, "Plans in Houston and N.Y.C. Would Tighten Promotion Rules," *Education Week,* April 29, 1998; Jeff Archer, "Approach High-Stakes Assessments with Caution, NRC Report Urges," *Education Week,* Sept. 9, 1998; Melanie Markley, "Governor Details Social Promotion Plan in Houston," *Houston Chronicle,* Jan. 15, 1998; Kathy Walt, "Non-Readers Shouldn't Go to Fourth Grade," *Houston Chronicle,* March 9, 1998, p. A13.

48. "Bush Seeks Funds for Early Reading Program to End Social Promotions," *Houston Chronicle,* Jan. 28, 1998, p. A23; Kathy Walt, "Governor Launches Quest to Quash Social Promotions in Texas Schools," *Houston Chronicle,* Jan. 26, 1999, p. A13; "Holding Back Kids in School Is Ill-Advised, Experts Warn," *Houston Chronicle,* Jan. 31, 1999, State, p. 1; Kathy Walt, "Bush Backs TAAS Appeals Process," *Houston Chronicle,* Jan. 31, 1999, State, p. 3.

49. Scott Baldauf, "Bad Scores? Sure, But No Flunking," *Christian Science Monitor,* June 10, 1998, p. 1; Markley, "New HISD Rules Designed to End Social Promotions"; Robert C. Johnston, "Waco Gets Tough with Summer School Effort," *Education Week,* Aug. 5, 1998.

50. "Social Promotion," *Sacramento Bee,* Sept. 8, 1998, p. B6; Anderson, "Anti-'Social Promotion' Bills Signed"; Nanette Asimov, "Why New Student-Promotion Policy May Flunk Out," *San Francisco Chronicle,* Nov. 24, 1998, p. A1.

51. Anne-Marie O'Connor, "Boyle Heights School in Eye of Social Promotion

Storm," *Los Angeles Times,* Jan. 27, 1999, p. A1; Kerry A. White, "L.A. to Ease Requirements for Promotion," *Education Week,* Dec. 15, 1999.

52. Alison Mitchell, "Clinton Urges State Action on Education," *New York Times,* March 28, 1996, p. B10; Brownstein, "Clinton Calls for End to 'Social Promotion'"; Ronald Brownstein, "Both Parties Take Similar Paths as Nation Travels Road to Innovation," *Los Angeles Times,* March 8, 1999, p. A5; "Clinton Plan Sets the Right Tone," *Star Tribune,* Jan. 21, 1999, p. A16; Marjorie Coeyman, "Repeating a Grade Gains Favor in Schools," *Christian Science Monitor,* April 6, 1999, Features section.

53. Rosalind Rossi, "Getting Students on Track," *Chicago Sun-Times,* Jan. 24, 1999, p. 12.

54. Ethan Bronner, "Union Chief Criticizes Pupil Promotion Policy," *New York Times,* Sept. 10, 1997, p. A21; Gayle Fallon, "Failing Texas Children," *Houston Chronicle,* Jan. 11, 1998, Outlook, p. 1.

55. Rothstein, "Where Is Lake Wobegon, Anyway?"

56. Brownstein, "Clinton Calls for an End to 'Social Promotion'"; John W. Gonzalez, "Minority Leaders Fear Rise in Dropouts under Bush Plan," *Houston Chronicle,* Feb. 27, 1999, p. A35.

57. "Retaining Kids No Answer"; Archer, "Approach High-Stakes Assessments with Caution."

58. Gary Hart, "Ending Social Promotion: Panacea or Fiasco?" *Sacramento Bee,* March 8, 1998, p. FO2; Richard Whitmire, "Report: Tests Shouldn't Be Sole Yardstick in Promoting Students," *Sacramento Bee,* Sept. 4, 1998, p. A11.

59. Lori Olszewski, "Raising Standards for Students," *San Francisco Chronicle,* Dec. 18, 1997, p. A22; Louis Sahagun, "L.A. School District Curtails Plan to End Social Promotions," *Los Angeles Times,* April 17, 1999, p. A1.

60. Robert M. Hauser, "What If We Ended Social Promotion?" *Education Week,* April 7, 1999.

61. Lorrie A. Shepard, "Repeating a Grade is Demoralizing, Doesn't Improve Achievement," *Cleveland Plain Dealer,* Feb. 8, 1999, p. B9; Karl Alexander, "Does Retention Help Students? Kids Benefit from the Extra Year," *Cleveland Plain Dealer,* Feb. 8, 1999, p. B9.

62. Millicent Lawton, "AFT Report Assails Schools Promotion, Retention Policies," *Education Week,* Sept. 17, 1997.

5. Does More Money Make Schools Better?

The second epigraph is a quotation from Rob Greenwald, Larry V. Hedges, and Richard D. Laine, "Interpreting Research on School Resources and Student Achievement: A Rejoinder to Hanushek," *Review of Educational Research* 66 (3), Fall 1996, pp. 411–416.

1. James W. Guthrie, "School Finance: Fifty Years of Expansion," *Future of Children* 7 (3), Winter 1997, pp. 24–29.

2. Donna L. Terman and Richard E. Behrman, "Financing Schools: Analysis and Recommendations," *Future of Children* 7 (3), Winter 1997, pp. 8–9.

3. Paul A. Minorini and Stephen D. Sugarman, "School Finance Litigation in the Name of Educational Equity: Its Evolution, Impact, and Future," in Helen F. Ladd, Rosemary Chalk, and Janet S. Hansen, eds., *Equity and Adequacy in Education Finance: Issues and Perspectives* (Washington, D.C.: National Academy Press, 1999), pp. 34–35.

4. Richard A. Rossmiller, "Federal Funds: A Shifting Balance?" in Julie K. Underwood and Deborah A. Verstegen, eds., *The Impact of Litigation and Legislation on Public School Finance: Adequacy, Equity, and Excellence* (New York: Harper & Row, 1990), pp. 3–4.

5. David Nasaw, *Schooled to Order: A Social History of Public Schooling in the United States* (New York: Oxford University Press, 1979), pp. 50–59; David Tyack and Elizabeth Hansot, *Learning Together: A History of Coeducation in American Public Schools* (New Haven: Yale University Press, 1990), p. 57.

6. Reed Ueda, *Avenues to Adulthood: The Origins of the High School and Social Mobility in an American Suburb* (New York: Cambridge University Press, 1987), p. 37; Tyack and Hansot, *Learning Together,* pp. 60–85.

7. John G. Augenblick, John L. Myers, and Amy Berk Anderson, "Equity and Adequacy in School Funding," *Future of Children* 7 (3), Winter 1997, p. 65; Terman and Behrman, "Financing Schools," p. 6.

8. Joel Perlmann, *Ethnic Differences: Schooling and Social Structure among the Irish, Italians, Jews and Blacks in an American City, 1880–1935* (New York: Cambridge University Press, 1988), pp. 17–18.

9. David B. Tyack, *The One Best System: A History of American Urban Education* (Cambridge, Mass.: Harvard University Press, 1974), pp. 272–275; James D. Anderson, *Education of Blacks in the South, 1860–1935* (Chapel Hill: University of North Carolina Press, 1988).

10. Guthrie, "School Finance," pp. 25–34; Tyack, *One Best System,* pp. 274–276.

11. Diane Ravitch, *The Troubled Crusade: American Education, 1945–1980* (New York: Basic Books, 1983), pp. 4–42.

12. Tyack, *One Best System,* pp. 274–276; Rossmiller, "Federal Funds," pp. 8–21; Guthrie, "School Finance," pp. 26–29.

13. Augenblick, Myers, and Anderson, "Equity and Adequacy in School Funding," pp. 65–66; Terman and Behrman, "Financing Schools," pp. 8–11.

14. James S. Coleman et al., *Equality of Educational Opportunity,* U.S. Department of Health, Education, and Welfare (Washington, D.C.: U.S. Government Printing Office, 1966), pp. 3–7.

15. Ibid., pp. 290–325.

16. Frederick Mosteller and Daniel P. Moynihan, eds., *On Equality of Educational Opportunity* (New York: Vintage Books, 1972), contains one of the most interesting arrays of responses to the Coleman Report.

17. Helen F. Ladd and Janet S. Hansen, eds., *Making Money Matter: Financing America's Schools.* (Washington, D.C.: National Academy Press, 1999), pp. 71–72.

18. William E. Sparkman, "School Finance Challenges in State Courts," in Underwood and Verstegen, eds., *Impact of Litigation and Legislation,* pp. 193–197.

19. Julie K. Underwood and Deborah A. Verstegen, "School Finance Challenges in Federal Courts: Changing Equal Protection Analysis," in Underwood and Verstegen, eds., *Impact of Litigation and Legislation,* pp. 177–189.

20. Richard F. Elmore and Milbrey Wallin McLaughlin, *Reform and Retrenchment: The Politics of California School Finance Reform* (Cambridge: Ballinger Publishing Company, 1982), pp. 3–38. The authors point out that "judicially initiated reform" that orders legislatures to fix a problem usually means that the group that created and maintained a problem is then being told to fix it (see p. 18).

21. Ibid., pp. 35–39.

22. Ibid., pp. 32–42.

23. *Serrano v. Priest* 487 P.2d 1241 (1971); James Gordon Ward, "Implementation and Monitoring of Judicial Mandates: An Interpretive Analysis," in Underwood and Verstegen, eds., *Impact of Litigation and Legislation,* p. 236; Elmore and McLaughlin, *Reform and Retrenchment,* pp. 6, 35–51.

24. *Serrano v. Priest* 557 P.2d 929 (1976); Elmore and McLaughlin, *Reform and Retrenchment,* pp. 51–167; Ward, "Implementation and Monitoring of Judicial Mandates," pp. 236–239.

25. Elmore and McLaughlin, *Reform and Retrenchment,* pp. 51–167; Ward, "Implementation and Monitoring of Judicial Mandates," pp. 236–239.

26. Ward, "Implementation and Monitoring of Judicial Mandates," pp. 236–239; Elmore and McLaughlin, *Reform and Retrenchment,* pp. 169–190; Minorini and Sugarman, "School Finance Litigation in the Name of Educational Equity," pp. 48–50.

27. Philip Hager, "High Court Will Review Ruling on School Spending," *Los Angeles Times,* Sept. 3, 1986, p. 3; William N. Evans, Sheila E. Murray, and Robert M. Schwab, "The Impact of Court-Mandated School Finance Reform," in Ladd, Chalk, and Hansen, eds., *Equity and Adequacy in Education Finance,* pp. 74–75.

28. *San Antonio Independent School District v. Rodriguez* 93 S. Ct. 1278 (1973); Minorini and Sugarman, "School Finance Litigation in the Name of Educational Equity," p. 39; Underwood and Verstegen, "School Finance Challenges in Federal Courts," pp. 177–178; Elmore and McLaughlin, *Reform and Retrenchment,* pp. 51–60.

29. *San Antonio Independent School District v. Rodriguez* (1973); Underwood and Verstegen, "School Finance Challenges in Federal Courts," pp. 177–178; Elmore and McLaughlin, *Reform and Retrenchment,* pp. 51–60.

30. Underwood and Verstegen, "School Finance Challenges in Federal Courts," pp. 177–185; Terman and Behrman, "Financing Schools," p. 6; Minorini and Sugarman, "School Finance Litigation in the Name of Educational Equity," pp. 39–40.

31. Underwood and Verstegen, "School Finance Challenges in Federal Courts," pp. 179–183; Sparkman, "School Finance Challenges in State Courts," p. 194.

32. Sparkman, "School Finance Challenges in State Courts," pp. 198–202; National Research Council, *Making Money Matter,* pp. 78–80.

33. Richard G. Salmon and M. David Alexander, "State Legislative Responses," in Underwood and Verstegen, eds., *Impact of Litigation and Legislation,* pp. 252–253.

34. Salmon and Alexander, "State Legislative Responses," pp. 255–263.

35. William E. Camp, David C. Thompson, and John A. Crain, "Within-District Equity: Desegregation and Microeconomic Analysis," in Underwood and Verstegen, eds., *Impact of Litigation and Legislation,* pp. 280–281.

36. Eric A. Hanushek, "Throwing Money at Schools," *Journal of Policy Analysis and Management* 1 (1), 1981, pp. 19–22.

37. Ibid., pp. 22–28.

38. Ibid., p. 26.

39. Hanushek, "Throwing Money at Schools," pp. 26–32; Morton Hunt, *How Science Takes Stock: The Story of Meta-Analysis* (New York: Russell Sage Foundation, 1997), p. 54.

40. Eric A. Hanushek, "The Impact of Differential Expenditures on School Performance," *Educational Researcher* 18 (4), May 1989, pp. 45–50; italics in the original.

41. Hunt, *How Science Takes Stock,* p. 55.

42. Ibid., p. 60.

43. Larry V. Hedges, Richard D. Laine, and Rob Greenwald, "Does Money Matter? A Meta-Analysis of Studies of the Effects of Differential School Inputs on Student Outcomes," *Educational Researcher* 23 (3), April 1994, pp. 5–6.

44. Ibid., pp. 5–13.

45. Eric A. Hanushek, "Money Might Matter Somewhere: A Response to Hedges, Laine, and Greenwald," in *Educational Researcher* 23 (4), May 1994, pp. 5–8.

46. Larry V. Hedges, Richard D. Laine, and Rob Greenwald, "Money Does Matter Somewhere: A Reply to Hanushek," *Educational Researcher* 23 (4), May 1994, pp. 9–10.

47. Rob Greenwald, Larry V. Hedges, and Richard D. Laine, "The Effect of School Resources on Student Achievement," *Review of Educational Research* 66 (3), Fall 1996, pp. 361–386.

48. Eric A. Hanushek, "A More Complete Picture of School Resource Policies," *Review of Educational Research* 66 (3), Fall 1996, pp. 397–408.

49. Richard J. Light and David B. Pillemer, *Summing Up: The Science of Reviewing Research* (Cambridge, Mass.: Harvard University Press, 1984), pp. 4, 74–75.

50. Some of Hanushek's arguments seem disingenuous and have a heavily political tone. For example, his misleading description of school finance lawsuits in his articles in the 1980s is something of a straw man. He claims that the plaintiffs in these court cases, some of which were described earlier in this chapter, believe that more money will automatically improve schools. But school finance cases are based on the belief that schools in disadvantaged school districts should receive the same kinds of resources that middle-class school districts do; funding is a necessary prerequisite to improvement in such schools, and an issue of fairness, not a solution by itself.

51. Sparkman, "School Finance Challenges in State Courts," p. 211; Ward, "Implementation and Monitoring of Judicial Mandates," pp. 239–240.

52. Sparkman, "School Finance Challenges in State Courts," p. 211; Minorini and Sugarman, "School Finance Litigation in the Name of Educational Equity," pp. 50–51; Ward, "Implementation and Monitoring of Judicial Mandates," pp. 239–243.

53. Ward, "Implementation and Monitoring of Judicial Mandates," pp. 239–243; Priscilla Van Tassell, "Two Suits Attack Constitutionality of Financing for Schools," *New York Times,* Dec. 27, 1981, Section 11, p. 1.

54. Ward, "Implementation and Monitoring of Judicial Mandates," pp. 242–243; *Abbott v. Burke* 477 A.2d 1278 (1984); Joan Verdon, "Poor Schools versus Rich; A Historic Lawsuit to Even Up the Score," *Record,* Jan. 2, 1987, p. B1; Priscilla Van Tassell, "School Financing Challenged at Trial," *New York Times,* Oct. 5, 1986, Section 11, p. 1; *Abbott v. Burke* 495 A.2d 376 (1985); *Abbott v. Burke* 575 A.2d 359 (1990).

55. *Abbott v. Burke* (1990); Verdon, "Poor Schools versus Rich"; Van Tassell, "School Financing Challenged at Trial"; Debra H. Dawahare, "Kentucky May Hold Answer to What Lies Ahead."

56. Kathleen Bird, "Abbott Revisited: It's Déjà Vu All Over Again," *New Jersey Law Journal,* June 20, 1991, p. 4; Kathleen Bird, "Adversary's Expert Boosts School-Funding Plaintiffs," *New Jersey Law Journal,* July 13, 1992, p. 3; Jennifer P. Heimmel, "State's Quality Education Act Is Declared Unconstitutional," *New Jersey Lawyer,* Aug. 1, 1994, p. 19; Jennifer P. Heimmel and E. E. Mazier, "CEIFA is Held Unconstitutional as to Special Needs Districts," *New Jersey Lawyer,* May 19, 1997, p. 57; *Abbott v. Burke* 643 A.2d 575 (1994).

57. *Abbott v. Burke* 693 A.2d 417 (1997); Ronald Smothers, "Forcing Change in Aid to Schools," *New York Times,* May 17, 1997, p. 21; Heimmel and Mazier, "CEIFA Is Held Unconstitutional"; Molly J. Liskow, "Whole-School Reform

Ordered for NJ Special Needs Districts," *New Jersey Lawyer,* May 25, 1998, p. 48; Padraic Cassidy, "School-Funding Dispute Flares Up Anew, This Time over Regulations," *New Jersey Law Journal,* Aug. 30, 1999, p. 5; Cheryl Winokur, "Court Gives Its Final Word in Abbott, Adopting State Reform Plan," *New Jersey Law Journal,* May 25, 1998, p. 5.

58. Augenblick, Myers, and Anderson, "Equity and Adequacy in School Funding," pp. 67–68.

59. *Rose v. Council for Better Education, Inc.,* 790 S.W. 2d 186; Jacob E. Adams, "School Finance Policy and Students' Opportunities to Learn: Kentucky's Experience," *Future of Children* 7 (3), Winter 1997, p. 81.

60. Adams, "School Finance Policy and Students' Opportunities to Learn," pp. 79–87.

61. Minorini and Sugarman, "School Finance Litigation in the Name of Educational Equity," pp. 59–60.

62. Laura Laughlin, "State Pursues Fairer School Funding Plan," *Phoenix Gazette,* Sept. 23, 1994, p. A1.

63. Minorini and Sugarman, "School Finance Litigation in the Name of Educational Equity," pp. 52–53; Tony Marcano, "Suit by Schools Seeks Balance in State Funding," *Los Angeles Times,* Nov. 29, 1990, p. A3; Catherine Gewertz, "127 School Districts Suing to Overhaul State Funding System," *Los Angeles Times,* April 8, 1992, p. A3; "Funding Gaps between Districts Still Exist, Despite Court Decision," *Fresno Bee,* April 15, 1994, p. A1.

64. Minorini and Sugarman, "School Finance Litigation in the Name of Educational Equity," p. 62.

65. Terman and Behrman, "Financing Schools," p. 9; Minorini and Sugarman, "School Finance Litigation in the Name of Educational Equity," p. 62.

66. Terman and Behrman, "Financing Schools," p. 14; Penny L. Howell and Barbara B. Miller, "Sources of Funding for Schools," *Future of Children* 7 (3), Winter 1997, pp. 43–45; *Roosevelt Elementary School District No. 66 v. Bishop,* 877 P.2d 806 (1994); Ed Foster, "State's School Funding Voided," *Arizona Republic,* July 22, 1994, p. A1; Hal Mattern, "School Aid Plan Called 'Repackage,'" *Arizona Republic,* Feb. 19, 1998, p. B1.

67. Minorini and Sugarman, "School Finance Litigation in the Name of Educational Equity," p. 35.

68. Guthrie, "School Finance," p. 35; Evans, Murray, and Schwab, "Impact of Court-Mandated School Finance Reform," pp. 77–82; Augenblick, Myers, and Anderson, "Equity and Adequacy in School Funding," p. 68.

69. Terman and Behrman, "Financing Schools," p. 7.

70. Minorini and Sugarman, "School Finance Litigation in the Name of Educational Equity," p. 62.

71. Ibid., p. 63.

Conclusion

1. Richard F. Elmore and Milbrey Wallin McLaughlin, *Reform and Retrenchment: The Politics of California School Finance Reform* (Cambridge, Mass.: Ballinger Publishing Co., 1982), p. 2.
2. Maris A. Vinovskis, "The Federal Role in Educational Research and Development," in *Brookings Papers on Education Policy 2000* (Washington, D.C.: Brookings Institution, 2000), pp. 359–380. Maris A. Vinovskis, "Missing in Practice? Systematic Development and Rigorous Program Evaluation at the U.S. Department of Education," paper presented at the Conference on Evaluation of Educational Policies, American Academy of Arts and Sciences, Cambridge, Mass., May 13–14, 1999.
3. Michael B. Katz, *Reconstructing American Education* (Cambridge, Mass.: Harvard University Press, 1987), pp. 134–135.

Suggested Readings

Some educational issues, such as Head Start, have been written about in great detail for many years; others, such as social promotion, have received little attention outside of academic circles until recently. Many of the sources I rely on (aside from media accounts) are very academic or heavily statistical, or both, and thus not appealing to most readers. Here I would like to list a few of the more accessible works on the educational issues covered in this volume, with some comments on how approachable each book is and where the author of each stands. Of course, any reader interested in pursuing one of these topics in detail should also consider making use of the endnotes, which contain the major evaluations and much of the relevant scholarly writing.

First, if you want to learn more about evaluation, Carol H. Weiss's *Evaluation* is an invaluable guide to the many different aspects of evaluation. Weiss writes beautifully, and is as knowledgeable about evaluation as anyone. For someone interested in the history of evaluation from the 1960s to the 1980s, *Foundations of Program Evaluation: Theories of Practice* by William R. Shadish, Jr., Thomas D. Cook, and Laura C. Leviton traces the work and thought of seven major figures in the field, including Weiss. *Foundations of Program Evaluation* is a more difficult read than *Evaluation,* and more geared toward philosophical issues, whereas Weiss's *Evaluation* contains a thoroughly practical discussion. James Popham's *Educational Evaluation* is a very useful textbook that focuses specifically on how to evaluate education.

There is a great deal of literature on Head Start. Much of the best pro–Head Start literature was written or edited by Edward Zigler, one of the program's founders. His *Head Start: The Inside Story of America's Most Suc-*

cessful Educational Experiment, written with Susan Muenchow, is a good place to start. For a more technical discussion of various preschool programs and their evaluations as of the early 1980s, *As the Twig Is Bent,* by the Consortium for Longitudinal Studies, remains unmatched. For information on attempts to provide follow-up to Head Start in programs such as Follow Through and Even Start, three chapters in Maris Vinovskis's *History and Educational Policymaking* are invaluable.

Most of the literature on bilingual education is biased in one direction or the other. One pro-bilingual book that is relatively balanced and insightful is James Crawford's *Bilingual Education: History, Politics, Theory and Practice.* Crawford's coverage is comprehensive, and he generally avoids letting his own position get too much in the way. The most thoughtful scholarly proponent of bilingual education is Kenji Hakuta, a psychologist whose 1986 classic *Mirror of Language* remains highly worth reading. Among critics of bilingual education, Christine Rossell and Keith Baker's *Bilingual Education in Massachusetts* is an intelligent and approachable work that makes a number of good points against how bilingual education is currently practiced. Rosalie Pedalino Porter's *Forked Tongue: The Politics of Bilingual Education* is a more passionate indictment of bilingual education; it is highly readable and based on Porter's own negative experiences with the bilingual "bureaucracy."

Most of the writing on class size is technical. One exception is Charles Achilles's *Let's Put Our Kids First, Finally: Getting Class Size Right.* The next best are the dueling Department of Education reports issued ten years apart, Tommy Tomlinson's *Class Size and Public Policy* and Jeremy Finn's *Class Size and Students at Risk.* These reports reflect the argument beautifully, including the difference between Finn's reliance on very specific evidence and Tomlinson's reliance on broad arguments of questionable relevance.

Social promotion has been written about less than any of the other topics in this book. Most of what does exist is technical. Lorrie Shepard and Mary Lee Smith's edited volume, *Flunking Grades,* is a bit dated, and some of the articles are difficult, but much of it is accessible and still relevant; there is probably no better place to start. For a more recent work that presents a nuanced argument in support of social promotion, see Karl Alexander, Doris Entwisle, and Susan Dauber's *On the Success of Failure.*

Most of the literature on school funding is highly academic. One obvious exception is Jonathon Kozol's *Savage Inequalities,* which is a moving and passionately written account of schools with limited funding. Richard Elmore and Milbrey McLaughlin's *Reform and Retrenchment* is a superb telling of the battles over school funding in California in the late 1960s and 1970s. The best introduction to the subject, although somewhat rough going in places, is *Making Money Matter: Financing America's Schools*, commissioned by the National Research Council and edited by Helen Ladd and Janet Hansen. All of the chapters are worthwhile, some are very readable, and the volume as a whole presents the many issues related to school funding more completely and sensibly than anything else currently available.

Index

257